ROUTLEDGE LIBRARY EDITIONS:
EDUCATION

EFFECTIVE SCHOOLS IN
DEVELOPING COUNTRIES

EFFECTIVE SCHOOLS IN DEVELOPING COUNTRIES

Edited by
HENRY M. LEVIN AND
MARLAINE E. LOCKHEED

Volume 8

LONDON AND NEW YORK

First published in 1993

This edition first published in 2012
by Routledge
2 Park Square, Milton Park, Abingdon, Oxon, OX14 4RN

Simultaneously published in the USA and Canada
by Routledge
711 Third Avenue, New York, NY 10017

Routledge is an imprint of the Taylor & Francis Group, an informa business

British Library Cataloguing in Publication Data
A catalogue record for this book is available from the British Library

ISBN 13: 978-0-415-61517-4 (Set)
eISBN 13: 978-0-203-81617-2 (Set)
ISBN 13: 978-0-415-66835-4 (Volume 8)
eISBN 13: 978-0-203-81645-5 (Volume 8)

Publisher's Note
The publisher has gone to great lengths to ensure the quality of this reprint but
points out that some imperfections in the original copies may be apparent.

Disclaimer
The publisher has made every effort to trace copyright holders and would
welcome correspondence from those they have been unable to trace.

Printed and bound by CPI Group (UK) Ltd, Croydon, CR0 4YY

Effective Schools in Developing Countries

Henry M. Levin
and
Marlaine E. Lockheed
Editors

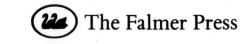 The Falmer Press

(A Member of the Taylor & Francis Group)
London • Washington, D.C.

UK   The Falmer Press, 4 John St, London WC1N 2ET
USA   The Falmer press, Taylor & Francis Inc., 1900 Frost Road, Suite 101,
        Bristol, PA 19007

First published 1993

The findings, interpretations, and conclusions expressed in this publication are those of the authors and do not necessarily represent the views and policies of the World Bank or its Board of Executive Directors or the countries they represent.

A catalogue record for this book is available from the British Library

ISBN 0 75070 173 0 cased

Library of Congress Cataloging-in-Publication Data are available on request

Jacket design by Caroline Archer

Typeset in 9.5/11pt Bembo by
Graphicraft Typesetters Ltd., Hong Kong

Printed in Great Britain by Burgess Science Press, Basingstoke on paper which has a specified pH value on final paper manufacture of not less than 7.5 and is therefore 'acid free'.

Contents

Chapter 1

Creating Effective Schools

Marlaine E. Lockheed and Henry M. Levin

Developing countries face a host of common problems in providing sufficient education of high quality to their youth. Typically, these general challenges break down into matters of participation, effectiveness and resources. For example, almost all countries in the developing world 'guarantee' that children of primary age, usually between the ages of 6 and 11, will be provided with a public education. In the poorest countries, however, this goal has not been met, and it seems to grow farther from reach as high birth rates stretch national fiscal and organizational capacity to provide more school spaces. Although a high proportion of students begin primary school, relatively few complete it. In rural areas the majority often obtain no more than two or three years of schooling. And studies of student achievement show that little is learned, far too little to master the technical requirements for being productive in an industrialized society. Since these skills are taught almost entirely within the context of schools in developing countries, it is possible to conclude that schools in developing countries are ineffective.

This volume brings together eight case studies which describe a variety of initiatives to create more effective schools for children of poverty, especially in the third world. The initiatives were identified through a search that sought nominations from colleagues internationally and reviewed published and unpublished documents; both qualitative and statistical studies were examined. Countries include Brazil, Burundi, Colombia, Ghana, Nepal, Sri Lanka, Thailand, and United States. Each initiative was developed independently to address unique challenges and situations. One would hardly expect them to have identical features. It is interesting — and important — to find that they do, in fact, share a set of common features with respect to provision of necessary inputs, existence of facilitating conditions and will. While there is commonality among the effective schools, there is individuality as well. In fact, a major feature that the various initiatives have in common is that each is adapted to local circumstances; flexibility appears to be the key to effectiveness. Taken as a group, the features of the approaches described in this volume might be viewed as a basis for considering the development of effective schools strategies in other contexts.

This chapter sets the framework for the remainder of the chapters in this volume. Here, we review the pressing problems that schools in developing countries must address and why school improvement is so essential, trace the history of 'effective schools' research and practice, describe the necessary inputs required for buildings to be schools and the necessary organizational and professional conditions for schools to work, and end with a discussion of what are necessary conditions for producing change.

Pressing Problems

Schools in developing societies face problems of relatively low school participation in terms of enrollments of eligible age groups; low levels of school completion, even at the primary level; and low levels of achievement (Lockheed and Verspoor, 1991). To some degree their lack of effectiveness is not a mystery, for resources sufficient to provide even the most rudimentary conditions for success often are lacking.

Participation

In the development decade of the sixties with its great optimism about economic growth, family planning, and educational expansion, universal primary education seemed to be around the corner. Instead, much attention during that decade was devoted to the expansion of secondary and tertiary schooling and the directions that those levels of schooling should take. But, in the nineties it is clear that much of Sub-Saharan Africa and parts of Latin America and Asia have not and will not come close to meeting universal primary participation for the foreseeable future (World Bank, 1990). In fact, some of these countries are farther from this goal today than they were a decade ago. According to estimates based on Unesco data, school places were available for fewer than 65 percent of primary school children in low-income developing countries, other than China and India, in 1985. Since many of these school places were filled by children repeating a grade, the median proportion of children of primary school age who were enrolled in school in these countries was only 50 percent, leaving an estimated 145 million children out of school.

School participation data do not tell the entire story. There remain serious problems of inequity in the provision of education. Masses of children from impoverished populations, who are at the margins of both economic and political power, are relegated to an inadequate system of public schooling, while the children of families of wealth and power are sent to so-called 'private' schools, which in developing countries are often heavily subsidized by public funds. In many countries, poor children have difficulty learning because they are taught in a language that is not their 'mother tongue', often by teachers who themselves are not fluent in the language of instruction (Eisemon et al., this volume). Moreover, schools for the poor do not provide the educational and social mobility that is associated with the popular image of education as a liberating force. School quality is poor and educational expectations are low, resulting in educational achievement that is so low as to provide little hope of escape from poverty.

Effectiveness

Schools are also unable to retain students throughout the primary cycle. Fewer than 70 percent of those who enter school in developing countries reach the final year of the primary cycle (Lockheed and Verspoor, 1991), and dropout occurs early in the cycle. In virtually all countries, dropout rates for girls are higher than those for boys, and they are higher for students in rural areas than for students in urban areas.

Schools affect students dropping out by, in some cases, encouraging repetition and by providing educational services of poor quality. On average, repetition rates in low and lower-middle income countries are 2–5 times higher than those in upper-middle and high income countries. Repetition is not equally likely at all grade levels. In some countries, nearly all students spend two years in first grade, often because teachers expect them to do so (Schiefelbein, 1975). In other countries, repetition is more acute in the terminal year, when students are preparing for their selection examinations for the next level of education (Eisemon *et al.*, this volume).

The most serious problem, however, is that even those who complete their education have learned very little, as has been shown repeatedly (Lockheed and Verspoor, 1991; IEA, 1988; Robitaille and Garden, 1989). While students often successfully memorize and repeat what is written in their textbooks or on the blackboard, they lack proficiency in reading, writing and computational skills, and seem to lack the skills required to apply what has been learned to new situations. This is a problem because it is the cognitive skills children develop in school — not simply their exposure to schooling — that are determinants of their subsequent productivity in the labor force (Boissiere, Knight and Sabot, 1985; Jamison and Moock, 1984).

Resources

Finally, the available resources that many developing countries are able or willing to allocate to education are inadequate for meaningful change to improve effectiveness. The costs of a modest school program for all primary age children in the poorest countries vastly exceed available national resources (this is not the case for 'middle income' countries, however). Expenditures per student, when adjusted for inflation in price levels, are declining. Relative to school spending in the industrialized world, annual recurrent public educational expenditures in developing countries are low — on average, $30 per primary student and $111 per secondary student in the mid-1980s, versus $1551 and $1811, respectively, in industrialized countries (Lockheed and Verspoor, 1991; Komenan, 1987).[1]

As a result, schools in developing countries often lack the most basic resources needed for education such as qualified teachers, facilities, and textbooks. Double and triple shifts of a few hours are the norm in some regions; the number of days in the school year has been reduced; and teachers' salaries have declined so much that fully qualified teachers are often a luxury and teacher turnover and attendance are problematic. Even with low salaries, almost all of the school budgets are spent on personnel, so there is little left for school textbooks and other instructional materials — less than $1 in low-income countries at the primary level, versus $52 in industrialized countries (Lockheed and Verspoor, 1991). Accordingly, the search for solutions to improve schooling in developing countries must begin with the attempt to provide at least minimum levels of essential school inputs.

Marlaine E. Lockheed and Henry M. Levin

Traditional Routes to Improvement

Traditional educational policy has sought out potential improvements at the margins of the educational system rather than its core. Such alterations have generally been piecemeal, leaving intact the infrastructure of institutions that are failing to serve the needs of their students. Typical of such policies have been those that provide additional inputs: more teacher training and retraining, more and better instructional materials, smaller class size, and selected educational technologies such as television and computers. In developed countries, the record of success for such incremental changes is meager. For example, Hanushek (1986) reviewed hundreds of studies of the effects of material inputs on student achievement in the United States, and concluded that variations in material input available in schools were unimportant in explaining differences in achievement among students. However, in developing countries, the record is significantly more positive, largely because of the low base from which schools are currently operating (Fuller, 1987; Lockheed and Verspoor, 1991; Harbison and Hanushek, 1992).

Beginning in the seventies, educational reformers began to argue that schools did not work for poor children because they were simply not designed to meet their needs. That is, the very nature of existing schools served to undereducate, miseducate, and fail students from marginalized populations (Carnoy, 1972; Illich, 1971). The underfunding of these schools was at least as much a symptom of the problem as it was a cause. In the US, simply providing more resources was not likely to make the substantial change in the character of education that was needed to succeed. Some critics argued that unless the operation of schools was shifted from a 'monopolistic' state to a competitive marketplace, it would not be possible substantially to improve matters (Coons and Sugarman, 1978). Others argued that within the public school system, 'effective schools' could be created. In general, the term 'effective schools' was used to refer to the types of schools that research had shown to be successful.

A Brief History of 'Effective Schools' Research and Practice

The origins of the effective schools literature can be traced back to the sixties in terms of general concerns with school effectiveness, but it took a particular form in the seventies. The notion of creating a different kind of school that would be more effective with children from marginalized or poverty backgrounds is found in many places. Most research on effective schools, however, has been conducted in the developed countries of North America and Europe. As a reform movement, the effective schools movement is largely based on research and reform strategies that were established in the United States and United Kingdom.

Research in the United States

The coining of the effective school movement is usually associated with the work of Edmonds (1979) and Brookover and Lezotte (1979). These authors raised the question of why there are some — albeit only a few — schools that seem to get good educational results for at-risk or marginalized students. They hypothesized that if they could identify those schools, they could ascertain how they differed from the more typical school educating at-risk children. They could then create school reforms based on effective school practices so that ineffective schools could be transformed into effective ones.

With achievement test scores as the criteria, the first 'effective schools' studies were statistical analyses of schools that were supposed to be serving student populations that were similar in race and socioeconomic status. Statistical 'outlier' schools that were performing much better and much worse than average were identified. Next, the researchers studied the two groups of schools to find out how they differed. Although different researchers came out with slightly different lists of characteristics, the most commonly cited list from these first studies is that compiled by Edmonds (1979). Edmonds identified the following five characteristics of effective schools:

(a) strong leadership of the principal;
(b) emphasis on mastery of basic skills;
(c) a clean and orderly school environment;
(d) high teacher expectations of student performance;
(e) frequent assessments of student progress.

Notably absent are differences in the material resources available to effective and ineffective schools.

Edmonds and his colleagues began to disseminate these results widely at educational conferences, and they were accepted as the basis for educational reform by large numbers of school authorities. The unusually receptive response to the results by educational practitioners seems to be related, in part, to the argument that they were based upon sophisticated statistical inquiry and, in part, to their appeal to common sense. In any event, US schools sought out training in effective school practices. The success of this proliferation is evidenced by the fact that the General Accounting Office of the US published a report in 1989 that found that 41 percent of the nation's school districts claimed to follow effective schools principles, and another 17 percent reported that they were planning to do so (US General Accounting Office, 1989).

What is unique about the effective schools strategy is its emphasis on transformation of the entire school, rather than on a specific aspect of curriculum or instructional strategies, or school organization. More typically school improvement has focused on the adoption of a large number of piecemeal changes which are often unconnected. Thus, a new reading series might be adopted; class size might be reduced; computers might be brought into the classroom; teachers might be retrained in providing mathematics instruction, and so on. But, the effective schools approach argued that research proves that effective schools for at-risk students are different in systematic ways from ineffective ones; and that the core characteristics of effective schools could be imparted to ineffective ones to increase their effectiveness through school-wide transformation rather than piecemeal reform.

Compelling as the effective schools movement has been to educators, researchers found much to criticize. First, the critics analyzed test performance of students and found inconsistent results from grade-to-grade and from year-to-year in terms of which schools were statistical outliers. That is, if the analysis were done in a particular grade and a particular year, a school might be shown to be statistically effective; for another grade or for another year, the same method-ology would show the school to be ineffective. Second, the statistical methods for identifying effective schools were also challenged, with different techniques identifying different outlier schools (Aitkin and Longford, 1986; Madaus, Kellaghan, Rakow and King, 1987, Raudenbush and Bryk, 1986; Reynolds, 1982; Zirkel and Scott, 1987). For example, outliers based on school mean achievement scores differed from those based on individual scores nested within schools; differences were also found when scores were adjusted for differences between students in terms of social class background and test scores upon intake. Third, the characteristics of effective schools were charged as being excessively vague, particularly when one was trying to replicate them in other schools. Finally, the empirical basis for the effective schools claim was weak. A search for evidence of schools that had improved student achievement by following the recommend-ations of effective schools research was unable to find a single documented case based upon acceptable evaluation methods (Felton, 1990). This absence is rather remarkable when one considers that over half of US school districts had adopted or planned to adopt the approach.

In the early 1980s, a 'second wave' of effective schools literature began to emerge, and the list of common characteristics of effective schools also changed. The most frequently cited list, compiled by Purkey and Smith (1983), identified nine organizational and four process characteristics. The organizational charac-teristics were:

(a) school-site management;
(b) instructional leadership;
(c) staff stability;
(d) curriculum articulation and organization;
(e) schoolwide staff development;
(f) parental involvement and support;
(g) schoolwide recognition of academic success;
(h) maximized learning time; and
(i) district support.

The process characteristics were:

(j) collaborative planning and collegial relationships;
(k) sense of community;
(l) clear goals and high expectation;
(m) order and discipline.

One recent statistical analysis of schools in a metropolitan area of the US found that these 'effective schools' characteristics — particularly teacher involvement in decisions and parental involvement in schools — were modestly associated with higher student achievement (Witte and Walsh, 1990).

Research in the United Kingdom

During the 1970s, a group of British researchers studied both elementary and secondary schools to identify the more 'effective' ones. The secondary school study was the first to be published (Rutter *et al.*, 1979), followed by the elementary school study, which appeared almost a decade later (Mortimore *et al.*, 1988). Both studies followed students over time; studied their teachers, classrooms, and schools through direct observation; surveyed teachers, parents, and students; and evaluated the connections between school and home influences and student test scores. They concluded that there are a range of school practices that can elevate the performance of students, regardless of socioeconomic background. These studies stressed features characteristic of the second wave of US effective schools studies.

The elementary school study found the following to be features of 'effective schools:

(a) purposeful leadership of the staff by the headteacher;
(b) involvement of the deputy head;
(c) involvement of teachers;
(d) consistency amongst teachers;
(e) structured sessions;
(f) intellectually challenging teaching;
(g) a work-centered environment;
(h) limited focus within sessions;
(i) maximum communication between teachers and pupils;
(j) record keeping;
(k) parental involvement; and
(l) positive climate.

At the secondary level, Rutter and his colleagues concluded that effective schools had the following characteristics:

(a) group management in the classroom;
(b) high expectations and standards;
(c) positive teacher models;
(d) feedback on performance;
(e) consistency of school values; and
(f) pupil acceptance of school norms.

Both of the UK studies asserted that schools with similar student intakes showed very different educational results and that these school characteristics explained the vast differences in effectiveness. However, these studies were not associated with the same type of explosive school effectiveness movement that was witnessed in the US where there was a concerted attempt to transform schools into those with effective schools characteristics. Instead, this line of research generated an explosion of new statistical techniques for examining school effects from a multi-level perspective (Goldstein, 1987; Longford, 1987).

Developing Country Research

Although little research on effective schools has taken place in the developing world, the statistical studies that have been undertaken have benefitted from the above developments in analytical techniques. Virtually all recent 'effective schools' research from developing countries has adopted multi-level statistical techniques (Creemers, Peters and Reynolds, 1990; Lockheed and Bruns, 1990; Lockheed and Longford, 1989; Raudenbush and Willms, 1991; Reynolds, Greemers and Peters, 1988; Riddell, 1989). As a result, these studies are less subject to some of the methodological criticisms that were levelled at the earlier effective schools research.

One important finding emerging from the few 'effective schools' studies in developing countries is the importance of material imputs on achievement in economically impoverished countries. Hanushek's conclusion about the importance of material inputs in economically advantaged countries simply do not apply. If they did, millions of children in developing countries would continue to lack textbooks, teachers with even basic education and training, or school buildings with desks and chairs. However, variations in the availability of material inputs at the school level are correlated with between-school variations in achievement in developing countries; provision of certain types of basic necessities is essential (Fuller, 1987; Lockheed and Verspoor, 1991). For example, controlling for student socio-economic background and initial level of achievement, Lockheed and Longford (1989) found that, in Thailand, achievement was higher in schools with more educated teachers, more frequent use of textbooks and an enriched curriculum. In Zimbabwe, Riddell and Nyagura (1991) found that achievement was higher in schools with more textbooks, less teacher turnover and a higher percentage of trained teachers. Other conclusions about the organizational and process characteristics of 'effective schools' — particularly conclusions drawn from the second wave of research — appear to have more relevance in developing countries.

From the earliest reviews, scholars have been quick to point out that recognizing an effective school is not the same thing as creating one (Purkey and Smith, 1983; Holmes, Leithwood and Musella, 1980). Efforts to create 'effective schools' through implementing a set of unrelated discrete changes — the 'checklist' approach described by Levin (1991) — were generally unsuccessful. Comprehensive change for school improvement is generally recommended, with some scholars arguing for incremental change (Verspoor, 1989) and others pressing for dramatic restructuring (Levin, 1991). Common to both approaches is the *will* to change, and this is the aspect of creating effective schools we address in this volume.

Creating effective schools is significantly more difficult in developing countries than in developed countries, because schools in developing countries lack even the basic minimum inputs necessary for them to function as schools at all, while schools in developed countries are adequately provisioned. We argue that creating effective schools in developing countries requires all three elements: basic inputs, facilitating conditions and the will to change.

Solutions I: Necessary Inputs

One reason that schools in developing countries are ineffective is that they lack certain material and non-material school inputs that are necessary to promote student learning: curriculum, instructional materials, learning time, and teaching (Lockheed and Verspoor, 1991). Without these necessary inputs, schools are not able to function at all. Yet many schools in developing countries are not supplied with a well-developed curriculum, sufficient instructional materials for students, adequate teaching and learning time, and educated and trained teachers (Lockheed, this volume). The effective schools described in this volume, however, manage to provide students with these necessary instructional inputs, despite otherwise impoverished circumstances.

Curriculum

While official primary school curricula are remarkably similar worldwide in terms of subjects taught and amount of time allocated officially to each (Benavot and Kamens, 1989), the curriculum in many developing countries is poor in terms of both scope and sequence. Frequently, the curriculum content is not developed across grades with appropriate steps from one concept to another. Often it lacks suitable connection with situations familiar to students. To address these problems, programs in Brazil (CIEPS) and Colombia (Escuela Nueva) developed curricula that were appropriately paced and sequenced, integrated across the primary grades and supported with textbooks that used examples from students' own experiences.

Instructional Materials

Over the past decade, research has demonstrated a consistent effect of textbooks on student achievement in developing countries (Heyneman, Farrell and Sepulveda-Stuardo, 1981). Where textbooks are available and used by teachers, learning is greater. The effective schools in this volume also tend to be adequately supplied with instructional materials (an exception is Burundi). The Escuela Nueva program provides a variety of instructional material to children, including study guides for children and a school library with basic reference materials. In Thailand, high achieving schools were those which received sufficient contributions from their local communities to purchase sets of supplementary text materials for the curriculum (including teachers' guides, exercises and practice quizzes). At the Gonakelle school in Sri Lanka, the teachers distribute supplementary readers for students to read individually or in groups, and discuss such written materials as newspapers and greeting cards with students. In adult literacy programs in Thailand and Nepal reading materials were distributed and village reading centers were established.

Time for Learning

Large differences in the availability of academic learning time are associated with substantial differences in how much children learn in school (Margo, 1986).[2] One of the common approaches of the schools in this volume is to increase dramatically the amount of time that students have available for study. In Brazil, the CIEPs students stayed all day at school. In Burundi, teachers combined shifts to increase the number of periods of instruction students receive in mathematics and other subjects examined in the *concourse national*, and schools with combined shifts had higher achievement. Repetition also lengthens the amount of time available to study a particular subject, and this, too, was related to higher achievement in Burundi. For adult literacy, a successful approach is to schedule instruction at times when children (or adults) are available to attend such as early in the morning or late afternoon or evening.

Teaching Practices

A fourth common feature of these schools is their attention to increasing student involvement in learning through teaching practices that encourage active student learning. Adult literacy programs in Nepal and Thailand encouraged discussion of problems of the community. In Colombia, classrooms include 'learning activity centers' that encourage group work and discussion among students. The pedagogy of the CIEPs schools stressed dialogues and debates among students and teachers. In all cases, the premise is that students learn more when they are actively engaged in the learning process, not when they are passive recipients of teacher lectures.

Solutions II: Facilitating Conditions

The availability of material and non-material inputs is only a precondition for effective schools. These schools must then marshall these resources effectively to see that they are used well. This typically involves community participation, school based professionalism and flexibility.

Community Involvement

Community–school relationship. Community involvement is central to effective schools. The community may increase the school's resources by providing in-kind contributions and by participating in school activities. In Thailand, for instance, education receives substantial support from communities through direct contributions, donations at school social gatherings, and contributions to schools through the temple, as Tsang and Wheeler discuss.

The school, in turn, can contribute resources to the community by addressing community needs in its programs and getting students to work on community problems and projects. In an effective educational program, the community is an asset to the school and vice versa. Meeting community needs, such as increasing adult literacy, proved to be a way of building support for children's education and the schools.

Parent involvement. Even more important than the support of the community as a whole is the involvement and support of parents. Every program described in these chapters was concerned with parent involvement and took steps to encourage it. In some cases, such as the CIEPs of Rio de Janeiro (Leonardos, this volume), program leaders were aware that they still had a long way to go in building parent support. Despite strenuous effort to involve parents, many were still negative about the program. Perhaps many parents and community members have rejected the program, Leonardos surmises, because it was imposed on them rather than planned with them as involved partners from the start.

School-based Professionalism

Schools are more effective when they choreograph their own activities (within the framework of a larger effective schools program) instead of being expected merely to follow a formula or script sent down from higher levels. A corollary of this school-based approach is that the school takes responsibility for students' success or failure — a fundamental tenet of the Brazilian CIEPs (Leonardos, this volume), the Accelerated Schools and other effective schools in the US (Levin, this volume), and the reform movement in Thailand (Bennett, this volume). The roles of the principal and teachers are also different in a school-based system.

Principal leadership. With so many important decisions made at the school level, the principal has a crucial role in school effectiveness. The principal's impact was evident in the Gonakelle School in Sri Lanka (Little and Sivasithambaram, this volume) where the principal expanded the school, created linkages with other schools in the vicinity, and mobilized strong community support for the school. In Thailand, Tsang and Wheeler found that principals were the key to many aspects of school improvement and to the impact of school clusters. Because of the important roles played by principals, providing training for them has been found to promote school improvement, as it has in Sri Lanka.

Teacher collegiality and commitment. In effective schools, teachers typically are decision makers and play important roles in shaping the school. In Brazil, Leonardos found a sharp contrast between a CIEP school, where teamwork and collegiality characterized the relationships among teachers and the principal, and a conventional school where teachers did their work individually and had a distant, hierarchical relationship with the principal. In Thailand, Tsang and Wheeler report, principals of improving schools promoted shared decision making within the school and greater collaboration among teachers.

One component of making schools more effective usually means improving teachers' skills and knowledge. In addition to training in subject matter and teaching skills, teachers may need to learn about a new program — its philosophy and strategies — as in Brazil's CIEP program and Colombia's Escuela Nueva (Colbert, Chiappe and Arboleda this volume). In developing countries, particularly in remote areas, effective teacher training may include developmental skills, such as agriculture or primary health care, as in the Nepal and Thailand cases described by Bennett.

Accountability. As more decisions are placed in the hands of individual schools and teachers, this autonomy must be balanced with accountability; schools and teachers must show that they can produce results. One implication of this is a need for improved assessment, as pointed out by Eisemon *et al.* and by Tsang and Wheeler.

In addition, classroom and school supervision and support have roles to play in improving school quality and accountability. In Sri Lanka's Badulla Integrated Rural Development Project, the role of supervisor shifted from inspector and monitor to supporter and advisor. A support mechanism that proved popular among Sri Lankan teachers was a program of visits to schools where they observed and assisted with the work of other teachers with greater experience and skill. The importance of effective school and classroom supervision was also emphasized by Eisemon *et al.* based on their findings in Burundi.

Flexibility

What works for one group of children and parents in one community will not necessarily work everywhere. While nearly everyone would agree with this statement in principle, it is more difficult to reach consensus on what is best for particular groups of children. For instance, do disadvantaged children require a slowed down program or an accelerated one? Is a high level of grade repetition always bad, or does it sometimes serve a useful purpose? These chapters demonstrate that the answers to such questions often are not straightforward and obvious. But if a common theme is struck, it is the importance of flexibility and adapting to local needs.

Relevant curricula. Several authors question the use of standard curricula designed for middle-class, urban children in rural and other disadvantaged areas. Bennett stresses the importance of a curriculum that is relevant to students' lives and practical for their futures. The Accelerated Schools in the US seek to build on the cultural strengths of students and families. Central to the Brazilian CIEPs' philosophy is acknowledging the students' culture throughout the curriculum, in both the academic and extracurricular portions of the day. The Colombian Escuela Nueva replaces an 'urban-biased' curriculum with a curriculum attuned to the lives of rural children.

Some programs contend that separate teaching of the various academic subjects diminishes the relevance of the curriculum. As Bennett writes about Thailand: 'This subject-based curriculum created a discontinuity between life at home, which centered around the family and community, and life at school, which was divided into a drop of Thai, a drop of mathematics, a drop of social studies, and other compartmentalized subjects'. The reformed Thai curriculum integrated language, math, health and hygiene, nutrition, and other areas in themes such as 'myself' or 'my family'.

Moving from a fragmented to an integrated curriculum was also a major feature of Rio de Janeiro's CIEPs. All subjects were linked together by their common aspects, and children were encouraged to see connections and relationships; extracurricular activities were integrated closely with the main curriculum. The Badulla project in Sri Lanka also included integrated lesson units.

Adjustments in level or pace. The Accelerated Schools Program in the US challenges the assumption that programs for poor children should move more slowly than programs for middle-class children in order to compensate for their educational disadvantage. Levin argues that, in fact, they should move at an accelerated pace. However, accelerated curricula require major changes in organization and instructional strategies in order to succeed. When centrally developed curricula are too demanding for a particular group of students because organizational and instructional techniques are not altered, the results may not be desirable. For instance, Burundi teachers confronted with a very advanced curriculum (Eisemon *et al.*, this volume) reacted by neglecting the teaching of practical subjects.

Organizational flexibility. Making the best use of resources is very important in developing countries, and one mechanism for doing so is school clusters. Bennett describes the use of clusters in Nepal, and Tsang and Wheeler discuss clusters in Thailand. Some of the purposes of school clusters were served by demonstrative schools and 'micro-centers' in Colombia and teachers' centers in Sri Lanka. To increase the effectiveness of schools in rural areas of Colombia, the Escuela Nueva program uses a flexible promotion mechanism adapted to the lives of rural children, who advance from one grade to another at their own pace. In addition, a multi-grade approach with one or two teachers handling all five grades makes it possible to provide complete primary schooling in places that now have only incomplete schooling. To meet the needs of Brazilian working parents and expose students to a variety of activities, the CIEPs provide a full-day program, some ten hours divided equally between instruction and extracurricular activities.

Pedagogical flexibility. Schools may also choose or adapt pedagogical methods to meet the needs of the students they serve. Two examples are active student participation and small group learning. Although both have been found to be beneficial for all kinds of students, their use may be particularly important in certain cases. In the Escuela Nueva, for instance, small groups not only foster children's ability to cooperate in solving problems, but also dovetail with the flexible pacing that allows children to work at different levels within the same classroom. Determining the optimal language of instruction for children of various ages and for different subjects is another area where school-level flexibility can enhance student achievement. Many developing countries use an official language of instruction that differs from the mother tongue. In some cases, early grades are taught in a mother tongue and later grades in an official language of instruction. In other cases, instruction occurs in the official language at all grades. In yet other cases, some subjects are taught in an official language while others are taught in the mother tongue. Inappropriate language of instruction may harm students, as argued by Bennett and by Eisemon *et al.*

Solutions III: The Will to Act

We have set out certain characteristics that seem to be common across a variety of effective schools. But the mere fact that we know to a great extent what is needed does not mean that these requirements will be satisfied. A major determinant of whether schools will adopt these requirements is the will or commitment by governments and communities to create effective schools. The notion of will or commitment is a complicated one. It goes beyond wishes or desires to leadership and even sacrifice. That is, for governments, communities and households to provide adequate resources requires that they sacrifice other amenities for which those resources can be used. It requires that resources move from the public bureaucracies into classrooms. It means that parents must reinforce school goals in the home and community and must set high expectations for their own children. It means that school personnel must view all children as being educable and must work together to make the fulfillment of that vision a reality. Finally, it means that schools have a vision of a future for all of their children that they will not swerve from in spite of the obstacles.

Vision

This commitment requires leadership at every level of society and with the support of a broad constituency of political parties, government bureaucracies, businesses, parents and students. It requires visionary spokespersons at all levels who will continue to push the vision and serve as the educational conscience of society. It requires leadership in the mass media to keep the vision constantly before society and to monitor progress towards that vision and the performance of national and community leaders. In the absence of this will to change, the knowledge base for effective schools that we have described will stay dormant, never emerging from its chrysalis to transform the schools. This type of leadership and mass mobilization may require nothing short of a mass social movement with charismatic leadership to overcome the inertia of the educational system and traditional practices. Such movements will need to be catalyzed in different ways in different societies depending upon such matters as political alignments, potential coalitions, institutional arrangements, and cultural traditions.

Decentralized Solutions

Effective schools appear to require a high degree of school-level responsibility and authority, with accountability to parents and local community. School decentralization programs that shift responsibility from central bureaucracies to local districts and schools are one strategy to promote effective schools.

There are, of course both advantages and disadvantages to decentralization. Centralization is efficient for achieving scale economies or national consistency in activities such as textbook production or teacher training. Even in decentralized systems, central government inputs and financing are necessary to ensure equity and to set standards for appropriate service levels and outcomes. But since teaching and learning occur in the classroom and in schools, increasing the authority of teachers and school administrators to design programs that meet local needs appears a promising strategy to improving learning.

One strong argument for moving from centralized decision making to greater local and school-based control is to design programs that meet the needs of specific communities and groups of children. The innovative programs described in this volume demonstrate that effective schools are tailored to the specific needs — and strengths — of children and their communities.

How to develop local autonomy and responsibility is a question that has confronted education development specialists for decades. One strategy that has been attempted in Thailand relies upon increasing local accountability for success:

monitoring the achievement of students and reporting to school headmasters their school's performance in relationship to other schools. Another strategy is providing school improvement funds that can be spent on a veriety of 'approved' educational materials at the discretion of the school. Local financing also increases the legitimacy of the local community to exercise control over the school. The cases reviewed in this book provide insight into how some programs for developing effective schools have worked.

Summary

Virtually all of the versions of and strategies for effective schools that are contained in this volume were initiated independently to address particular challenges and situations. What is remarkable is the agreement among the strategies. We conclude this chapter by summarizing these areas of accord as a basis for considering generic approaches to developing schools that will be more effective.

Central philosophy. The most effective schools are characterized by a central philosophy that provides a guiding spirit to the design and implementation of results. The reforms seem to be inspired by a serious and persistent set of educational concerns towards which a profound transformation of schools seems to be the only solution. The philosophy of each effective schools movement is cohesive, overarching and holistic rather than being a collection of piecemeal and incremental changes. This philosophy is embodied in a movement which has a spiritual and reformist appeal as opposed to the more traditional technocratic and mechanical approach to school improvement. This means that an effective schools movement must go beyond a mere checklist to an organic approach that encompasses these features in a natural way rather than mere 'add-ons' to existing schools.

Overall strategy. The overall strategy is to use the central philosophy to design an ideal school and school program. This ideal is used as a basis for a comprehensively conceived curriculum, training program, materials, administration support, and uniform approach to school change at a macro-level. At the same time, local flexibility, adaptations, and variations are encouraged to meet local needs within the overall program boundaries.

Community involvement. Community involvement is central to the ideal of the effective school in two ways. First, the community is expected to contribute local resources to the school through the provision of in-kind contributions and voluntary participation in school activities. In addition, families have particular responsibilities to support and reinforce the education of their children. Second, the school is expected to contribute resources to the community by addressing community needs in its programs and getting students to work on community problems and projects. The community is expected to be an asset to the school and vice versa.

Empowerment. A principal emphasis is placed on empowering teachers, students, parents, and the community to take responsibility for making educational decisions and for the consequences of those decisions. At the heart of the educational philosophy is the view that a meaningful education requires active participation among all who are involved in the process rather than following a script or formula set out by higher levels. Schools are expected to choreograph their own activities within the framework of the larger effective schools program

Active learning. The emphasis on student learning is to shift from a more traditional passive approach in which all knowledge is imparted from teachers and textbooks to an active approach in which the student is responsible for learning. Effective schools approaches emphasize self instruction, the use of manipulative and objects around which activities are built, problem solving, and meaningful applications. Active learning also means the application of learning activities to the local context.

Focus. Effective schools tend to delineate the scope of their programs, often focussing on accomplishing well a narrow set of objectives rather than addressing ineffectively a much larger set of goals. The Coalition for Effective Schools in the US stresses that 'less is more'. This view is also found in accelerated schools where acceleration often means to cover fewer topics and activities in depth rather than more topics in rapid profusion. The Escuela Nueva is clear about its four curriculum areas. Each of the programs seems to emphasize a clear and manageable focus rather than a proliferation of goals.

Teacher expectations. Either explicitly or implicitly, each of the approaches is premised on high teacher expectations. The view is that students can succeed if the right conditions and support are provided to ensure their success. This view is embodied in the central philosophies of the programs as well as in the training and curriculum.

Funding and resources. In most developing countries, where the school resources are below the threshold to sustain regular schooling programs, additional resources must be found. These can come from the community and parental efforts as well as from national budgets. Effective school reforms must partially address this problem by freeing up resources that can be reallocated to meet more pressing needs. For example, one major multi-country project, Impact, was premised on raising student to teacher ratios by increasing self-instruction, low-cost educational technologies, and community participation (Cummings, 1986). Another major source of additional resources comes from reducing high rates of retention (Harbison and Hanushek, 1992). Clearly, if students do not have to repeat grades, those resources can be used to expand enrollments and improve educational quality. But the shortage of resources must be addressed systematically to make schools more effective.

Notes

1 Thus, it is not surprising that current attempts to create effective schools in industrialized countries focus primarily on restructuring school organization and pedagogy. In some cases more resources are needed, but it is widely viewed that

the greatest gains in educating marginalized or at-risk populations can be accomplished without additional resources.
2 Small increases in academic learning time do not show as substantial effects, although they are often positive (Brown and Saks, 1987; Levin and Tsang, 1987).

References

AITKIN, M. and LONGFORD, N. (1986) 'Statistical modelling issues in school effectiveness studies', *The Journal of the Royal Statistical Society Series A (general)*, **149**, 1, pp. 1–43.

BENAVOT, A. and KAMENS, D. (1989) *The Curricular Content of Primary Education in Developing Countries*, World Bank Policy, Planning and Research Work Paper WPS–237, Washington, DC, World Bank, Education and Employment Division.

BERMAN, P. and MCLAUGHLIN, M.W. (1977) *Federal Programs Supporting Educational Change: Factors Affecting Implementation and Continuation*, Santa Monica, CA, Rand Corporation.

BOISSIERE, M., KNIGHT, J.B. and SABOT, R.H. (1985) 'Earnings, schooling, ability and cognitive skills', *American Economic Review*, **75**, 5, pp. 1016–30.

BROOKOVER, W. and LEZOTTE, L. (1979) *Changes in School Characteristic Coincident With Changes in Student Achievement*, East Lansing, MI, College of Urban Development, Michigan State University.

BROWN, B.W. and SAKS, D.H. (1987) 'The microeconomics of the allocation of teachers' time and student learning', *Economics of Education Review*, **6**, 4, 319–32.

CARNOY, M. (1972) *Schooling in a Corporate Society*, New York, Longman.

COONS, J. and SUGARMAN, S. (1978) *Education by Choice*, Berkeley, CA, University of California Press.

CREEMERS, B., PETERS, T. and REYNOLDS, D. (Eds) (1990) *School Effectiveness and School Improvement*, Amsterdam, Swets and Zeit.

CUMMINGS, W. (1986) *Low-Cost Primary Education: Implementing an Innovation in Six Nations*, Ottawa, Canada, International Development Research Centre.

EDMONDS, R. (1979) 'Effective schools for the urban poor', *Educational Leadership*, **37**, pp. 15–24.

FELTON, M.K. (1990) *The Effective Schools Movement: A Review of Its Research and Implementation*, unpublished Senior Thesis, Honors Program in Education, Stanford University.

FULLER, B. (1987) 'Raising school quality in developing countries: What investments boost learning?', *Review of Educational Research*, **57**, 3, pp. 255–92.

GOLDSTEIN, H. (1987) *Multilevel Models in Educational and Social Research*, New York, Oxford University Press.

HANUSHEK, E. (1986), 'The economics of schooling: Production and efficiency in public schools', *Journal of Economic Literature*, **23**, pp. 1141–77.

HARBISON, R. and HANUSHEK, E. (1992) *Educational Performance of the Poor: Lessons From Rural Northeast Brazil*, New York, Oxford University Press.

HEYNEMAN, S., FARRELL J. and SEPULVEDA-STUARDO, M.A. (1981) 'Textbooks and achievement in developing countries: What we know', *Journal of Curriculum Studies*, **13**, 3, pp. 227–46.

HOLMES, M., LEITHWOOD, K.A. and MUSELLA, D.F. (Eds) (1980) *Educational Policy for Effective Schools*, New York, Teachers College Press.

ILLICH, I. (1971) *Deschooling Society*, New York, Harper and Rowe.

INTERNATIONAL ASSOCIATION FOR THE EVALUATION OF EDUCATIONAL ACHIEVEMENT (IEA) (1988) *Science Achievement in Seventeen Countries*, Oxford, Pergamon Press.

JAMISON, D.T. and MOOCK, P.R. (1984) Farmer education and farm efficiency in Nepal. The role of schooling, extension services and cognitive skills', *World Development*, **12**, pp. 67–86.

KOMENAN, A. (1987) *World Education Indicators*, World Bank Education and Training Department Discussion Paper 88, Washington, DC, World Bank, Population and Human Resources Department

LEVIN, H. (1991) 'Effective Schools in Comparative Focus', in ALTBACH, P., ARNOVE, R. and KELLY, G. (Eds) *Emergent Issues in Education: Comparative Perspective*, Albany, NY, State University of New York Press.

LEVIN, H.M. and TSANG, M.C. (1987). 'The economics of student time', *Economics of Education Review*, **6** (4), pp. 357–64.

LOCKHEED, M.E. and BRUNS, B. (1990) *School Effects on Achievement in Secondary Mathematics and Portuguese in Brazil*, World Bank Policy, Research and External Affairs Working Paper WPS-525, Washington, DC, World Bank, Education and Employment Division.

LOCKHEED M.E. and LONGFORD, N. (1989) *A Multi-Level Model of School Effectiveness in a Developing Country*, World Bank Discussion Paper 69, Washington, DC, World Bank.

LOCKHEED, M.E. and VERSPOOR, A.M., with others (1991) *Improving Primary Education in Developing Countries*, New York, Oxford University Press.

LONGFORD, N.T. (1987) 'A fast-scoring algorithm for maximum likelihood estimation in unbalanced mixed models with nested random effects', *Biometrika*, **74**, pp. 817–27.

MADAUS, G., KELLAGHAN, T., RAKOW, E.A. and KING, D.J. (1987) The sensitivity of measures of school effectiveness, *Harvard Educational Review*, **49**, 2, pp. 207–30.

MARGO, R-A. (1986) 'Educational achievement in segregated school systems: The effect of "separate-but-equal"' *American Economic Review*, **76**, 4, pp. 794–801.

MORTIMORE, P., SAMMARS, P., STOLL, L., LEWIS, D. and COB, R.E. (1988) *School Matters*, Berkeley, University of California Press.

PURKEY, S.C. and SMITH, M.S. (1983) 'Effective schools : A review', *The Elementary School Journal*, **83**, 4, pp. 427–52.

RAUDENBUSH, S. and BRYK, A.S. (1986) 'A hierarchical model for studying school effects', *Sociology of Education*, **59**, pp. 1–17.

RAUDENBUSH, S.W. and WILLMS, J.D. (Eds) (1991) *Schools, Classrooms and Pupils: International Studies of Schooling From a Multilevel Perspective*, New York, Academic Press.

REYNOLDS, D. (1982) 'The search for effective schools', *School Organization*, **2**, 3, pp. 215–37.

REYNOLDS, D., CREEMERS, B. and PETERS T. (Eds) (1988) *School Effectiveness and Improvement*, Amsterdam, Swets and Zat.

RIDDELL, A.R. (1989) 'An alternative approach to the study of school effectiveness in third world countries', *Comparative Education Review*, **33**, pp. 481–97.

RIDDELL, A.R. and NYAGURA, L.M. (1991) *What Causes Differences in Achievement in Zimbabwe's Secondary Schools?* World Bank Policy, Research and External Affairs Working Paper WPS-705, Washington DC, World Bank, Population and Human Resources Department.

ROBITAILLE, D.F. and GARDEN, R.A. (1989) *The IEA Study of Mathematics II: Context and Outcomes of School Mathematics*, Oxford, Pergamon Press.

RUTTER, M., MAUGHAN B., MORTIMORE, P., OUSTON, J., with SMITH, A. (1979) *Fifteen Thousand Hours*, Cambridge, MA, Harvard University Press.

SCHIEFELBEIN, E. (1975) 'Repeating: An overlooked problem in Latin American Education', *Comparative Education Review*, **19**, 3, pp. 468–87.

US GENERAL ACCOUNTING OFFICE OF THE US CONGRESS (1989) *Effective Schools*

Programs: Their Extent and Characteristics, Washington DC, US Government Printing Office.

VERSPOOR, A. (1989) *Pathways to Change: Improving the Quality of Education in Developing Countries*, World Bank Discussion Paper 53, Washington, DC.

WITTE, J.F. and WALSH, D.E. (1990) 'A systematic test of the effective schools model', *Educational Evaluation and Policy Analysis*, **12**, 2, pp. 188–212.

WORLD BANK (1990) *Primary Education: A World Bank Policy Paper*, Washington, DC, World Bank.

ZIRKEL, P.A. and GREENWOOD, S.C. (1987) 'Effective schools and effective principals: Effective research?', *Teachers College Record*, **89**, 2, pp. 255–67.

Chapter 2

The Condition of Primary Education in Developing Countries

Marlaine E. Lockheed

Schooling in developing countries takes place under conditions that are very different from those in developed countries. At the primary level, students in developed countries are likely to go to school in modern well-equipped buildings and have a curriculum that is well thought out in terms of scope and sequence. On average they have 900 hours a year of learning time, $52 a year of non-capital material inputs, and a teacher with sixteen years of formal education. Moreover, these students will share a teacher with fewer than twenty other children, most or all of whom have good health and nutritional status. In many low-income countries, by comparison, students are likely to go to a shelterless school or have class in a poorly constructed and equipped building, and their curriculum is likely to be poorly designed. On average they have only 500 hours a year of learning time, $1.70 a year of non-capital material inputs, and a teacher with ten years of formal education. Typically, the student will share a resource-poor learning environment with more than fifty other children, many of whom are chronically undernourished, parasite-ridden and hungry.

One consequence of these differences is that the job of education is significantly more difficult in developing countries than in developed countries. Yet some schools are effective in developing conditions conducive for learning. They are able to provide: (a) curriculum that is appropriate in terms of scope and sequence, (b) adequate instructional materials, (c) adequate learning time, and (d) effective teaching practices. Most schools in developing countries, however, do not have conditions favorable to learning.

The Curriculum

The Official Curriculum

International summaries of research demonstrate that students learn the content of the curriculum they are taught (Fraser *et al.*, 1987). In primary schools, the official curriculum is remarkably similar worldwide. A recent study of curricular emphases in 130 countries, including 94 low and middle income countries, found that primary curricula not only contained the same subjects, but gave them the same relative importance (Benavot and Kamens, 1989). This consistency in

Table 2.1   Percentage of curriculum devoted to 10 major content areas, by GNP per capita

Curriculum Content	GNP Per Capita Level			
	Low	Lower Middle	Upper Middle	High
	%	%	%	%
Language	37	34	36	34
Math	18	17	18	19
Science	7	9	8	6
Social Studies	8	10	9	9
Moral	5	6	4	5
Music and Art	9	8	11	13
Physical Education	7	6	7	9
Hygiene	1	2	2	1
Vocational Subjects	6	7	3	1
Other	3	3	2	3

Source: Lockheed and Verspoor (1991)

curricular emphases was found across countries, without regard to level of economic or educational development (Table 2.1). Moreover, the relative emphasis of the primary curriculum has been consistent across countries since the early 1960s. In primary schools, over 50 percent of available time is used for acquisition of language skills and mathematics. Science, 'social studies', and aesthetics are given equal weight, about half that of mathematics and one-fourth that of language; other areas receive less attention. This reflects the commonly agreed upon central objectives of primary education: imparting both basic and higher-order literacy and numeracy skills.

The curricular content of primary education shows one important difference between less developed and more developed countries. While all countries spend about 36 percent of instructional time on language instruction, in low and lower-middle income countries this time is divided between instructional time for an indigenous language and instructional time for a non-indigenous language. The result is that less time is available for instruction in either language. More developed countries concentrate instruction in a single indigenous language (e.g., French in France). Language policy and bilingual education are politically sensitive and complex topics, but an important consequence of multiple language instruction is decreased attention to a single language, which could result in a slower rate of literacy acquisition in multilingual as compared with monolingual countries.

The Curriculum as Implemented

Official, intended curriculum only establishes broad guidelines for instruction. Actual curriculum implementation is carried out by teachers using instructional materials, principally textbooks. In textbooks, the scope of the subject matter to be taught is defined and its sequence for instruction is laid out. Textbooks are the major — if not *only* — definition of the curriculum in most developing countries.

Unfortunately, the curriculum as presented in textbooks often suffers from poor instructional design, particularly the scope and sequence of the material. This is important because inappropriately targeted curriculum (either too difficult or too easy) can result in student frustration and failure. A recent study of the scope and sequence of textbooks for grades 1, 3 and 5 in fifteen countries found that the material in both mathematics and textbooks was too difficult at the earlier grades (Cope, Denning and Ribeiro, 1989). In the upper grades, mathematics texts were too difficult, but the material of reading texts was too easy and failed to develop problem-solving skills appropriately. The overly challenging content of the first grade books could explain high rates of repetition in the earlier grades in developing countries.

Textbooks also suffer from factual inaccuracies, inappropriate illustrations and poor choice of text language and script. In Pakistan, for example, textbooks contain a high proportion of factual and grammatical errors, significant gaps between the actual textbooks produced and the specifications, as set out by the Curriculum Bureau of the Textbook Board. They are characterized by poor language grading from one level to another and even between books for different subjects at the same level. Teachers in Pakistan surveyed for their opinions regarding textbooks reported that the books were overly difficult for their students, putting too much burden on children and making them feel uneasy. In particular, because the children could not read fluently the Arabic style Nasakh script used in the textbooks, the children failed their examinations unless the teachers read the textbooks for them and summarized and shortened their lessons (Government of Pakistan, 1983).

Textbooks also appear to lack materials that reinforce the development of higher order thinking skills: problem solving skills and critical thinking. For example, Cope, Denning and Ribiero (1989) found that the majority of the material in fifth-grade books would be more appropriate for students in grades 2 or 3; very little of the material required the students to use the book to 'learn the new'. While teachers can adjust their teaching practices to elicit thoughtful consideration of the text, textbooks that require more than memorization of problem solutions (as in mathematics texts) or that concentrate on using written language to solve 'real world' questions and problems would also encourage the development of higher order thinking skills. Such curriculum reforms are rarely implemented and evaluated in developing countries, but one study from Nigeria found that students exposed to a 'problems approach' curriculum not only learned more facts, but also had better comprehension of the material and were better able to apply the knowledge to new problems (Ogundare, 1988).

Instructional Materials

Instructional materials are key ingredients in learning. They provide information, organize the presentation of information in terms of scope and sequence, and provide students opportunities to use what they have learned. Learning materials that are known to enhance student achievement are textbooks, teacher guides, and other software.

Textbooks

Because textbooks typically deliver the curriculum, they are regarded as the single most important instructional material. As Altbach (1983) notes, 'Nothing has ever replaced the printed word as the key element in the educational process and, as a result, textbooks are central to schooling at all levels'. Sufficient availability of textbooks can ensure that instructional time is not wasted as teachers and students copy text on and off blackboards. Over the past decade, researchers have documented the consistently positive effect of availability of textbooks and other instructional materials on student achievement in developing countries (Heyneman, Farrell and Sepulveda-Stuardo, 1981; Heyneman and Loxley, 1983).

For example, Nicaraguan students in classes randomly assigned to receive textbooks scored significantly higher, by about one-third of a standard deviation, on a test of mathematics achievement than students in classes with no supplementary materials (Jamison, Searle, Galda and Heyneman, 1981). In the Philippines, first- and second-grade children were supplied with textbooks under two different conditions: a student to textbook ratio of 2:1 and a student to textbook ratio of 1:1. A comparison group was drawn from students in school the previous year when the ratio of students to textbooks was 10:1. The effect of having textbooks was substantial, with students in both textbook conditions scoring about one-third of a standard deviation higher on tests of science, mathematics and Filipino than the comparison group (Heyneman, Jamison and Montenegro, 1984). A study of student learning in Brazil examined the effects of adding various 'school quality' elements, e.g., textbooks, to poor rural schools over a five-year period (1981–1985). In schools that received textbooks, second- and fourth-grade students scored significantly higher on tests of mathematics and Portuguese than students in schools lacking textbooks (Armitage *et al.*, 1986; Harbison and Hanushek, 1992).

In the past, there has been a serious lack of textbooks. Textbooks were often not provided to students at all, or their availability was such that the majority of students lacked regular access to them. For example, in Central African Republic the national student to textbook ratio for the French text was 10–20:1 (Paxman, Denning and Read, 1989). In the Philippines, prior to a massive investment in textbooks, the student to textbook ratio was 10:1 (Heyneman, Jamison and Montenegro, 1984). In Brazil, prior to the implementation of a World Bank assisted project to increase material inputs in rural schools, only 23 percent of all schools had received a grade 1 textbook (Armitage *et al.*, 1986); in the Dominican Republic, fewer than 20 percent of eighth-grade students in public schools had mathematics textbooks (Luna and Gonzales, 1986); in Botswana, fewer than 20 percent of primary school students had access to science or social studies textbooks (Ministry of Finance and Development Planning, 1984). One survey in Malawi found that fewer than 30 percent of primary students had their own textbooks (Mundangepfupfu, 1988).

Reducing the student to textbook ratio has been a central element of investments in educational quality in many developing countries for the past decade, and successful projects include the Philippines, which reduced the student-textbook ratio to 2:1 and Northeast Brazil, which tripled the number of primary schools receiving grade 1 textbooks (Armitage *et al.*, 1986; Heyneman, Jamison and Montenegro, 1984). Textbook availability in developing countries has improved substantially, often as a result of donor activity, but significant rural–urban differences in textbook availability remain. Little is known about how frequently the available textbooks are used by teachers, but it appears that provision of textbooks does not guarantee their use. For example, one study of approximately 500 schools in the Philippines reported that 32 percent of fifth-grade science teachers used textbooks frequently, while another study of 127 primary classes in Botswana reported that teachers used textbooks only 12 percent of the time (Fuller and Snyder, 1989; Lockheed, Fonacier and Bianchi, 1989).

Availability of textbooks depends, to some extent, on their physical quality (Paxman, Denning and Read, 1989). Many developing countries opt for low-quality production to reduce unit costs. Low physical production standards, combined with state subsidies, can bring textbook prices within the reach of many poor parents. However, the useful life of such textbooks is short, often measured in months, and many parents either have to buy books several times during a year or have their children go without books. In the Paxman, Denning and Read (1989) study of textbook quality in twenty developing countries, the physical quality of books was found to be acceptable in only half the countries studied.

Teacher Guides

Teacher guides that are well integrated with the textbook or other instructional materials can have a positive impact on student achievement. Particularly effective are guides that include information on both what to teach and how to teach it, diagnostic tests to assist teachers in monitoring student learning and in modifying the daily lessons accordingly, suggestions on classroom management practices, and activities for classroom use. Teacher guides also assist teachers in boosting student learning to higher cognitive levels by suggesting good exercises and questions. Unfortunately, teacher guides for textbooks are seldom available in developing countries. For example, a study in Guinea-Bissau found that there were no teacher manuals for any grades other than grade 1. A survey in Malawi reported that fewer than 15 percent of teachers surveyed had received a teacher guide for any subject other than English. In rural Brazil only 44 percent of teachers had received teachers guides in 1983 (Mundangepfupfu, 1988; Armitage et al., 1986). As many teachers' themselves were educated in schools lacking good textbooks, they may need additional assistance in integrating textbooks into their instructional program.

Other 'Software'

Other instructional materials that facilitate the teaching and learning process are those that (a) assist the teacher to communicate knowledge, such as chalkboards and chalk, (b) enable the student to practice what has been taught, such as pencils and paper, or (c) do both (Baker, 1988). While most educators agree that learning aids are invaluable, the impact of specific aids has rarely been studied. As a result, few instructional materials have been clearly shown to improve student learning, and where research has been conducted, the effects are not uniformly positive.

Table 2.2   Percentage of surveyed classrooms with various instructional materials in Brazil (1985) and Somalia (1984)

Instructional materials	Brazil (1985)	Somalia (1984)
Exercise books/student notebooks	100	89
Pencils	89	93
Textbooks for all students	91	41
Blackboard	n.a.	93
Chalk	95	95
Maps	n.a.	23
Science equipment	n.a.	9
Globe	n.a.	11
Dictionary	n.a.	3
Library	n.a.	4
Visual aids	n.a.	28

Source: Lockheed and Verspoor (1991)

For example, in Brazil, a package of writing materials (chalk, notebooks, pencils, erasers and crayons) was effective in boosting fourth-grade mathematics achievement, but had no effect on reading (Harbison and Hanushek, 1992). The effect on mathematics achievement was undoubtedly due to increasing children's opportunity to practice mathematics.

In general, availability of simple instructional materials in developing countries has increased considerably. For instance, most classrooms in developing countries are supplied with a blackboard. In most developing countries, parents provide their children with basic schooling materials, such as pencils and paper. However, other instructional materials, including such items as dictionaries, globes and maps, are frequently absent from primary classrooms (Table 2.2).

Time for Learning[1]

Research from a variety of countries has shown that the amount of time available for academic studies, as well as how effectively this time is used by students and teachers, is consistently related to how much children learn in school. The effect of additional time is particularly imporatant for earlier grades; estimates of the time elasticities of achievement at the second grade are in the neighborhood of 0.25 for mathematics and half that in reading (Brown and Saks, 1987). Moreover, time is more important for enhancing achievement of low performers; the productivity of time varies inversely with children's initial level of learning.

In general, the more time devoted to instruction, the more students learn. For example, more teacher instructional time and more student reading time were associated with greater science learning in Iran, India and Thailand (Heyneman and Loxley, 1983); more teacher instructional time was associated with greater mathematics learning in Nigeria (Lockheed and Komenan, 1989). While in-school learning time is valuable for all students, it has been found especially important for poor students, whose out-of-school time for learning is limited. For example, a 1981 study of factors related to ninth-grade mathematics achievement in Indonesia found that time spent on classroom assignments was the most significant predictor of achievement for poor rural students, the second most

Marlaine E. Lockheed

Figure 2.1   Length of primary school cycle in 169 countries, 1985

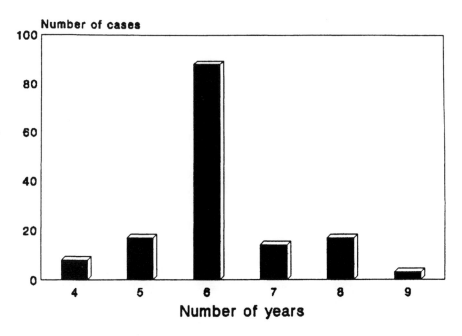

Number of cases

Number of years

Source: Lockheed and Verspoor (1991)

significant predictor for poor urban students, but was only eighth in importance
for middle-class urban students (Suryadi, Green and Windham, 1981).

The annual number of hours available for children to study any subject in
school is determined by three factors: the length of the official school year in
hours, the proportion of these hours assigned to the subject, and the amount
of time lost through school closings, teacher absences, student absences and
miscellaneous interruptions. Additional available time for study can be provided
by after-school study periods and assignment of homework. The proportion of
time children use effectively ('time on task') is determined both by their motivation and by the teacher's management of available time.

Official Time for Learning

The official primary school cycle in most countries worldwide is six years (Figure
2.1), and the official academic year for primary grades 1–6 averages approximately 900 instructional hours in length (Table 2.3) and increases somewhat
according to the economic status of the country. In some developing countries,
however, the official academic year is substantially shorter than average, for
example, 610 hours in Ghana, while in others it is longer, for example, 1070
hours in Morocco.

Since curricular emphasis at the primary level is relatively consistent across
countries, with approximately 35 percent of available time spent on literacy and

Table 2.3   National averages of annual official hours of instruction by GNP per capita

Country's GNP per capita	Hours		
	Total	Literacy	Numeracy
Low	870	322	157
Lower middle	862	293	147
Upper middle	896	323	161
High	914	311	174

Source: Lockheed and Verspoor (1991)

18 percent spent on numeracy, the official number of hours available for instruction in these subjects is similar for developed and developing countries. That is, official curricula in low-income countries allocate on average 322 hours to literacy and 157 hours to numeracy, which is about the same as the official time allocated to these subjects in industrialized countries, 311 hours and 174 hours, respectively.

Actual Time for Learning

However, time loss for unscheduled school closings, teacher and student absences, and disruptions results in the actual time for learning being significantly less than the official time. For example, in Haiti, the 1984 school year had 162 days, short by international standards of 180 days, but made significantly shorter by unofficial closings and delayed openings. The school day often began late; teachers frequently were absent on Tuesday and Friday market days; and forty-eight public holidays were celebrated, instead of the twenty-eight holidays built into the school year. The result was a functional school year of seventy days, 43 percent of the official year and 40 percent of the international standard. Another example is from Malawi, where the school year is 192 days, but one-third of these days are scheduled during the rainy season, when instruction is all but impossible during a rainstorm (the teacher cannot be heard above the noise of the rain on the school's tin roof) and roads are impassable, so many children do not go to school.

Teacher absences due to administrative procedures are also common in developing countries; for example, many teachers need to travel considerable distances to be paid, while others are assigned to teach long distances from their homes. Both situations can contribute to teacher absences. Teacher strikes in some countries also leave many schools not functioning; months of time can be lost, as in the case of Brazil in 1988. Teacher absences also result from maternity leave policies that do not provide for substitute teachers. For example, observers in Burundi noted that in one sixth-grade class, students had missed about two months of instruction when their teacher took maternity leave; a month passed before a substitute was placed in the classroom, and then the substitute soon became ill and left without further replacement (Eisemon and Schwille, 1991).

One observational study of instructional time in Indonesia examined national and local official time, as well as actual time; not only was the local official school

Table 2.4   National official, local official and actual instructional time in Indonesia, 1978, in hours per week

Grade	Hours		
	National	Local	Actual
1–2	26	13	9
3	33	22	n.a.
4–6	36	24	18

Source: Lockheed and Verspoor (1991)

week shorter than the national official school week, but the number of hours actually taught was significantly fewer than either (Table 2.4).

When the school day itself is shortened, as it typically is in a double-shift situation, instructional time is affected. A reduction in the length of the school day can have different effects on instructional time for particular subjects. At the one extreme, it can shorten instructional time in all subjects equally; one consequence of this approach is to reduce the hours of instruction in key subjects below acceptable norms. At the other extreme, retaining previous levels of instructional time in key subjects, such as reading or mathematics, could necessitate reducing or eliminating time allocated to other subjects, such as art, needlecraft or 'vocational' subjects. In Burundi, for example, reductions in total instructional time due to double shifting necessitated reducing the number of hours devoted to practical agriculture and home economics from four hours to one hour a week; 92 percent of instructional time at grade 6 was devoted to the four subjects examined in the secondary school entrance examination (Schwille, Eisemon and Prouty, 1989).

Effective Teaching

The role of teachers has long been recognized as central to the delivery as well as to the quality of education. It usually has been assumed that the academic and professional training of teachers has a direct and positive bearing on the quality of teaching performance and consequently on the achievement of students (Avalos and Haddad, 1981; Schiefelbein and Simmons, 1981). Effective teaching is determined by both subject matter knowledge and pedagogical skills.

Subject Matter Knowledge

Evidence from developed countries shows a strong positive effect of teachers' subject matter knowledge on student achievement. Only a few studies from developing countries have examined this question; however, the results are consistent (Fuller, 1987). For example, the English language proficiency of teachers in Uganda was found to have a positive effect on student achievement in both language and mathematics (Heyneman and Jamison, 1980). And teachers' achievement on a secondary school-leaving examination was correlated with their second-grade students' achievement in Iran (Ryan, 1972). Teachers' level of formal education is often used as an indicator of their subject matter knowledge. Although the impact of teachers' years of education on their students' performance is not consistent in all studies (Fuller, 1978), teachers with less than secondary education do appear to be less effective than those with complete secondary education. For example, in Pakistan, students of teachers with secondary education outperformed students of teachers with only primary education on tests of mathematics and science (McGinn, Warwick and Reimers, 1989).

Because of shortages of qualified personnel, in many countries 'non-qualified' persons are recruited as primary teachers (Dove, 1986). Such reduction in standards occurs most often in periods of rapid expansion of primary school capacity. The result is that teachers with incomplete secondary education often staff primary schools. For example, in Nepal a third of all teachers lack post-primary education, and in ten out of thirty-three Sub-Saharan African countries for which data are available, the majority of primary teachers lack complete secondary education. In Nigeria only five years of primary education were required for entry to teacher education in 1981; this was the lowest minimum educational requirement of all African countries at the time (Zymelman and DeStefano, 1988). Where teacher education requirements are low, many primary school teachers have a weak background in the subjects they are teaching, particularly in upper primary grades.

Teachers' Pedagogical Practices

Teaching is a complex enterprise and requires that teachers have command of a wide range of instructional strategies. These strategies include those for teaching specific subjects and those for managing the classroom. At a bare minimum, effective teaching involves (a) presenting material in a rational and orderly fashion at a pace appropriate to the students' age; (b) requiring active student participation; (c) providing students opportunities to practice and apply what they have learned, particularly in relationship to their own experience; (d) monitoring and evaluating student performance; and (e) giving appropriately paced feedback on student performance.

Active student participation. A variety of techniques can be used to generate active participation by students. One method found to be effective in preschool and the early grades of primary school is a carefully sequenced curriculum in which lessons are presented in small hierarchical steps, with teachers presenting a bit of information followed by children repeating the information and answering questions about the material; teachers give prompt feedback for student responses (Bereiter and Engelmann, 1966; Becker and Engelmann, 1978). For teaching some 'basic skills', e.g., multiplication tables, a drill-and-practice format may be effective; in other cases, teachers need to ask questions that stimulate students' thinking. The important thing is to use available classroom time as intensively as possible. Several studies that have examined the long-term effects of this type of systematic instruction have concluded that positive academic effects are retained through secondary school, with students achieving higher levels of academic performance, lower dropout and repetition, and greater probability of graduation than comparison groups of students taught with less active student participation (Stallings and Stipek, 1986). Young children, as well as older ones, need to practice comprehension and application; listening to stories and interpreting what has been read to them is also important.

In addition to basic skills, higher order skills need to be developed more intensively. For reading, this involves comprehension and application skills; in mathematics, it involves applying skills to new problems. To facilitate comprehension and knowledge acquisition, active student involvement is again essential and can be encouraged by asking students to think about the relationships between the text they are reading and their experience and knowledge (Wittrock, 1986). Research indicates that having children actively relate to the text sharply enhances their understanding of what they have read. For example, in one study of low-achieving Hawaiian primary school students, children were asked to state in their own words several events in their lives that related to stories read to them by their teachers. After one year of this type of instruction, children scored 40–60 percentile points higher in reading than control groups of students (Au, 1977).

Practice. Opportunities for students to rehearse what is taught are provided through such teaching practices as assigning individual worksheets (at home, in class, during a study hall), homework, or group work and discussion. Worksheets and homework are effective, but they require either additional materials or out-of-class time that may not be available. A more promising technique for developing countries is group work, principally due to its known cost-effectiveness. Small cooperative group learning involves four to six students working together on a learning task (such as a science project). The task can be divided so that each member works on a different part, or all members of the group can work on all parts of the task jointly. In formal evaluations of cooperative learning programs in developed countries, significant gains in achievement were observed for all group members, but particularly for initially low achieving students (Cohen, 1986; Sharan and Shachar, 1988; Slavin *et al.*, 1984). Recent research in the Philippines also found that group work led to higher levels of student achievement in science, with students in classes using group work outscoring students in ordinary classes by 57 percent (Lockheed, Fonacier and Bianchi, 1989). Cross-age peer tutoring, an instructional alternative that entails the use of older students as tutors of younger students, also increases student opportunities for practice; it has been found to be highly effective in developed countries and has been employed selectively in developing countries. For example, the Colombian Escuela Nueva claims to have adapted its group learning techniques from the schools of nineteenth century Lancaster, England. In experimental studies, overall learning gains were substantial for both tutors and tutees; cross-age peer tutoring has also been found to be one of the most cost-effective educational practices (Levin and Meister, 1986). In all cases, the students' active participation provides opportunities for them to relate to the material and to make conceptual sense of it.

Monitoring and evaluation. Teachers discover what students already know and what they still need to learn by monitoring student work through such means as essays, quizzes and tests, homework, classroom questions, and standardized tests.

They use student errors on tests and in class as early warning signals to point out and correct learning problems before they worsen. Studies demonstrating the effectiveness of monitoring and evaluating student performance are beginning to emerge from the developing country literature, and the results are consistently positive (Arriagada, 1981; Lockheed, Fonacier and Bianchi, 1989). For example, frequency of teacher evaluations (progress reports) was positively related to achievement in Colombia; teacher time spent correcting tests and exercises was related to achievement in Argentina and Colombia; teacher time spent discussing exercises was related to science achievement in Paraguay; teacher time spent monitoring and evaluating student performance was related to mathematics achievement in Swaziland. In the Philippines, students frequently tested in their classes outperformed students in conventional classes by one-quarter of a standard deviation. Monitoring performance at the classroom level is particularly important and should be distinguished from national programs of performance testing, particularly where the main objective is selection.

Feedback. Research from developed countries on the effects of classroom tests and quizzes indicates that their effectiveness is closely linked to the immediacy of the feedback provided to students. Students of teachers who provide immediate feedback on their quizzes outperform students whose teachers provide delayed feedback (Kulik and Kulik, 1988). Immediate feedback to students on their performance also enhances motivation.

Actual Teaching Practices

At present, much teaching in developing countries is characterized by teaching practices that are not conducive to student learning: (a) whole class instruction emphasizing teacher lectures, student copying from the blackboard, and few opportunities for students to ask questions or otherwise participate; (b) student memorization of texts with few opportunities to actively work with the material; and (c) little ongoing monitoring and assessment of student learning through homework, classroom quizzes or tests. While in US classrooms 40 percent of teacher time is devoted to lecturing and 19 percent to student participation (Pfau, 1980), active student participation is rarely encountered in classrooms in developing countries. For example, in Nepal, 78 percent of fifth-grade science instruction was lecturing and less than 7 percent was student participation (Pfau, 1980). In Thailand, 54 percent of fifth-grade mathematics instruction employed teacher lectures, explanations or demonstrations; another 30 percent of the time was spent on written seatwork; only 4 percent of the time was used for oral work of any kind, including discussion (Nitsaisook, cited in Avalos, 1986). In Botswana, 54 percent of the observed instructional time was spent with students listening to the teacher lecture, and another 43 percent of the time was spent in oral recitation (not to be confused with discussion) (Fuller and Snyder, 1989). In Jamaica, observers noted that 59 percent of classroom time was taken up by teacher talk, with teachers dominating the lessons and posing few 'open ended' questions (Jennings-Wray, 1984).

Group work, which encourages discussion, is rarely encountered. In Nepal, no group work was observed; in the Philippines, only 10 percent of fifth-grade science teachers reported using small groups for instruction (Lockheed, Fonacier and Bianchi, 1989). But group work is infrequent in the US as well, occurring only 10 percent of the time in fifth-grade classrooms (Lockheed and Harris, 1982). Classroom assessment is not prevalent in many developing countries. For example, in the Philippines, only 29 percent of fifth grade science teachers reported using tests frequently (Lockheed, Fonacier and Bianchi, 1989). In Nigeria, only 10 percent of primary school teachers used 'continuous assessment' techniques (Ali and Akubue, 1988), and in Botswana students were observed taking tests only 1 percent of the time (Fuller and Snyder, 1989).

The Consequences of Ineffective Primary Education

Although the objectives of primary education include developing the cognitive competencies of students, few schools in developing countries achieve this goal, largely because of the previously identified poor schooling conditions. As a result, there are three undesirable consequences: too few children complete primary school in developing countries; students who do complete school are often poorly educated; and, consequently, the adult labor force is uneducated.

Too Few Primary School Completers

Despite relatively high gross enrollment rates worldwide, including developing countries, fewer than 60 percent of those who enter school in the low income countries and only about 70 percent of those who enter school in the lower-middle income countries reach the terminal year of the primary cycle (Lockheed and Verspoor, 1991); moreover, primary school completion rates have declined over the past decade in the poorest countries. As a result, illiteracy remains widespread, and fewer than 30 percent of adults in the labor force have completed primary school.

Low completion rates result from high early dropout, which is related to poor academic achievement and high rates of repetition. On average, repetition rates in low and lower-middle income countries are two to five times higher than those in upper-middle and higher income countries, as indicated in Table 2.5.

Table 2.5   Median repetition rates, 1965–85, by GNP per capita of country

Country's GNP per capita	Year				
	1965	1970	1975	1980	1985
Low	21.7	20.9	17.0	15.6	16.3
Lower middle	19.0	15.8	11.4	11.7	10.6
Upper middle	10.3	11.4	9.3	6.5	7.5
High	0.0	1.6	2.5	2.0	1.5

Source: Lockheed and Verspoor (1991)

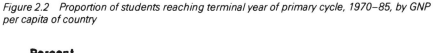

Figure 2.2   Proportion of students reaching terminal year of primary cycle, 1970–85, by GNP per capita of country

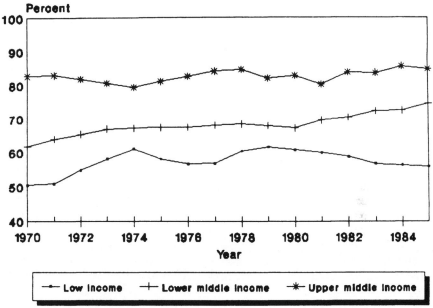

Source: Lockheed and Verspoor (1991)

The highest repetition rates are found in the lowest income countries. For example, of twelve countries reporting primary level repetition rates of 20 percent or more in 1985, 60 percent are low income countries.

Grade repetition is not equally likely at all grade levels. In some countries, nearly all students spend two years in first grade which leads to an over-representation of students in the first grade. For example, over 40 percent of all students enrolled in grades 1–5 in Ethiopia, Bhutan, Nepal, Bangladesh, Haiti, Chad, and Lao are enrolled in grade 1 (Lockheed and Verspoor, 1991). In many African countries, children also repeat the terminal year of primary school intentionally, in order to increase their preparation for the secondary level entrance examination.

Undereducated Primary School Completers

Second, even those who complete their education in developing countries typically have learned very little, with many students in low income countries failing to reach either national or international standards of cognitive performance in mathematics, science and reading comprehension. While national standards for subjects such as social studies (history, geography), morals or aesthetics will vary considerably from country to country, most countries — at least officially —

intend that the primary curriculum should impart lasting literacy and numeracy skills, as well as a general 'scientific' understanding of the world. Yet many children who are in the upper grades of elementary school in low and lower-middle income countries have not learned the skills expected by their national curriculum.

Since the early 1960s, the International Association for the Evaluation of Educational Achievement (IEA), a non-government organization of research institutions, has conducted studies of educational achievement in approximately 40 countries worldwide.[2] Results from these studies indicate that students in some low and lower-middle income countries have not learned as much of their national curriculum as expected. On tests of mathematics, reading and science — key areas of the primary school curriculum — students in developing countries have performed poorly, answering correctly only about 40 percent of the questions on the various tests (Table 2.6 presents average test scores for national random samples of students in countries participating in IEA studies.) In all cases, students were tested on a set of questions that reflected their own national curriculum, but were common to the curricula of all countries participating in the study. Thus, poor performance indicates that students were not reaching national (as well as international) standards for achievement.

The first IEA reading comprehension test was administered to sixth-grade students in nine industrialized and five developing countries; the median score across all countries was 68 percent correct. Heyneman (1980) reported that in three of the least developed countries, the scores were 34 percent (Malawi), 39 percent (Iran), and 53 percent (India). Similarly, in 1981, eighth-grade students from twenty-six industrialized and three developing countries took an IEA mathematics test with simple arithmetic problems as well as more complex problems using algebra (Livingstone, 1985). The median score across all countries was 50 percent correct for arithmetic and 43 percent correct for algebra. Students from the three developing countries solved 39 percent of the arithmetic problems and 31 percent of the algebra problems. In 1983, students in ten industrialized and six upper-middle income and two lower-middle income countries participated in a test of science achievement at the primary level (IEA, 1988). Across all eighteen countries, the median score for general science was 54 percent correct. Scores for upper-middle income countries ranged from 47 percent correct to 64 percent, roughly comparable to the range in scores for developed countries. Students in Nigeria and the Philippines, which were the only participating low or lower-middle income countries, performed less well (33 percent and 40 percent correct, respectively).

These country-level averages hide significant within-country variation between schools. For example, average science scores for public primary schools in the Philippines ranged from 17 percent to 88 percent correct, with average scores of sixty-seven schools (15 percent of those tested) exceeding the international median score (Lockheed, Fonacier and Bianchi, 1989). It is probably the case that in every developing country there are schools in which children complete primary education having mastered the skills targeted in the curriculum. However, not all differences between schools with respect to student achievement are due to the schools themselves. Some schools with good student performance in fact have recruited unusually talented students; many such schools are high quality private schools with students from families that can afford the

Table 2.6   Cross-national comparisons of achievement in mathematics, reading, and science

	Percentage of correct answers			
	Reading comprehension grade 6	Arithmetic grade 8	General science grade 6	General science grade 4–6
High Income				
Australia	—	—	—	54
Canada (Eng.)	—	56	—	57
Canada (Fr.)	—	—	—	60
Francophone Belgium	74	57	48	—
Flemish Belgium	65	58	53	—
England and Wales	71	48	56	49
Finland	74	46	57	64
France	—	58	—	—
Germany	—	—	51	—
Italy	65	—	55	56
Japan	—	60	61	64
Luxembourg	—	45	—	—
Netherlands	69	59	48	—
New Zealand	—	46	—	—
Norway	—	—	—	53
Scotland	70	50	51	—
Sweden	72	41	60	60
United States	67	51	61	55
Average	70	52	55	57
Upper-Middle Income				
Hong Kong	—	55	—	47
Hungary	70	57	53	60
Iran	39	—	32	—
Israel	—	50	—	50
Korea	—	—	—	64
Poland	—	—	—	50
Singapore	—	—	—	47
Average	55	54	43	53
Low and Lower-Middle Income				
Chile	61	—	36	—
India	53	—	36	—
Malawi	34	—	42	—
Nigeria	—	41	—	33
Philippines	—	—	—	40
Swaziland	—	32	—	—
Thailand	—	43	47	—
Average	49	39	40	36

Source: Lockheed and Verspoor (1991)

tuition (Jimenez, Lockheed, Luna and Paqueo, 1991). While there are good public schools, which teach children successfully under difficult conditions, in most developing countries there are simply too few such schools. The result is that many students in developing countries do not acquire sufficient numeracy and literacy skills needed for functioning effectively in their own society. Particularly

Marlaine E. Lockheed

Table 2.7   Mean years of education by age group, for 65 countries, by GNP per capita, 1980

GNP per capita	Age			
	15–19	25–29	35–39	45–49
Low	2.4	2.9	2.3	1.7
Lower middle	5.5	4.8	3.7	2.7
Upper middle	8.5	9.0	7.8	6.9
High	9.4	10.1	9.0	8.0

Source: Lockheed and Verspoor (1991)

weak is reading *comprehension*, which is a necessary skill. When education does not produce literacy sufficient to understand such written material as directions on commercial fertilizers or pesticides, serious environmental and health dangers may result (Eisemon, 1988).

Uneducated Adult Labor Force

Because of low participation rates and high rates of repetition and dropout, which lead to low rates of primary level completion, those presently constituting the adult labor force in developing countries have obtained very few years of formal education (Table 2.7). The average adult 15 years and older in low income countries has completed fewer than three years of formal education, which is inadequate for acquiring sustained literacy and numeracy (Horn and Arriagada, 1986). As a result, the vast majority of the adult labor force in developing countries is unprepared to respond to technological change, whether in techniques for subsistence farming, industrial production, or communications.

Few Scientists and Engineers

The adult labor force of most developing countries consists predominantly of subsistence farmers. Few adults work in the formal labor sector, and of those who do, fewer have high level skills, particularly in areas such as science and engineering. Countries with a greater number of scientists and engineers, especially if they are involved in research and development, have a much greater possibility of adapting and developing new technologies (Rosenberg, 1982). Indeed, the countries that have shown the greatest advances in technology creation and adoption in recent years are those with the highest ratios of scientists and engineers. As indicated in Figure 2.3, low and middle income countries produce relatively few scientists and engineers. These countries need to develop the scientific personnel who will understand fully the latest technological advances coming out of the industrialized countries and be able to adapt and apply them for local production of goods and services.

The consequences of poor education are clear. The challenge is to change the conditions of learning from those that inhibit achievement to those that accelerate achievement. It can be done. Schools throughout the developing world have been

Figure 2.3   Scientists and engineers in research per 100,000 inhabitants, by GNP per capita

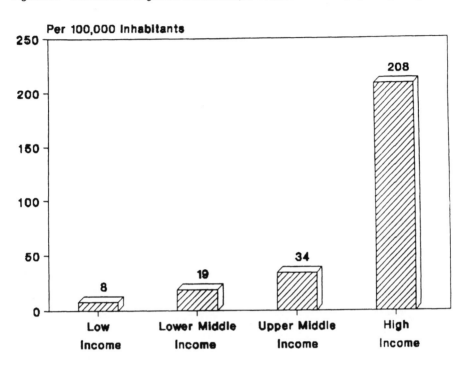

Per 100,000 Inhabitants

Source: Lockheed and Verspoor (1991)

effective in enhancing children's learning. The process undoubtedly requires additional resources, but the gains can outweigh the costs (Harbison and Hanushek, 1992). The challenge is to concentrate on children's learning as a reachable goal.

Notes

1 'Learning time' is used here to mean the number of actual student–teacher contact hours; 'time on task,' which includes an element of student motivation, is included in learning time.
2 IEA achievement tests, specifically developed for cross-national comparisons, examine the extent to which students have learned an agreed-upon curriculum; they also examine the degree to which the curriculum is taught.

References

ALI, A. and AKUBUE, A. (1988) 'Nigerian primary schools' compliance with Nigeria national policy on education: An evaluation of continuous assessment practices', *Evaluation Review*, **12**, 6, pp. 625–37.

ALTBACH, P. (1983) 'Key issues of textbook provision in the Third World', *Prospects: Quarterly Review of Education*, **13**, 3, pp. 315–25.

Marlaine E. Lockheed

ARMITAGE, J., BAUTISTA-NETO, J., HARBISON, R., HOLSINGER, D.B. and LEITE, R. (1986) *School Quality and Achievement in Rural Brazil*, Washington, DC, World Bank, Education and Training Discussion Paper EDT 25 (updated tables).

ARRIAGADA, A.M. (1981) *Determinants of Sixth Grade Student Achievement in Colombia*, Washington, DC, World Bank, Education Department (processed).

AU, K. (1977) *Cognitive Training and Reading Achievement*, paper presented at the meeting of the Association for the Advancement of Behavioral Therapy, Atlanta, Georgia.

AVALOS, B. (1986) *Teacher Effectiveness: An Old Theme with New Questions*, paper presented at International Movement Toward Educational Change (IMTEC) Seminar on the Quality of Teaching in Lesser Developed Countries, Bali, Indonesia.

AVALOS, B. and HADDAD, W. (1981) *A Review of Teacher Effectiveness Research in Africa, Latin America, Middle East, Malaysia, Philippines and Thailand: A Synthesis of Results*, Ottawa, International Development Research Centre (IDRC).

BAKER, V. (1988) *Blackboard in the Jungle: Formal Education in Disadvantaged Rural Areas, A Sri Lankan Case*, Delft, The Netherlands, Eburon.

BECKER, W.C. and ENGELMANN, S. (1978) *Analysis of Achievement Data on Six Cohorts of Low-Income Children from 20 School Districts in the University of Oregon Direct Instruction Follow Through Model* (Technical Report T8-1), Eugene, Oreg., University of Oregon, Follow Through Program.

BENAVOT, A. and KAMENS, D. (1989) *The Curricular Content of Primary Education in Developing Countries*, Washington, DC, World Bank, PPR Working Paper No. 237.

BEREITER, C. and ENGELMANN, S. (1966) *Teaching Disadvantaged Children in the Preschool*, Englewood Cliffs, NJ, Prentice-Hall.

BIANCHI, P., CARNOY, M. and CASTELLS, M. (1988) *Economic Reform and Technology Transfer in China*, Stanford, Calif., Stanford University, Center for Educational Research at Stanford (CERAS).

BOTSWANA MINISTRY OF FINANCE AND DEVELOPMENT PLANNING (1984) *Botswana Education and Human Resources Sector Assessment*, Washington, DC, USAID.

BROWN, B.W. and SAKS, D.H. (1987) 'The microeconomics of the allocation of teachers' time and student learning', *Economics of Education Review*, **6**, 4, pp. 319–22.

COHEN, E. (1986) *Designing Groupwork*, New York, Teacher's College Press.

COPE, J., DENNING, C. and RIBEIRO, L. (1989) *Content Analysis of Reading and Mathematics Textbooks in Fifteen Developing Countries*, London, Book Development Council (processed).

DOVE, L. (1986) *Teachers and Teacher Education in Developing Countries*, London, Croom Helm.

EISEMON, T.O. (1988) *Benefiting from Basic Education, School Quality and Functional Literacy in Kenya* (Comparative and International Education Series, Vol. 2), Oxford, Pergamon.

EISEMON, T.O. and SCHWILLE, J. (1991) 'Should schools prepare students for secondary education or for self employment? Addressing a dilemma of primary schooling in Burundi and Kenya', *Elementary School Journal*, **92**, pp. 23–39.

FRASER, B.J., WALBERG, H.J., WELCH, W.W. and HATTIE, J.A. (1987) 'Syntheses of educational productivity research', *International Journal of Educational Research*, **11**, 2, pp. 145–252.

FULLER, B. (1987) 'Raising school quality in developing countries: What investments boost learning?', *Review of Educational Research*, **57**, 3, pp. 255–92.

FULLER, B. and SNYDER, C. Jr. (1989) *Vocal Teachers, Silent Pupils? Life in Botswana Classrooms*, paper presented at the annual meeting of the Comparative and International Education Society, Boston, Massachusetts.

GOVERNMENT OF PAKISTAN (1983) *Draft Comprehensive Report: Primary Education Report*, Islamabad, Pakistan.

HARBISON, R. and HANUSHEK, E. (1992) *Educational Performance of the Poor: Lessons from Rural Northeast Brazil*, New York: Oxford University Press.

HARTLEY, M. and SWANSON, E. (1984) *Achievement and wastage: An analysis of the retention of basic skills in primary education*, Washington, DC, World Bank RPO (Processed).

HEYNEMAN, S. and JAMISON, D.T. (1980) 'Student learning in Uganda: Textbook availability and other factors', *Comparative Education Review*, **24**, 2, pp. 206–20.

HEYNEMAN, S. (1980) *The Evaluation of Human Capital in Malawi*, Washington, DC, World Bank, PPR Working Paper No. 420.

HEYNEMAN, S., FARRELL, J. and SEPULVEDA-STUARDO, M. (1981) 'Textbooks and achievement in developing countries: What we know', *Journal of Curriculum Studies*, **13**, 3, pp. 227–46.

HEYNEMAN, S. and LOXLEY, W. (1983) 'The effect of primary-school quality on academic achievement across twenty-nine high- and low-income countries', *The American Journal of Sociology*, **88**, 6, pp. 1162–94.

HEYNEMAN, S., JAMISON, D.T. and MONTENEGRO, X. (1984) 'Textbooks in the Philippines: Evaluation of the pedagogical impact of a nationwide investment', *Educational Evaluation and Policy Analysis*, **6**, 2, pp. 139–50.

HORN, R. and ARRIAGADA, A.M. (1986) *The Educational Attainment of the World's Population: Three Decades of Progress*, Washington, DC, World Bank, Education and Training Discussion Paper EDT 37.

HUSEN, T., SAHA, L.T. and NOONAN, R. (1978) *Teacher Training and Student Achievement in Less Developed Countries*, Washington, DC, World Bank, Staff Working Paper No. 310.

INTERNATIONAL ASSOCIATION FOR THE EVALUATION EDUCATIONAL ACHIEVEMENT (IEA) (1988) *Science Achievement in Seventeen Countries. A Preliminary Report*, Oxford, Pergamon.

JAMISON, D.T., SEARLE, B., GALDA, K. and HEYNEMAN, S. (1981) 'Improving elementary mathematics education in Nicaragua: An experimental study of the impact of textbooks and radio on achievement', *Journal of Educational Psychology*, **73**, 4, pp. 556–67.

JENNINGS-WRAY, Z.D. (1984) 'Implementing the "integrated approach to learning": Implications for integration of the curricula of primary schools in the Caribbean', *International Journal of Educational Development*, **4**, pp. 265–78.

JIMENEZ, E., LOCKHEED, M., LUNA, E. and PAQUEO, V. (1991) 'School effects and costs for private and public schools in the Dominican Republic', *International Journal of Educational Research*, **15**, 5, pp. 393–410.

KOMENAN, A. (1987) *World Education Indicators*, Washington, DC, World Bank, Education and Training Discussion Paper EDT 88.

KULIK, J. and KULIK, C.L. (1988) 'Timing of feedback and verbal learning', *Review of Educational Research*, **58**, 1, pp. 79–97.

LEVIN, H. and MEISTER, G. (1986) 'Is CAI cost-effective?', *Phi Delta Kappan*, **67**, 10, pp. 745–49.

LIVINGSTONE, I. (1985) *Perceptions of the Intended and Implemented Mathematics Curriculum*, International Association for the Evaluation of Educational Achievement (IEA).

LOCKHEED, M., FONACIER, J. and BIANCHI, L. (1989) *Effective Primary Level Science Teaching in the Philippines*, Washington, DC, World Bank, PPR Working Paper WPS 208.

LOCKHEED, M. and HARRIS, A.M. (1982), 'Classroom interaction and opportunities for cross-sex peer learning in science', *Journal of Early Adolescence*, **2**, 2, pp. 135–43.

LOCKHEED, M. and KOMENAN, A. (1989) 'Teaching quality and school effects on student achievement in Africa: The case of Nigeria and Swaziland', *Teaching and Teacher Education*, **5**, 2, pp. 93–113.

LOCKHEED, M. and VERSPOOR, A.M., with BLOCH, D., ENGLEBERT, P., FULLER, B., KING, E., MIDDLETON, J., PAQUEO, V., RODD, A., ROMAIN, R. and WELMOND, M. (1991) *Improving Primary Education in Developing Countries*, New York, Oxford University Press.

LUNA, E. and GONZALES, S. (1986) *The Underdevelopment of Mathematics Achievement: Comparison of Public and Private Schools in the Dominican Republic*, Santiago, Centro de Investigaciones UCMM (processed).

McGINN, N., WARWICK, D. and REIMERS, F. (1989) *Policy choices to improve school effectiveness in Pakistan*, paper presented at the VII World Congress of Comparative Education, Montreal, Canada.

MUNDANGEPFUPFU, M. (1988) *School Quality and Efficiency in Malawi*, report of the pilot of the primary school quality survey, Lilongwe, Malawi, Ministry of Education and Culture.

OGUNDARE, S.F. (1988) 'Curriculum development: A description of the development of the national curriculum for primary social studies in Nigeria', *Educational Studies*, **14**, 1, pp. 43–50.

PAXMAN, B., DENNING, C. and READ, A. (1989) *Analysis of Research on Textbook Availability and Quality in Developing Countries*, London, Book Development Council (processed).

PFAU, R. (1980) 'The comparative study of classroom behaviors', *Comparative Education Review*, **24**, 3, pp. 400–14.

ROSENBERG, N. (1982) *Inside the Black Box: Technology and Economics*. Cambridge, England, Cambridge University Press.

RYAN, J.W. (1972) *Educational Resources and Scholastic Outcomes: A study of rural primary schooling in Iran*, doctoral dissertation, Stanford University, Stanford, California.

SCHIEFELBEIN, E. and SIMMONS, J. (1981) *Determinants of School Achievement: A Review of Research for Developing Countries*, Ottawa, International Development Research Centre (IDRC).

SCHWILLE, J., EISEMON, T.O. and PROUTY, R. (1989) *Between policy and students: The reach of implementation in Burundian primary schools*, BRIDGES Project Paper presented at the Annual Meeting of the Comparative and International Education Society, Boston, Massachusetts.

SHAEFFER, S. (1979) *Schooling in a Developing Society: A Case Study of Indonesian Primary Education*, doctoral dissertation, Stanford University, Stanford, California.

SHARAN, S. and SHACHAR, H. (1988) *Language and Learning in the Cooperative Classroom*, New York, Springer-Verlag.

SLAVIN, S., LEAVEY, M.B. and MADDEN, N.A. (1984) 'Combining cooperative learning and individualized instruction: Effects on student mathematics achievement, attitudes, and behaviors', *Elementary School Journal*, **84**, 4, pp. 409–22.

STALLINGS, J. and STIPEK, D. (1986) 'Research on early childhood and elementary school teaching programs', in WITTROCK, M.C. (Ed.) *Handbook of Research on Teaching*, New York, Macmillan.

SURYADI, A., GREEN, M. and WINDHAM, D. (1981) *Teacher Quality as a Determinant of Differential Mathematics Performance Among Poor Rural Children in Indonesian Junior Secondary Schools* (processed).

WITTROCK, M.C. (1986) 'Students' thought processes', in WITTROCK M.C. (Ed.) *Handbook of Research on Teaching*, New York, Macmillan.

ZYMELMAN, A. and DeSTEFANO, J. (1988) *Teacher Salaries in Sub-Saharan Africa*, Washington, DC, World Bank Discussion Paper No. 45.

Chapter 3

How Can Schooling Help Improve the Lives of the Poorest? The Need for Radical Reform

Nicholas Bennett

Raising world consumption to US levels would multiply the combustion of fossil fuels fifty times, the use of iron a hundred times, the use of other metals two hundred times. By the time these levels are reached the standards in the US would again have tripled, and the population would also have tripled. Such projections lead to results as absurd as the premises from which they come.

Everett Reimer

Those who work with their minds rule, those who work with their hands are ruled.

Mao Tse Tung

I hear and I forget, I see and I remember, I do and I understand.

Mencius

Politicians, educational administrators, and aid bureaucrats the world over express shock and dismay over the low intake of poor children from remote rural areas and urban slums by schools and over the high dropout rates of these children from the early grades. In one developing country after another, intake and enrollment rates have stopped expanding and begun to stagnate or even fall. This decline has been most rapid among the poor in the most backward and disadvantaged areas. Analysts bemoan the decreasing average unit costs, the high proportion of 'unqualified' teachers, and the lack of even basic textbooks. They suggest that if resources could be increased, or training expanded, or textbooks provided, all would be well in the kingdom of the school. Those of us who have spent time in backward and resource poor areas realize that these might be necessary conditions for effective education, but they are certainly not sufficient conditions.

We all carry our own philosophical baggage, our own view of what kind of development is possible and desirable, and our own ideas of what role education and schooling should play in this development. Some feel that one of the prime functions of schooling is to make children literate, even though in many parts of the world there is nothing to read and no reason to write. But would we teach people to swim who live in a desert? Others believe that schooling is justified as it opens the minds of children to the modern world — a modern world in which the majority will inevitably remain on the periphery. Still others feel that schooling provides some equality of opportunity to enter the secure, the salaried, the governing positions in a society, even though research shows that this equality of opportunity has never existed.

In my view, the function of the school is to provide children with the knowledge, skills, and attitudes that will enable them to cope more effectively with the environment in which they will find themselves when they leave school. Schooling can play a role in teaching literacy, but can only do this if the environment can be literalized at the same time. Schooling is useful if it opens children's eyes to a wider world, but not if it makes them neglect the world of their parents and the world where they are destined to live. Schooling can help some children attain élite positions in society, but it will do more harm than good if it gives children the idea that they are failures and destroys their pride in their community and culture.

We talk about a school system as if it were a uniform system with a uniform product. But there are many of us who, in visiting schools, have spent a morning basking in the sunshine of a middle-class school — with neat well-fed children in white socks, well-equipped classrooms, lively teachers, and an active Parent-Teacher Association. And in the afternoon, a mile or so away, we are horrified to see pot-bellied dirty children, crouched in the warmest corner of a damp hovel; surrounded by scraps of paper and a tired teacher. Both are financed by the same government, a part of the same system.

We all are aware that throughout the world the school system is a loaded lottery. Even if equivalent resources were available for educating the rich and the poor, because the media, the content and the evaluation processes are more attuned to the middle class, such children inevitably perform better than the economically disadvantaged in this lottery. In the real world, however, more and better public resources are available for the education of the rich than of the poor.

In every third world country where I have worked, there is a dualistic society. The middle class and those who aspire to the middle class have a certain view of the world and aspirations based on those of the developed, materialistic West. The poor have values and aspirations closer to the traditional society. This dualism is most apparent in ex-colonial countries where the élite aspires to a nuclear family, a car, a large concrete house and a three-piece suit; to hospital treatment, to a university education, and even to a foreign language. Quite obviously, however, there is no way in which the mass of the population will be able to achieve this Western-oriented lifestyle in their lives or even in the lifetimes of their children or grandchildren. Thus, current school systems in developing countries, which are almost always cheap carbon copies of Western systems with their hidden middle-class curricula, tend to alienate the disadvantaged even further from their own roots and from their potential for self-created social and economic advancement.

In the school system of virtually all developing countries, the Western middle-class value orientation is obvious. In first grade in Thailand, 'Ama took an apple to school', even though the only apples were expensive Australian imports in Bangkok; in higher primary grades, telephones were used in educational materials. In Nepal, 'Sushilla took a bus to the zoo' in fifth grade, even though 60 percent of the children living in the mountains had never seen a wheel (one child, when asked, said 'a bus is a kind of porter'). In Cote d'Ivoire, primary texts are full of French markets and 'my time in Paris'. Such curricula can only alienate the majority of children, who do not come from middle-class families, from their culture and communities. In the most pernicious cases, where schooling is in a foreign language, children are alienated from their very roots.

Perhaps even more serious in any attempt to achieve the fantasy of equality is the lack of effort on the part of the curriculum developer to take account of the learning achievements of the disadvantaged. In Nepal, for example, it is assumed that children who enter primary school have a familiarity with the alphabet. In Ghana, because of automatic promotion, there are many schools where not one sixth grade student can even read 'BAD', let alone the texts which are similar in complexity to those found in British schools. In a hill tribe area in Northern Thailand, I have visited a school where most children could mouth the text, but not understand a single word.

It is not only the curriculum developer who fails to recognize the realities of his or her own society and culture, but also the educational administrator. In most third world countries there is a uniform school year. It is typically in tune with the school year in a metropolitan Western country and thus takes no account of the demand for the child's labor in peak farming seasons, which obviously differs from region to region. An extreme case is Cote d'Ivoire, which has not only a long vacation in synchrony with that in France, but also a $2\frac{1}{2}$ hour lunch break, despite the distance of children's homes from school. It is not surprising that most children from disadvantaged areas have far fewer contact hours than the administration assumes. For example, in Nepal, the official school year is 220 days, but all rural and poorer urban schools close at the slightest excuse; few are open more than 140 days. Because few children manage to attend for more than half this time due to their economic and family responsibilities — the opportunity cost of attending school is very high for these children — actual time spent in school by the rural child is only one-third of the norm. Further, since teachers in remote rural areas are frequently absent from their classrooms, instructional time for the disadvantaged is even more severely limited.

Even the location of the school is selected for the convenience not of the child but of the bureaucrat — close to a road, but distant from the nearest village. In towns as well, schools typically are not located in the slums where the poor live; supervisors do not want to go to these areas. Since the children of the disadvantaged have to spend a long time travelling to and from school, the opportunity cost of schooling is increased.

A few decades ago in developing countries children who completed school usually managed to find paid employment. This was a benefit that most parents could understand. But now children who have completed secondary education, or even the university, cannot find jobs. This situation, combined with the fact that many young people who pass through school shun farming or other manual work, convinces parents that there is little point in sending their children to school. In an extreme case in Northern Thailand, parents have even been known to move their houses so that they no longer fall within a compulsory education area.

In Ghana 70 percent of adults are illiterate; in Nepal the figure is around 80 percent. How can one expect that these illiterate parents will be active in the management of their children's schools, and an effective pressure group to ensure that adequate resources are provided for children's schooling? Without pressure, it is unrealistic to assume that resources will be shifted from the schools serving more affluent groups to those serving the poor. Thus, it is likely that the current imbalance will continue, with governments giving the better schools allocations of up to ten times the amount they give to some schools in poor rural areas.

From a political standpoint, it can be difficult to establish a special program, or even a single special school, to provide an effective education to deprived children. Because one of the stated functions of the school is to promote national unity, any departure from the national curriculum tends to be highly suspect. Moreover, one of the unstated functions of the school is to maintain the existing socio-economic order. Consequently, attempts of teachers to be involved with their students in larger local issues can lead to serious consequences. I have known several teachers in Thailand who have been driven out of the profession, or even killed, for such political activity. Thus, it is necessary to tackle the system as a whole rather than trying to take on the problems of individual schools.

From this long litany of problems and constraints, it initially might seem impossible to provide any meaningful education for the poor. But the very fact that the system is so rife with problems and so blatantly inefficient has brought the political leadership in country after country to recognize the necessity of reform. It has been possible to convince political leaders that a system that takes six or more years to make only a small proportion of children numerate and literate, and little else, must be extremely inefficient and wasteful and must be reformed. Within the framework of such reforms it is possible to design a system in which middle-class children improve their performance in literacy and numeracy skills, while at the same time the poor are able to gain essential life skills from their time in school.

Three Movements of Education Reform

Over the past twenty years I have been involved in three major education reform movements: (1) the reform of the school system with associated non-formal education in Thailand throughout the 1970s; (2) the education for rural development program in the Seti Zone in the far West of Nepal during the first half of the 1980s; and (3) the ongoing education reform movement in Ghana. The three movements have at least four elements in common. First, they all assumed that to achieve effective education of children, parents must be motivated and involved. In the Thai and Nepali programs, adult functional literacy, combined with a literalization of the environment, was an integral element; in Ghana, community participation was key. Second, each of the three movements was convinced that in order to break down the barrier between society and the school, at least in the early years, the maternal language must be the medium of instruction. Third, all three attempted to make schooling more relevant and more useful to the future life of children in differing socio-economic environments. Finally, all the movements were designed to improve pedagogic efficiency without increasing costs.

Thailand

The catalyst for the Thai reforms was the development of a functional adult literacy program with a problem-solving orientation. Despite the fact that from 1960

Thailand had a national enrollment rate in primary school of over 93 percent of the age group, in 1970 at least 28 percent of the adult population were not functionally literate. Illiteracy was particularly high in the poverty-stricken North-east of the country (bordering Laos and Kampuchea), among the non-Thai speaking hill tribes (bordering Laos and Burma), among urban slum dwellers, and among Malay-speaking southerners. Most of these groups were regarded as posing a security threat to the government.

To prepare functional literacy materials, a process was developed involving villagers in different parts of the country. First, key problems were identified, their causes analyzed, and possible solutions identified. Each problem became one sheet of a loose-leaf primer, each sheet illustrated on one side, with a key word or slogan, and on the other side a short text. This loose-leaf approach had the advantage of flexibility since different sheets could be used in different parts of the country; it also motivated participants to attend each class to obtain the next sheet. A lesson included intense discussion around the picture, reading of the text, and practice in writing and calculation related to the text. Each class met at a convenient place in the village for three hours in the evening five days a week, at a time selected by the participants, thus keeping the opportunity cost to the adult as low as possible.

With this approach, extraordinary results were achieved. A substantial level of literacy was achieved within six months, and within a year participants were able to pass the primary school grade 4 examination that was the key to many doors in the society, such as obtaining a government job or a driving license. Literacy was also maintained through the establishment of Village Reading Centers wherever classes were held. So successful was the program that it was extended (with far less functional content) to the end of high school. Non-formal participants were able to graduate with a certificate equivalent to grade 12 through only six years of study, three hours each evening for five days a week. The success of this program led to a very critical analysis of the way primary and secondary school children had been taught, and resulted in a major curriculum reform of the entire school system. The motto of the reform was 'Teach children, don't teach books'.

Perhaps the key element of this reform was to break away from the past system in which children from first grade were taught a plethora of different academic subjects. This subject-based curriculum created a discontinuity between life at home, which centered around the family and community, and life in school, which was divided into a drop of Thai, a drop of mathematics, a drop of social studies, and other compartmentalized subjects. In the reform, the teaching of separate subjects was largely discarded during the first four years of schooling. Instead, when a child entered school, the first term was spent on studying 'myself' integrating language, math, health and hygiene, nutrition, and other areas. Next came 'my family', 'my school', 'my community', 'my district', and by the end of fourth grade, 'my nation'. These integrated themes, of course, had to be supplemented by drills in Thai and math. Since something was learned every day, even those children who dropped out after a year or two benefited from their time in school. In addition, the community was expected to provide local skilled craftsmen or progressive farmers as volunteer teachers to discuss and demonstrate their occupation and skills at their respective places of work.

The textbook was no longer the main teaching material; instead, a series of teachers' guides, supplementary readers, and kits for practical work became paramount. The reform was introduced with a massive training program for administrators, educators, and teachers, and with a grouping or clustering of schools for further training and support. Children actually began to enjoy their schooling, to take pride in their communities, and to learn skills useful in their lives. Much to the surprise of middle-class citizens, who had looked on this reform with much trepidation, Thai and mathematics scores were higher with this new system than with the old, despite reduced instructional time focused explicitly on those areas. Even more importantly, scores in the impoverished North-east of the country improved significantly.

This reform did not help much in increasing access of the poor to higher levels of schooling, but it did help ensure that many of the rural poor gained more from their time in school than previously had been the case. There still remained parts of the country where there was no schooling, or no effective schooling — in the Islamic South, in the hill tribe areas, and among urban slum dwellers. Different approaches were used for each of these groups, with varying degrees of success.

In the Islamic areas in the South, Government agreed to support the Koranic schools that existed in most communities, as long as the communities accepted that at least half the day would be devoted to the national curriculum, suitably adapted to include gradual introduction of the Thai language. This offer was combined with a massive functional literacy campaign using the same loose-leaf conscienticization approach discussed above, which started in Malay and gradually moved into Thai. The approach was successful in bringing Thais into the mainstream of national life and helped eliminate a separatist insurgency. It was much harder to provide any effective education for the hill tribes since neither the children nor the adults were motivated to spend time in formal learning. They had always felt exploited by the Thais and lived a partially nomadic existence, involved in shifting cultivation, often of opium.

After some study, it was determined that what these hill people wanted was medicines to cure their common illnesses. To meet this need, functional literacy teachers were trained in primary health care, as well as the culture and language of the tribes; each was provided with a kit of basic pharmaceuticals and sent to live in a particular village. Gradually, the teachers became accepted by the villagers and started to run functional literacy classes for the village children and, as soon as possible, for the adults. Again, the flexible loose-leaf materials were used, starting in the local language and leading into Thai. These functional education/health centers were grouped around a hill tribe development center, which not only offered more sophisticated health care, but also provided a special school designed to prepare a few graduates from each village center for eventual entry into secondary schools. This program has had mixed success, but at least large numbers of tribes people now are more able to cope with their Thai neighbors than they were a decade ago.

It has been most difficult to provide effective education for urban slum children or their parents. There was little sense of community, massive social problems, and a much greater need to make money immediately in any way, than was the case in the rural areas. It was only through the efforts of a few highly dedicated social workers, who have touched the hearts of the élite, that any progress has been made. Progress usually has been achieved through outside inputs and influences, and, while cognitive skills have been taught, most children have not gained life skills to help them cope with their difficult surroundings.

What lessons can be learned from this process of reforming the education system so that the majority of Thais received a reasonably effective basic education? First, we can see that such a systematic reform takes many years before results are achieved. It took nine years from first conception just to transform the curriculum in four grades of primary school, and a further five or six years to spread these same new ideas to peripheral groups. Second, it was essential that school and non-formal reform programs progressed in tandem. Third, it was essential to design a uniform system and structure that also allowed for a great deal of flexibility and differentiation. Fourth, it was important to build the reformed system around the local community, culture, religion, language, and perceived needs of the people, and to integrate school and community. Fifth, as it is only primary schooling that all Thais can aspire to, it was necessary to design the primary school curriculum as terminal, and to build the curriculum of the higher levels on whatever knowledge and skills the primary graduate had gained. Finally, and perhaps most important of all, a strong political will to bring all citizens into the mainstream of society and development activity was essential. In Thailand, this political support was prompted by a desire to reduce the recruiting ground for communist insurgents.

Nepal

The Education for Rural Development in the Seti Zone project was designed around two facts: first, most development projects in that remote area had failed; and, second, the inhabitants of the far West would be unable in the foreseeable future to enter the mainstream of the Nepali economy and unable to compete effectively in the formal school system. The measure of effective education in such an area is not what children or adults learn, but what use they make of this learning in taking action to change the physical environment and reducing their suffering.

The project area was in the foothills of the Himalayas. It was not served by any roads, and the thousand or so villages could be reached only after days of arduous mountain trekking from the nearest airstrip or roadhead. It was a permanent food deficit area, with the rivers washing the fertile topsoil to the Terrai (plains) and on to India, and the people following. There were few households without at least one male member working in India, providing the only source of cash income for the family. It was a disaster-prone area with earthquakes, droughts and floods. Tuberculosis, goitre and intestinal parasites were endemic. The caste system was still in force, and women were valued little more than cattle.

At the start of the project, the school system was in a state of profound crisis and extreme inefficiency. Some children, largely upper-caste boys, were taught to read and write. Since the written word had no place in village life, many lapsed back into illiteracy shortly after leaving school. English was supposed to be taught from grade 4, though most teachers themselves could not speak a word of English. Science was taught as facts to be memorized rather than a way of thinking. Teaching of other subjects was similar; lessons were memorized only to be reproduced — often without understanding — in examinations.

Student attendance was very low and did not average more than fifty to sixty days throughout the year. There was a high rate of dropout: it was not uncommon to find about fifty students in grade 1, fifteen or so in grade 2, and only six or seven in grades 3, 4, and 5. Most village teachers took on teaching only as a part-time occupation, with farming or trading as their primary activity, and about 30 percent actually were absent on a given day. Few ever prepared a lesson; even trained teachers did not generally seem to use any teaching method other than reading from the textbook. School buildings were often little better than cow sheds, without furniture or any amenities. The only educational materials seen were textbooks. Usually, the school was built in an isolated place, on the top of a hill, far from the village. There was very little community participation in the affairs of the school, except for initial construction of the building. Visits by district supervisors were years apart.

Though the school system in the Seti Zone did not seem to be fulfilling any useful purpose, it had a far greater potential for promoting rural development than any other governmental system. There were ten times as many teachers actually living in the villages as all other government employees combined. Teachers could be retrained as community organizers and instructors in functional literacy, and each could learn a developmental skill, such as primary health care or agriculture. If this could be achieved and the focus could be shifted from trying to provide children with academic knowledge to creating opportunities for practical application, then schools could play a significant role in the transformation of the area.

It was possible to produce such a transformation partly because the area was far from the concerns of Kathmandu bureaucrats. One could tamper with the traditional role of the school without undue administrative interference. Moreover, many of the most serious problems could be solved with a minimum of external inputs. For example, if compost pits could be made, more of a better quality manure would be produced and crop yield increased. If latrines were built and used, intestinal problems could be reduced significantly. If fruit trees and vegetables were planted and the produce eaten, nutritional standards would improve. And if for every tree cut down, two were planted, the problem of fuel scarcities and soil erosion could be mitigated.

The first activity undertaken by the project was to carry out baseline research in the project area. What do the rural people learn traditionally, how, and when? What knowledge, attitudes, and practices exist among the villagers? What do teachers actually do, and what are they capable of doing? And, finally, what was the location and number of schools, teachers and students in the project area?

From this baseline research a whole series of new curriculum materials were developed by project staff living and working with villagers. Loose-leaf functional literacy materials for adults were designed to promote literacy, and the villagers were involved in twenty different development actions in 130 part-time (usually evening) study sessions. Loose-leaf functional literacy materials were developed around the life of one fictional village girl who performed all her normal daily functions, but each in a slightly improved way. Designed for out-of-school girls, these materials sought to promote literacy and pride and to involve the girls in fifteen different development actions in 150 early morning study sessions. Entertaining supplementary readers with development messages were prepared for village reading centers, along with wall newspapers. A series of highly intensive training programs for different categories of teachers were developed. These programs were residential, with teachers living and working together in resources centers, and ran from 8 a.m. to 10 a.m., seven days a week. The programs varied in length: twenty-one days for primary school teachers, thirty-five days for adult education teachers, thirty-five days for rural women who would run the program for out-of-school girls, ten days for teachers in primary health care, and ten months to train a cadre of teachers imbued with the project philosophy and skilled in community organizing, adult education, primary health care, and agriculture.

The three project districts were divided into thirty-five areas each centered around a resource center that became the core for training, supervision, distribution of materials and demonstration of new ideas. Forest and fruit tree nurseries were started, along with vegetable seed gardens. Designs were prepared for school buildings, smokeless cooking stoves, latrines, and protected springs, none of which required inputs that were not available locally. In every activity, the program strictly adhered to a principle of payment by results, and to a principle of only helping those who helped themselves. For example, adult teachers were rewarded only if evidence of the physical transformation of the village could be seen; and villagers constructing a school would be rewarded only after a certain stage of building was completed to an acceptable standard.

As of a year ago when I last visited the program, it was still having a highly positive impact on the socio-economic situation in the Seti Zone and could demonstrate visible progress in most of the immediate tasks that it had set itself. A total of thirty-five schools were functioning as resource centers serving the surrounding village schools, and training of teachers in supervision, teaching methods and development skills was in full swing. Around 100 new schools had been built, many equipped with compound walls (which allow fruit trees and vegetables to be grown) and piped water. Village reading centers and latrines have been constructed by villagers; medicines have been distributed, together with leaflets explaining the origin and cure of the most common diseases; and supplementary reading materials for students and adults have been produced. Thousands of adults have passed through literacy programs, and thousands of poor village girls have been given something beyond a life of suffering and drudgery. The diet is changing with the introduction of fruit and vegetables, and the incidence of intestinal parasites and scabies has been reduced. Most important of all, the people have been given hope — hope that by their own efforts they can create a better life for themselves.

In thinking back on the radical reform, which only affected one region of the country, it seems there are at least eleven steps that contributed to success:

- forming a team of highly dedicated technicians who were prepared (for relatively high rates of pay) to spend many years of their lives living and working with the poor;
- making the rural educational system more efficient and effective through turning key schools into resource centers which have supervised, trained, and improved the surrounding satellite schools;
- focusing all education resources and personnel on basic education;

- making the school itself both a demonstration center for development activities and a resource center to provide useful services, such as health care, to the local people;
- retraining the teachers in developmental as well as teaching skills and, in so doing, creating an *esprit de corps;*
- ensuring that the environment in every place any class was held was 'literalized', with the opening of a village reading center;
- reducing dramatically the content that was taught to children and adults, so that what was taught could be absorbed and applied;
- making it a rule never to be prescriptive in teaching, but rather to let adults and children discover their own problems and solutions;
- providing schools and non-formal groups with small but significant development inputs, such as seeds, fruit trees, water pipes, and medicines;
- paying teachers and other personnel only by results; and, most importantly,
- ensuring that the educational process would teach concepts not just theoretically but always through practical application as well.

In discussing an evaluation of the project, I wrote some time ago:

> We will not concern ourselves with what people have learned, or what they have memorized, or even with what certificate they have gained. What we will be concerned with in this final evaluation is the extent to which our project has affected the rural environment and the extent to which this can be done at a cost that can be borne by the Government in the longer run. If trees are planted, vegetables grown, toilets built, villages cleaned, health improved, new income sources developed, etc., and all these are achieved at a relatively low unit cost, then our project can be considered a success. If, however, we just make large numbers of people literate (without them using their literacy skills), increase enrollments in schools, reduce dropouts, without having any impact in rural environment, or on rural development, our project can be considered a failure.

Ghana

The educational reforms that have recently been launched in Ghana aim to ensure a much wider access to a more useful basic education, more rooted in the national culture. Of greatest significance to the theme of this book is the attempt to ensure a significant shift in educational resources provided by government from the rich to the poor and the attempt in basic education to ensure that children develop a manual as well as a mental literacy. Though it is still far too early to evaluate the impact of these reforms, they have resulted in a dramatic increase of more than 10 percent growth per annum in primary school intakes during the first two years of program implementation.

What is most interesting, however, is the strategy being used in implementation. The reform program was elaborated in 1973 and accepted as government policy in 1976. Because the middle class and élite groups were monopolizing both a large proportion of governmental resources for education, as well as most of the places in the higher echelons of the existing school system, there was strong opposition to the reform program. This opposition was so persistent that implementation was always postponed for one reason or another. Government thus decided to introduce the new system in 1987 without having prepared adequately for its implementation. This was a conscious decision to defeat the opponents of reform, with the strategy being to implement the new structure on a nationwide scale and solve the problems afterward. The strategy has succeeded, and the new system is in place, a system that puts a premium on practical skills and the expansion of effective access. Modifications are now taking place, and these are being followed by the launching of a massive action-oriented literacy program, which is drawing its inspiration from the experiences of school systems.

Conclusions

Perhaps only two conclusions can be drawn from these three examples. The first is that the political dimensions are crucial in any attempt to provide effective education for the disadvantaged. In almost every society it is the middle class who reap the greatest benefits from schooling, and consume the largest share of governmental educational resources. Many different technical solutions are possible, but only in a supportive political atmosphere can those technical solutions be put into practice. In Thailand, the key was the desire to remove the threat of communist insurgency. In Nepal, the far West was an area where most projects in the past had failed, and thus the Government was prepared to try almost anything. In Ghana, the Government's need to show that it truly was concerned with improving the life of the rural and urban masses (and not just in fulfilling IMF/World Bank macro-economic conditionalities) provided the opportunities to implement a reform that had been identified and approved more than a decade before. If we are to provide effective schooling for poor and disadvantaged children, we must first show how this advances the political interests of those with power, or at the very least, how it benefits at least one powerful group.

The second general conclusion is that once the political will is mobilized, there must be a radical reform, for radical reform is what is needed. The needs of the disadvantaged cannot be met merely by providing a watered-down version of schooling originally designed for the middle class. New curricula, new structures and new systems are needed, designed around the current problems of the poor and the skills and attitudes they will need to cope with their future lives. Any program that really serves the needs of the poor must challenge many of the sacred tenets of the school. Why should schooling be a full-time activity stretching over many years? Why are professional teachers and a school building required? Why should academic, theoretical subjects be taught, and why should teaching of the poor be directed at exams in which they will never really excel? Let us not forget that we want to educate the poor, not so that they will pass exams and eventually fail at higher levels, but so they gain skills, knowledge, attitudes and practices useful for their lives. This is the challenge we face.

Chapter 4

The New School Program: More and Better Primary Education for Children in Rural Areas in Colombia*

Vicky Colbert, Clemencia Chiappe and Jairo Arboleda

Introduction

For the first time, Colombia is in a position to comply with the Article of its Constitution which guarantees a primary education to all citizens. The country now has the technical, political and financial conditions necessary to universalize primary education, particularly in rural areas where low coverage and inefficiency of the system have persisted over decades.

In effect, the *technical conditions* are guaranteed in the New School ('Escuela Nueva') program designed and tested during a fourteen-year period and already implemented in 17,000 schools throughout the country, reaching more than 900, 000 children. The current government policies provided the necessary *political conditions*. The *financial conditions* have been created through the allocation of government resources, a loan from the World Bank, and the cooperation of UNICEF, all contributing to maintaining the quality of the New School program as it goes to full scale.

The first section of this chapter summarizes the background of the New School program, the context of rural education in Colombia in terms of qualitative and quantitative conditions, and previous efforts to provide better opportunities for schooling of rural children. The second section describes the components of the New School program, the innovations devised to go to scale and its evolutionary process. The third section discusses major evaluation results, the responsiveness of the system to Rural Primary Education, the value of the New School in the international context, and lessons for educational planners.

* The core of this article is based on three previous documents: V. Colbert and O. Mogollon (1977); V. Colbert (1987); and V. Colbert and J. Arboleda (1989). Clemencia Chiappe contributed ideas, especially in relation to lessons for planners. We also want to acknowledge the contributions of the following members of the Central Team of the New School: Oscar Mogollón, Hernando Gelvez, Pedro Pablo Ramírez, Luz Nelly Vásquez, and Heriberto Castro.

The Context of Rural Education in Colombia

Colombia experienced an accelerated expansion in primary education beginning in 1950. As a result, overall coverage rose to 92.8 percent by 1975 and has now stabilized, with 4,160,000 children currently enrolled in primary education. However, the distribution of this coverage reveals sharp differences between the various regions of the country and between urban and rural zones. In effect, it averages 81 percent in the rural areas and drops to levels between 60 and 72 percent in six of Colombia's thirty-three provinces (Ministry of Education, 1985).

At the beginning of the 1980s, the overall student retention at the primary level was 62 percent, but in the rural sector it was lower. During the period from 1968 to 1985, only one of every five children entering the first grade completed all five years of primary education.

Students in rural Colombia have 1.7 years of schooling on the average, while the average level of schooling in the urban sector is 3.8 years. In general terms, this puts rural children within the range of functional illiteracy. Promotion rates are also unsatisfactory, particularly with respect to transition from first to second grade. In 1985, this figure was 65 percent in the urban zone and just 45 percent in the rural areas. The highest repetition rates are also observed in these two grades: 17 percent in the urban zone and 20 percent in the rural zone. In short, the rural area is still behind the urban sector in access, success and achievement in primary schooling.

In addition, the qualitative deficiencies of the traditional rural education system include: greater use of passive pedagogical methods; use of urban-biased curricula that are inappropriate for rural children; lack of special training in multigrade techniques even though the majority of teachers must handle more than one grade; lack of educational materials to support learning processes for both teachers and students; rigidity of calendar and schedules; lack of parental and community involvement; and failure of the school to provide leadership within the community.

In view of these problems, Colombia appears to have a long way to go before it can meet the proposed goal of providing all five years of primary education to the entire school age population.

Previous Efforts: The Unitary School (1961–1974)

Many Third World countries with situations similar to that of Colombia have tried the Unitary School methodology to address the problems noted above. The Unitary School, promoted by UNESCO in 1961 in a meeting of Ministries of Education in Geneva, has the following characteristics. It is designed to permit the school to operate with only one teacher; instructional cards permit the teacher to work with several groups at once. Active learning enables children to advance at their own pace, and promotion is automatic. Complete primary education is provided where there is a demand for it. The Unitary School program is appropriate for areas with low population density. This approach differs from that of traditional schools where the most frequently used methods are memorization, copying lessons from the blackboard, and repetition in unison.

As a result of the Geneva meeting, Colombia began to develop a Unitary

School program under the guidance of UNESCO experts. In effect, the first demonstration of a unitary rural school for primary education was organized at the Instituto Superior de Educacion Rural (Institute of Rural Education) in Pamplona, Norte de Santander, under UNESCO Project 1 for Primary Educacion. The objective was to train teachers and supervisors in the Unitary School methodology.

In 1967, the Colombian government issued a decree promoting the Unitary School approach in all schools with one teacher, especially in the sparsely populated zones. To implement this legislation the Departments of Education in the provinces were required to train rural school teachers in this methodology. From this point to 1974, different innovations in relation to the unitary school took place in the country, some emphasizing individualized instruction, others non-formal community based adult education.

By the mid-1970s, the national scenario of the unitary school was characterized by different approaches and views on the problems of the rural school, each responding to different aspects of the problem. Consequently, it was difficult to reach consensus on a nationwide strategy, and universalization fell short.

The New School Program of the Colombian Ministry of Education

The New School program was organized in 1975 as a response to the persistent problems of the rural education in Colombia, which the Unitary School approach had attempted to address.

Definition and Assumptions

The New School is a system of primary education that integrates curricular, community, administrative-financial and training strategies. The program is designed to make it possible to provide complete primary education and to improve the effectiveness of the nation's rural schools.

Essentially, this system provides active instruction, a stronger relationship between the school and the community, and a flexible promotion mechanism adapted to the lifestyle of the rural child. Flexible promotion allows students to advance from one grade or level to another at their own pace. In addition, children can leave school temporarily to help their parents in agricultural activities, in case of illness, or for any other valid reason, without jeopardizing the chance of returning to school and continuing with their education.

The New School program started with two fundamental assumptions. The first was that improving educational effectiveness would require creative changes in the training of teachers, in the administrative structure, and in relations with the community. Accordingly, the program offers an integral response by developing four major components — curriculum, training, administration, and relationship to the community — and features concrete strategies for children, teachers, administrative agents and the community.

Second, the program assumes that it is essential from the outset to develop mechanisms that are replicable, decentralized, and viable technically, politically, and financially. In other words, the design of the system must include plans for going to scale.

Program Components and Objectives

This section presents for each component the technical innovations required to achieve the program objectives for children, teachers, administrative agents and the community as a whole.

Curriculum component. This component promotes active and reflective learning, the ability to think, analyze, investigate, create, apply knowledge and improve children's self-esteem. It incorporates a flexible promotion system and seeks to develop children's cooperation, comradeship, solidarity and civic, participatory and democratic attitudes. The New School curriculum emphasizes social relevance and inductive, concrete, active learning experiences for children.

The curricular elements that embody the New School approach are: study guides for children, a school library with basic reference material, activity or learning centers, and the organization of a school government. Each of these interrelated elements of the curriculum is described below.

Study guides. Study guides are self-instructional materials for children from grades 2 to 5 in four basic areas (natural science, mathematics, social studies, and language). The guides follow a methodology that promotes active learning, cognitive abilities, discussion, group decision making, and the development of application skills within the environment in order to create a viable link between the school and the community.[1]

Study guides contain a sequence of objectives and activities to be developed at the learning pace of the students; in this way, flexible promotion is developed. This objective replaces the idea of 'repeating a grade' and gives educational planners a valuable alternative for lowering school dropout and repetition rates. This concept of flexibly paced learning that is adapted to the child is a highly important learning variable in this model.

Study guides are designed to combine individual student work with group efforts. In the group interactions, children develop analytical skills and participate in decision making. The guides are organized sequentially and in such a way that they can be 'readily taught' by less qualified teachers or extended by more skilled teachers (Neumann, 1980).

Another important characteristic of the study guides is that they combine a core national curriculum with possibilities for regional and local adaptations made by the teachers during the training courses. The study guides can be produced at a national level, which considerably reduces printing costs, while the regional and local materials that are developed can be produced with simpler and less expensive technologies.

Adoption of self-instructional guides is a recognition of the need to assist teachers who have to handle more than one grade at a time. With textbooks or learning materials that are not self-instructional, it is extremely difficult for a teacher to support several groups of children in each grade. The study guides, are used by groups of two or three children, to encourage group work processes. In addition to having pedagogical advantages, this scheme is affordable. Another important feature of the guides is that they support the teacher's planning process of class activities and this is specially required for a teacher that has to work simultaneously with various class levels.

Learning activity centers. Learning activity centers, organized in the four basic curricular areas (mathematics, natural science, social studies, and language), contain materials to be elaborated by the children and/or objects from the community. The study guides direct children to specific activities and to observation and manipulation of concrete objects; the learning centers complement the study guides and support the designed activities, offering development. These centers also strengthen students' knowledge and appreciation of cultural elements of their community.

School government. The school government is an organization where children can be introduced to civic and democratic way of life. Children are organized in committees, and they learn group decision making, responsibility, and attitudes of solidarity, comradeship and cooperation. These school committees can be linked to community groups and projects. The school government is an essential element of the curriculum that facilitates social-affective and moral development and links the school with family and community.

School library. The school library is organized with general reference material, dictionaries, textbooks for curricular areas, children's literature, and books on rural community development topics. Complementing the study guides and learning centers, the library is essential for providing active learning and 'learning to learn' attitudes. Children learn to organize their library. A library committee of the school government is in charge of lending the books and taking care of them. Activities are organized throughout the school year to promote the school library as a center for cultural participation of the community.

Providing one library per school, with approximately 100 volumes, costing only US$225, is practical and financially feasible for the Government, which can acquire textbooks already available through private publishing companies. The New School materials and strategy, emphasizing study guides and libraries, have given the Colombian Government a tool for furnishing rural schools with educational materials published by the nation, as well as texts acquired from the private sector.

Teacher training and follow-up component. This component promotes in teachers a guiding and orienting role as opposed to one involving a mere transmission of knowledge. It also encourages a positive attitude towards new ways of working in rural education, the acceptance of the teacher's role as a leader and dynamic force in the community, a positive attitude towards the administrative agents and towards technical assistance.

Teachers are trained to handle adequately the New School curriculum elements described above. Moreover, they are taught to adapt the schedule or timetable to suit the requirements of flexible promotion, to adapt the guides to the child's level and environment, and to handle several grades at once.

This training and follow-up for teachers and administrative agents involve active in-service training workshops as opposed to informative courses. Group discussion motivating teachers to change and strengthening their commitment to the proposed changes is the key to promoting positive attitudes towards the New School program. Group discussion experiences in teacher training programs also help teachers to work with small groups in their own classrooms. This approach to teacher training is based on the conviction that if teachers are to develop classrooms in which children's learning is active, discovery-oriented, tied to the community, cooperative and creative, then the process of training teachers must have similar characteristics. Consequently, teacher training materials use an approach and process similar to those in the children's study guides.

The workshops are organized using the teacher's training manual *Hacia la Escuela Nueva* (Colbert and Mogollon, 1977) and designed so that the administrative agents work with the teachers, who in turn work with the children and apply the same active process they learned in the training workshop. These characteristics make training easily replicable. The training strategy also establishes a sequence that permits gradual innovation and corresponding changes of attitude in children, teachers, administrative agents and the community. Furthermore, training and implementation are interrelated. In effect, training consists of learning how to implement the program. Therefore, each component of the process has its own operative instruments to facilitate application.

A series of four basic workshops, one for administrative agents and three for teachers, over a year's time, are essential for correct implementation of the New School methodology. The procedure and sequence utilized for training teachers is described below.

Workshop for regional administrative agents. The workshop for the administrative agents — departmental supervisors, directors of school clusters (*nucleos*),[2] and the basic team of multiplier agents — has the following objectives: to develop the abilities to guide the application of New School techniques; to develop the abilities to follow up the classroom implementation of the program; and to modify the administrator's traditional roles so that he/she carries out the orientation function and serves as the teachers' immediate resource person with respect to the learning process. The administrative agents, in turn, present a similar workshop for the rural teachers.

Initiation workshops for teachers. The objectives of the eight-day initiation for teachers include: to develop teachers' abilities in applying the basic concepts and methodological principles of the New School; to develop the capacity to adapt the school to the effective use of small groups and activity centers; to mobilize the human and material resources of the community for the improvement of the school; and to gain an understanding of how to organize the school government to promote children's social-affective development.

Given the fact that the program encourages a relationship between the school and the community for mutual enrichment, it is expected that the teacher will create an adequate climate for innovation among community members before introducing changes in the school. Equally, the teacher is encouraged to stimulate children and community members to gather useful basic information about the community in order to increase the understanding of its history and its place in the immediate socio-economic environment and beyond. In this way, the school can become a source of basic information on the community to be used for the benefit of other institutions.

For each objective a unit was designed for the Teacher's Training Manual. The units include: 'The New School: The School and the Community', 'The Local Building', 'Learning Centers and Other Materials for the Learning Process in the Classroom', 'The School Government', and 'Methods of Group Work'. These units consist of various specific objectives developed through formative guides that follow a similar methodology to that used by children. This way the teachers approach the learning processes by doing and experimenting active learning themselves.

Workshop on the use and adaptation of children's study guides. This workshop takes place once the school is organized and the community has been informed and mobilized. It serves as a delivery system through which the Government provides free of charge a set of children's materials for each school. Two or three sets of materials, depending on the number of children, are given to each teacher during this event.

In the workshop teachers study the children's materials, learn to use them correctly, learn to use them with a multi-grade approach and flexible promotion mechanism, and introduce local innovations and adaptations. The 'open-ended' nature of the guides permits flexibility for local initiatives. In fact, this workshop is designed to provide the opportunity for planning the use of classroom units in a flexible manner, adapted to local and children's needs.

Workshop on organization of the school library. The objective of this workshop is to learn how to organize and use the school library in order to facilitate the active learning of the New School approach. As with the guides, the teachers receive the basic library of 100 titles at the end of the workshops.

Workshops for local follow-up. After each of the three different workshops, teachers have the opportunity to meet monthly to exchange ideas, analyze problems and discuss results. During the initial phase of the project, these workshops were coordinated by the supervisors of the New School, who had been previously trained to become multiplier agents. Each supervisor organized the teachers in his/her zone and performed a follow-up on those activities of the longer workshop that had been left to be implemented at the school and community levels.

These local follow-up workshops developed gradually based on demand and acceptance of the program in the different regions of the country. Once the program was adopted as the National Strategy to Universalize Primary Education in rural areas in Colombia in 1985, the local non-formal workshops acquired a more regular and systematic character and received the denomination of 'micro-centers' (Mogollon, 1986).

Demonstrative schools and micro-centers. Over time, a formal visit to a school that was a good example of the New School program became part of the initiation workshop. The formal visit to these 'demonstrative schools', characterized for their effectiveness in the application of the methodology and their operation as effective community centers, became a vital part of the training process. These visits motivated the teachers to apply what was learned in the workshops.

The demonstrative school became a complement to the training process and a way to ensure the quality of the model in the process of expansion. In the expansion phase, the micro-center became a participatory experience where teachers could evaluate, create, enrich their own experiences, innovate, criticize, analyze, and carry out projects for the improvement of the school and the community.

At present, these demonstrative schools and micro-centers are indispensable elements of a training strategy that has gone to scale and needs to maintain the correct implementation and educational effectiveness achieved through the original New School model and methodological principles. These elements have helped to develop and maintain an ongoing horizontal training network where problems can be analyzed and solved, thus providing continuous feedback to the system. This approach represents a decentralized, in-service, low-cost mechanism to maintain quality in the process of going to scale.

In summary, the training strategy gives the teachers the opportunity to implement and apply in their school and community what they learn during each workshop. As noted above, the training strategy establishes a sequence that permits gradual innovations, and it does not separate training from implementation. Rather, training consists in learning how to implement the program.

Finally, it will be useful to point out how the new approach differs from the traditional approach, particularly since past studies have tended to suggest that teacher training has little impact on student learning. Unlike many training programs, New School training focuses directly on encouraging teachers to adopt and initiate innovations; the training process consists of becoming familiar with the components of the new methodology and applying them in a real situation. This emphasis on application is new. In the traditional Colombian system, teachers' training typically involves theoretical courses on different areas of primary education.

The community component. This component encourages the mobilization of parents and community members for involvement in school activities. Some of these activities include becoming familiar with the new educational approach, helping to gather simple information on the community, improving the physical space, furnishing the classrooms, and helping to organize the library or the activity centers.

The program gives teachers the guidelines to prepare a community map, a family information register, a calendar of agricultural events, and various social and cultural monographs to increase the knowledge of the community. This is the first step toward a process of community development and is essential whether or not the teacher lives in the community. Thus, the school can become a source of basic information on the community to be used for the benefit of other institutions.

In addition, the written materials used by the students include topics relating to the community, which encourages children to apply what they learn in their everyday lives and to promote activities that contribute to overall community improvement. For example, the materials and activity centers give students experiences with cultural elements representative of the region (proverbs, folksongs, myths, legends, tales), and contribute to a cultural revitalization process (Ministry of Education, 1990a). The fact that children participate in health, sanitation, and nutrition activities with their parents and younger siblings also facilitates child-to-child interactions (Ministry of Education, 1990b).

In short, the community component of the curriculum promotes cooperation of parents with school activities, increases their satisfaction with the new system, and makes the school an integrating force in the community.

Administrative component. This component promotes a view of educational administration focused on orienting rather than controlling. Therefore, administrative agents are required to integrate pedagogical practices with their administrative functions. In this way, each agent can become an immediate resource person and technical support for teachers. It is assumed that if administrative agents adequately implement the practices of the new approach, their traditional role will be modified. Their ability to orient and organize teacher training processes and strategies will promote positive attitudes toward working with teachers and with the New School system.

The organizational structure of the New School program is as follows. At the national level a coordinator and a core group are in charge of designing the basic policies and technical strategies of the program as well as promoting, supervising and evaluating the correct implementation of all four components.

At the departmental (i.e., state) level there was a New School Committee and a team of multipliers (e.g., teacher trainers and supervisors). The Committee was formed by top managers of the Departmental Secretariat of Education, a delegate from the central Ministry for Finance Matters (Fondo Educativo Regional), the manager of the Departmental Training and Curriculum Center (Centro Experimental Piloto), and the Departmental Coordinator for the New School. The main role of this Committee was to plan the expansion of the program, especially the teacher training and implementation of schools. The implementation of this plan and its adaptation to the Department was the responsibility of the Coordinator and his team of multipliers. Furthermore, the administrative agents (rural primary supervisors), once trained, replicated the training with teachers and provided local follow-up through monthly workshops.

In the process of expansion from 1987, the administrative component has experienced several changes resulting from changes in the general structure of the educational sector. Some of these changes will be discussed in the next section.

Evolution of the New School Program: Stages in Going to Scale

The New School program went through three steps: local and departmental innovation, national implementation of the program, and universal application in all rural schools. These three stages, by and large, correspond to the approach of going to scale by expansion, one of the three approaches proposed by David Korten (1980) and discussed by Robert Myers (1984) in relation to education programs. The approach of expansion consists of three stages: learning to be effective, learning to be efficient, and learning to expand.

Learning to be Effective the first stage, occurred with the support of the Agency for International Development (AID) and consisted of the implementation of 500 schools in three regions: Norte de Santander, Boyaca, and Cundinamarca. During the period from 1975 to 1978, there was 'an acceptable level of fit between the beneficiaries (children, teachers, parents) and the working program model and the capabilities of the team' (Myers, 1984, p. 12). This stage included the design and production of materials for teachers and children; planning and implementation of the program, including administrative and financial organization in the departments; training and follow-up strategy for administrative agents and teachers; organization of delivery systems, reproduction and distribution of materials; implementation in the school and the community; and initial evaluation of the program.

Learning to be Efficient the second stage, from 1979 to 1986, took the program to 3,000 schools with the financial support of the Department, the Interamerican Development Bank, and private organizations of Colombia, such as the Coffee Growers' Federation and the Foundation for Higher Education (FES). This second stage, *learning to be efficient*, included replication of training at the national level and the use of teachers' manuals and children's study guides that had already been designed, thus reducing the input requirements per unit of output.

During this time the program produced a second and third version of children's materials and systematized training and financial processes. Furthermore, at the national level a core team was institutionalized within the Ministry of Education. At the department level, the organization of the program took place with a representative committee, a coordinator and a multiplier team.

During this stage the Development Plan started with resources provided by the World Bank. At the time the initiative was known in Colombia as the Plan to Develop Education in the rural areas and small-scale population centers (Ministry of Education, 1982). The Plan intended the expansion of the New School methodology and support to physical improvements of the schools, including rebuilding classrooms and providing safe drinking water, sanitary units and classroom furniture.

The World Bank project also resulted in two decisive initiatives with respect to the future of the New School. The first initiative concerned the need to calculate unitary costs per student and per school, and to conduct a detailed diagnosis of needs for a sampling of rural schools in Colombia. This information was used to develop a set of indicators that served to estimate the cost of applying the New School model throughout the country.

The inventory of needs with respect to these items was used to establish indicators that reflected the amount of service required in comparison with the total number of schools under consideration. For example, the indicator relating the number of required sanitary units to the total number of schools assessed was 0.51; in other words, in the expansion of the investment project one sanitary unit would be needed for approximately every two schools. The cost structure for the curriculum and training was determined on the basis of one teacher manual per teacher, one library per school, one set of self-instructional guides for three children, and the series of three training events. The experience of previous implementations was the main basis for determining the cost factors.

The present costs are as follows: average training cost per teacher in a year is US$82; the average school library US$150; in 1989, the cost of supplying one student with study guides for four subjects per grade level came to US$15. Actually, costs per student are reduced to a fourth of this amount because the same set of materials is used at the school during a four-year period.

Average cost per school was calculated by comparing the indicators with tables of unit costs for each of the services. This calculation not only facilitated adequate budgetary planning for schools included in the development plan, but also contributed to a well founded estimate of the investment needed to equip rural primary schools adequately throughout Colombia as part of a second national investment project.

The second initiative was a study of the educational sector designed to arrive at a medium-term policy proposal (Ministry of Education, 1988). A group of Colombian researchers took part in the study, which was spearheaded by the Planning Office of the Ministry of Education and directed by a noted Colombian researcher. This group included experts in educational administration and planning, educational economists and teachers; representatives of the National Planning Department and the Finance Ministry were also involved. Because these people were involved, the findings and policy proposals coming out of the study were discussed and accepted by a group of individuals with considerable potential for circulating the conclusions and outcome of this effort. The study concluded:

> The share corresponding to primary education declined continuously as of 1975, although the budgetary allocation increased slightly in real terms. Accordingly, attention to the population still denied access to primary education, which is found in rural zones and the less developed provinces, must involve a conscious effort that reverses the budgetary tendency of the last 10 years. Part of the problem is the difficulty of servicing the rural sector by increasing the number of classrooms and teachers, without a change in methods (Ministry of Education, 1988, p. 60).

A consensus was gradually developed with respect to policy priorities in the educational sector. This consensus eventually led to a landmark policy decision by the Government in 1985 to adopt the New School program as the strategy to universalize rural primary schooling in Colombia. By this time, the program had expanded to 8,000 schools throughout the country with a combination of financial resources from the national and departmental governments and from private institutions.

Learning to Expand the third stage of implementation, started in 1987 and continues today. The target is 27,000 rural schools by 1992. The 1985 government decision to promote this educational strategy was carried on to the new Administration in 1986. The New School became a top priority of the sector, one of the five pillars of the Government's plan to eradicate severe poverty.

In the process of expansion where an organizational capacity (rather than program) had to be built, a Universalization Plan was designed and put into action. Two new structures emerged: a Universalization Committee at the national and departmental levels and the school clusters (nucleos educativos). The objective of these mechanisms was to promote decentralization and institutional support.

However, the Universalization Committee became a superstructure to national and departmental levels, controlling the financial resources of the New School program. As a result of this, the Universalization Committee began to make decisions about the program based primarily on quantitative and financial concerns without sufficient consultation with the core technical team of the New School, both at the national and departmental levels.

In addition, the unevenness in the timing of developing school clusters created special situations for the core team of the program. Where implementation was rapid, the increased number of administrative agents created demand for training that exceeded the capacity of the New School program to respond. Where organization of the clusters did not take place or developed very slowly, there was inefficiency and uncertainty with respect to expansion and follow-up activities.

The implementation process was distorted when the number of days for the key training workshops was reduced or when study guides could not be delivered on time to be used in training. When these things happened, they weakened the experiential learning of the training approach and implementation, discouraged the teachers, and caused criticism of the program.

In Korten's model, learning to expand to the 27,000 rural schools requires constant attention to ensure an acceptable level of fit among organization, program and beneficiaries. But the numerous problems that emerge in implementation result in losses of effectiveness and efficiency. To a greater or lesser degree, this kind of reduction in effectiveness and efficiency is inevitable in going to scale.

However, organizational capabilities can be developed to help preserve the quality of the model. In effect, UNICEF's cooperation is intended to support new materials, training and follow-up activities, and to strengthen the managerial capacity of the New School administrative staff. This qualitative support is timely now that the country is engaged in a political and administrative decentralization process in which the municipality becomes the basic cell of a new social fabric. Such effort is essential to ensure the quality of the model, as it goes to full scale in the universalization of primary schooling in rural areas in Colombia.

Evaluation and Concerns for Replication

Evaluation of the Program

The impact of the program is now becoming evident, particularly when New Schools are compared with traditional ones. The growing demand for implementation of the New School system and the positive reaction of teachers, administrative agents, and communities participating in the program are the best indication of success.

Formative evaluations have been conducted at student and teacher levels at different periods of time. For example, it was found that the level of creativity among students of New Schools where a teacher is responsible for several grade levels does not differ significantly from rural schools where there is a teacher assigned to each grade (Rodriguez, 1978).

Children in the New School program were found to have a much higher level of self-esteem than those enrolled in rural schools where there is a teacher for each grade. The fact that self-esteem of girls equalled that of boys is particularly important; more participatory classrooms appear to help girls' self-esteem.

Complete schooling has been observed in schools implementing the program. The most recent evaluation done by Instituto SER indicates that 89.3 percent of teachers believed that the New School is superior to other traditional rural schools (Rojas and Castillo, 1988). In tests on socio-civic behavior, self-esteem, and selected subjects (mathematics for third grade and Spanish for third and fifth grades), New School children scored considerably higher than those in traditional rural schools.

Responsiveness of the System to Rural Primary Education

The New School responds to the needs of rural primary education in Colombia in the following ways:

- It offers a multi-grade approach that permits provision of complete primary schooling where incomplete schooling exists.
- With a multi-grade approach, one or two teachers can handle all five grades simultaneously.
- It reaches children, teachers, administrative agents and communities through its four interrelated components: curriculum, training, administration and community processes.
- The learning strategies help children develop their capacity to be active, creative, participatory and responsible. The program encourages their ability to think, create, analyze, and especially to apply in their communities what they learn.
- Through the school government, children learn civic and democratic attitudes and develop habits of cooperation, comradeship, solidarity, and participation. They learn to act with responsibility in the organization and administration of the school.
- Children work in small groups using self-instruction study guides and a small library furnished by the Government. The design of the study guide takes into consideration the learning pace of each child. The classroom is a dynamic work area with the library and learning centers supporting the activities developed by children and community.
- There is no grade repetition; promotion to the next objective or grade is progressive and flexible. Children can study and continue helping their parents at home. In this way, learning is recognized not simply as years of schooling but as the basis for applying within the community what is learned in school; the link is strengthened between basic education and individual and societal development.
- Materials are affordable, because one set is for two or three children, and each set lasts for several years. The materials include a core national curriculum with possibilities for local adaptation, and they also include individual and group work. The materials link the school with the community and integrate cognitive and social development.
- The program provides for a community library with a basic set of reference materials and approximately 100 books.
- The objectives and themes of the workbooks deal with the lives of children and their communities. These materials develop an essential set of

basic skills, attitudes, values and knowledge so that children continue to learn and to apply what they have learned in the community. For example, in relation to health and nutrition, the program covers child survival topics, and it is expected that children will communicate the information to parents and other adults in the community and contribute to their siblings' survival and development.

- The school operates as the center of information and as an integrating force for the community. Parents participate in school activities and school promotes actions that benefit the community.
- Teachers are facilitators; they guide, orient and evaluate learning. They are trained in workshops that follow methodologies similar to those they will later apply in working with their pupils.
- The in-service training of teachers is local, replicable and permanent. The follow-up to the training takes place through rural micro-centers in which groups of teachers interact and exchange the fruits of their teaching experience.

The New School in the International Context

Delegations from more than 15 countries from Latin America and Africa have come to study the New School program. Based on evaluations of New School teaching materials and classroom visits, UNESCO (1986) states that the program's 'achievements are of a very high level in absolute terms and constitute an experience of unquestionable international value'.

UNICEF and non-governmental organizations like Save the Children Federation are promoting the introduction of the strategies of the New School program to other countries in Latin America and the Caribbean. The New School program was presented in the World Conference Education for All as one of two roundtable sessions from Latin America.

Lessons for Educational Planners

Throughout the chapter, comments have been made with important implications for educational planners. In this final section, we list a series of factors for success in large-scale programs, identified in papers by David Korten (1980), Samuel Paul (1982), and David Pyle (1984), and applicable to the New School. Among the important factors for success that have been noted are these:

- Funds were always available for the larger effort.
- The political commitment was present.
- The demonstration model worked well in various regions simultaneously.
- The 'mystique' associated with the original project continued as the program grew.
- The charismatic, dedicated leadership that accounted for the small scale success was expanded.
- Appropriate administrative methods were in place.
- Information about the results of the pilot project was timely and appropriate for the people who counted.

- The transition from project to program was associated with a learning process in which errors were admitted, people participated in the planning and there was a clear link between knowledge-building and action.
- The roles of researchers, planners and administrators were combined in a well coordinated team
- The organizational capacity developed in the pilot project was preserved and drawn on as expansion occurred. The core team remained together and moved to new positions of leadership during the expansion period.
- Training was viewed as an ongoing process.
- Supervisors assumed the role of trainers of teachers, thus legitimizing the innovations in the classroom and its environment.

The New School from the Standpoint of Educational Planners

From the standpoint of educational planning, the New School offers a set of features that constitutes an innovative response and, in some respects, an improvement in accepted solutions to the problems of rural primary education found in most Third World countries. We have described these features in previous sections of the paper because of their importance to educational planners, who must evaluate innovations in terms of replicability and cost and must consider new factors or how certain aspects of past solutions must be modified. In the present case, that is, rural primary education in Third World countries, adequate service in terms of coverage and effectiveness is thought to depend on factors such as the availability of teachers in the rural area, educational materials, the number of effective school days, curricular relevance, class size, and ability of the teacher.

Lack of teachers is the first problem cited in any diagnosis of the rural primary education problem in Third World countries. Despite awareness of this problem, there has still not been sufficient emphasis on the standard by which the teacher shortage is measured. In Colombia, it was unclear whether the standard should be based on a student–teacher ratio or should be one teacher for each primary grade, regardless of the estimated number of students per grade.

In the Colombian case, it is becoming increasingly clear that efficiency is enhanced by determining the number of teachers based on the number of children within the area of access to a school; that is, within a distance that allows children to travel from home to school in a reasonable period of time. In some instances, the number of school age children may be insufficient to justify a teacher for every grade. For example, if only eighty school-age children live within an hour's travel time of School X, it is not efficient to assign to the school five teachers, one for each primary grade. Based on such considerations, the New School team developed a multi-grade classroom model.

In 1986, during the stage of 'learning to be efficient', when detailed information was made available on 2,258 rural schools in Colombia (6.8 percent of the total), the following profile was established:

Average student–teacher ratio	31.0
Average number of classrooms per school	1.2
Average number of teachers per school	1.9
Average number of students per school	62.3

These data on the student–teacher ratio provided additional justification for the multi-grade strategy.

It also is important to analyze the New School model as a response to problems with high dropout and repetition rates. In traditional primary schools, it is the teacher who imposes the pace of learning, based on the performance of the student body as a whole. Students requiring a slower pace become dropouts and repeaters. Such is the case in Colombia where, as in many other countries, students in rural zones often are obliged to drop out of school for short or long periods of time to help their families in the fields or at home. To respond to this situation, the New School developed the approach of flexible promotion that has been described.

The literature shows the availability of textbooks and instructional materials to be among the most important factors in schooling. Of course, certain methods for textbook design and use are better than others. Study guides such as those used by New School students are self-explanatory and can be employed by the teacher and student to guide the learning process, thus allowing the teacher to assume the role of a facilitator.

A series of textbooks for each subject and grade level could not have been introduced without a self-explanatory technique. For multi-grade situations, it is important to use the traditional type of text that requires teacher participation and is designed to complement a central activity (e.g., a lecture or teacher instructions). This type of scheme would not have been as appropriate in Colombia as the New School model, since most Colombian schools would not have more than two teachers for all five primary grades.

Another topic of consideration concerns the teacher-training process featured in the New School model. Educational literature talks about the low impact that teacher training has on student learning. However, as noted above, New School training focuses directly on encouraging teachers to adopt and initiate innovation. The training process familiarizes teachers with the components of the new methodology and develops their ability to apply these in a real situation.

Overall, we believe that the New School model meets most of the criteria outlined in the World Bank book, *Improving Primary Education in Developing Countries* (Lockheed and Verspoor, 1991). As a matter of fact, the curriculum has been improved by strengthening cognitive competence and social relevance; it has increased the quality and availability of textbooks and teachers' guides. Flexible promotion permits the dedication of adequate time to schooling, and in-service training of teachers supported with adequate and sufficient materials. Furthermore, the program enhances community–school relationships, which are extremely important for improving educational effectiveness in developing countries.

Notes

1 Two important efforts are under way to strengthen this curriculum component. One is a new set of study guides that make the New School curriculum even more socially relevant. The second is a specific project, 'Systematic Incorporation of Thinking Processes and Abilities in the New School', supported by the Organization of American States (OAS), and coordinated by Luz Nelly Vásquez, that provides more strategies and materials to promote cognitive abilities.

Vicky Colbert, Clemencia Chiappe and Jairo Arboleda

2 From 1975 to 1981, the administrative agents only included departmental supervisors and the team of multipliers. Since 1982 a new group of administrative agents was organized in the country, through decentralized 'school clusters'. This decentralized structure required additional efforts from Escuela Nueva to train the directors and incorporate them as part of the new administrative educational structure.

References

COLBERT, V. and MOGOLLON, O. (1977) *Hacia la Escuela Nueva* (The New School Manual), 7th ed., Bogota, Ministry of Education.

COLBERT, V. (1987) 'Universalización de la Primaria en Colombia — El Programa de Escuela Nueva', in *La Educacion Rural en Colombia*, Cali, Colombia, Foundation for Higher Education (FES).

COLBERT, V. and ARBOLEDA, J. (1989) *Universalization of Primary Education in Colombia — The New School Programme*, paper presented at the World Conference on Education for All, Jomtien, Thailand.

KORTEN, D. (1980) 'Community organization and rural development: A learning process approach', *Public Administration Review*, **40**, 5, pp. 480–511.

LOCKHEED, M., VERSPOOR, A., et al. (1991) *Improving Primary Education in Developing Countries*, New York: Oxford University Press.

MINISTRY OF EDUCATION (1982) *Plan de Fomento para la Educación en el Area Rural y los Centros Menores de Población*, Bogotá.

MINISTRY OF EDUCATION (1985) *La Eficiencia Interna del Sisteme Educativo Colombiano en el Nivel Primario (1961–1983)*, Bogatá.

MINISTRY OF EDUCATION (Planning Office) (1988) *Análisis del Sector Educativo, con Enfasis en sus Aspectos Administrativos y Financieros*, Bogota.

Ministry of Education (The New School Programme), Organization of American States, Valle del Cauca Autonomous Corporation, and United Nations Children's Fund (1990a) *La Recuperación Cultural y los Agentes Educativos*, Bogotá, Museo de Artes y Tradiciones Populares.

MINISTRY OF EDUCATION (1990b) *La Supervivencia y el Desarrollo Infantil para Maestros de Escuela Nueva*, Bogotá, UNICEF.

MINISTRY OF EDUCATION (The New School Programme) (1990c) *Los Micro Centros Rurales — Una Estrategia para Mejorar la Calidad de la Educaion Rural en Colombia*, Bogatá, (processed).

MYERS, R. (1984) *Going to Scale*, paper presented at the Second Interagency Meeting on Community Based Child Development, New York.

MOGOLLÓN, O. (1986) *El Micro Centro y el Proceso de Educación Permanente en Escuela Nueva*, Bogota, Ministry of Education (processed).

NEUMANN, P. (1980) *Publishing for Schools: Textbooks and the Less Developed Countries*, Washington, DC, World Bank Staff Working Paper No. 398.

PAUL, S. (1982) *Managing Development Programs: The Lessons of Success*, Boulder, Colo., Westview Press.

PYLE, D. (1984) *Life After Project. A Multi-Dimensional Analysis of Implementing Social Development Programs at the Community Level*, Boston, John Snow.

RODRIGUEZ, J. (1978) *El Logro en Matemáticas y Lenguaje en la Educación Primaria en Colombia*, Bogotá, Instituto SER DE Investigaciones.

ROJAS, C. and CASTILLO, Z. (1988) *Evaluación del Programa Escuela Nueva en Colombia*, Bogotá, Instituto SER DE Investigaciones.

UNESCO (1986) *Colombia: Aspectos de la Calidad de la Ensenanza Basica Primaria en Relacion con la Renovacion Curricular*, Education Financing Division, Paris (processed).

Chapter 5

CIEP: A Democratic School Model for Educating Economically Disadvantaged Students in Brazil?

Ana Cristina Leonardos

Introduction

During the first democratically elected state administration of Rio de Janeiro (1982–1986), the Integrated Centers of Public Education, or CIEPs, were created to respond to serious problems in public elementary education. In order to understand the rationale for the CIEPs and the reasons for the specific program features, it is important to look at the context within which these innovations were made.

The Plight of the Disadvantaged Student in Brazil

Out of the Brazilian population of approximately 150 million people, almost a third are children under 15 years of age, over half of whom live in poverty; 28 percent — over 13 million children — live in total deprivation (Jaguaribe et al., 1989). The low-income student population in Brazil faces many problems, including too few public schools, high repetition rates, low educational achievement, scarcity of funds and support, and the gulf between private and public schools.

About a quarter of Brazilian school-age children are not in school and will never enter, despite the fact that elementary education is compulsory and defined as a 'right of all' in the Brazilian Constitution (Costa, 1984). There are not enough schools in many rural and urban areas to accommodate the growing number of students. Classrooms are usually overcrowded, and the student–teacher ratio is very high (40:1). Fewer than half (46 percent) of the students enrolled in the first grade reach second grade, and only 17 percent reach eighth grade (Gatti, 1981; Rosenberg, 1981; Arns, 1978; Dias, 1979 [cited in Brandao et al., 1984]). Many existing primary school places are held by over-age students (Saraiva, 1984).

Resources allocated to primary school do not reflect the importance that the Government professes to give to primary schooling. For instance, an analysis of 1974 federal expenditures by school level shows that only 13 percent of the money was placed into elementary schools (Saraiva, 1984).

The expansion of primary education after 1964 increased the need for teachers, increased and raised total staff expense, but the higher expenditures were not sufficient to permit an increase in teacher salaries. Moreover, states and municipalities often do not deliver salary payment on time (Saraiva, 1984). Public school teachers frequently strike, demanding better salaries or, at least, salaries that keep pace with the high monthly inflation rates in Brazil.

In the elementary grades, the public school system enrolls 76 percent of Brazilian students, the majority of them from disadvantaged homes (Saraiva, 1984). Middle-class and affluent families usually can afford to enroll their children in private schools, where 80 percent of the students graduate (Castro and Sanguinetti, 1980 [cited in Brandao *et al.*, 1984]). 'Tracking' in Brazil is socio-economic and occurs more at the educational system level — public versus private — than at the school level. According to Levin (1984), 'this not only promotes a systematic difference in the quality of education in favor of privileged children, but also undermines any political support for public schools. As the upper classes do not need public schools' services, they can tolerate their low quality'. A vicious cycle is created in which private schools continue to obtain support and feel pressure to maintain their high standards, while public schools continue to lack support and encouragement to improve their standards. In this way, the public educational crisis contributes to the widening of social inequalities in Brazil.

Brazilian Public School System

In the extensive literature on the Brazilian public school system, the following aspects are salient: (1) cultural incongruence between the school curriculum and the students' background; (2) lack of integration across subject matter areas; (3) pedagogical approaches that emphasize individual rote memorization, dictations, and mechanical drills reinforcing the superficial acquisition of knowledge; (4) lack of specified program goals; (5) teachers' inadequate training; (6) teachers' negative views of students; and, finally, (7) lack of parental involvement in the schooling process.

The incongruence between the public school curriculum and the students' background has been noted by various authors. Castro and Sanguinetti (1980 [cited in Brandao *et al.*, 1984]) pointed out the disparity between test content and students' reality and the 'insurmountable distance between classroom culture and the culture of the student group'. In a study comparing the pedagogy used at elementary public schools attended by working class children in a Brazilian metropolitan center and at vocational schools (SENAI), Frigotto (1977) concluded that the curriculum and teaching methods of public schools 'mirrored those used by the élite schools, but given their distance from the culture of the children and the scarcity of material and human resources, the actual teaching and learning was only a parody of the ones used in the élite schools'. A comparative study by Tomaz da Silva (1984), which examined pedagogic practices employed in three schools serving different student populations in the urban area of Porto Alegre, Rio Grande do Sul (the southernmost state of Brazil), provides supporting evidence for Frigotto's findings. Da Silva concluded: 'It is true that the values and cultural resources of these children are in general dismissed by the school's pedagogy. What is offered in its place, however, is not dominant, mainstream knowledge, but a very much diluted and degraded version of it' (1984, p. 318).

First of all, the mere attempt to offer mainstream culture to low-income students shows that public schools disregard the fact that their student population does not possess the 'cultural capital' that would allow them to succeed in school (Bourdieu and Passeron, 1977). Second, in face of the problems arising from the cultural clash, teachers slow the pace. The children are seen as lacking competence because they have failed to acquire middle-class values and knowledge at home. By blaming the students, the school avoids educational responsibility for the disadvantaged student population and does not question the efficacy of its curriculum content, methods and means.

In addition to the clear conflict between the students' culture and school knowledge, poor curriculum design and poor pedagogy are widespread in the Brazilian public schools. Curriculum goals are not well specified; unlike vocational schools, public elementary schools typically have diffuse educational objectives (Frigotto, 1977; Costa, 1978). Further, the public school elementary curriculum lacks cohesiveness; knowledge within each subject matter area is fragmented, and students are not given the opportunity to make connections between different topical sub-areas.

With pedagogical practices consisting mostly of memorization and drills, students have great difficulty establishing links even within a subject matter area. Da Silva (1984) provides a vivid example of the type of pedagogy that can be found in public school classrooms.

> There was little oral interaction between teacher and students over instructional issues. The dominant type of schoolwork was solitary work in textbooks, workbooks, notebooks, and worksheets. Children were required to do filling-in types of exercises that called for short answers to factual questions. This typically followed a short and verbally economical introduction by the teacher of some new topic. In general, children went about their work without being monitored or receiving individual help. Verbal interaction between teachers and students was limited to procedural issues, control, and to economical question-and-answer sequences. There is little feedback. As a rule, the children's answers to the exercises went unchecked. A disjuncture between what was being taught and what was supposedly being learned appeared to exist.
>
> The extensive use of solitary drills and exercises excluded the use of other modes of teaching and types of activities. There was an impressing sameness to the type of work in these classrooms. Besides children working individually at their desks, short presentations of new topics by teachers, and occasional dialogues between the teachers and the pupils, little else, as far as schoolwork is concerned, could be seen there (p. 274).

Teachers' weak preparation to assume roles of responsibility in elementary public schools is another serious problem in the teaching of economically disadvantaged students. According to Saraiva (1984), Brazilian teacher training courses usually convey how to teach rather than what to teach. She also argues that these training institutions (*escolas normals*) are quite unlike the schools where the teachers will actually teach. Teachers working with low-income students are faced with a reality very different from their own, and they receive no training about how to adapt the curriculum to the local students' culture, reality and needs.

For the most part, Brazilian public school teachers tend to view low-income pupils as lacking in intelligence, creativity, affection and motor skills. Da Silva's (1984) study provides evidence that teachers' views and attitudes differ according to the students' background. He compares the views of teachers working with low-income students to those of teachers at a school with an upper-class clientele (Hill School):

> First and foremost, the teachers' views were based on an implicit theory that attributed most of the problems they faced in their daily teaching to the class characteristics of the children and their families. In an obvious contrast with the prevalent attitude at Hill School, where the uniqueness and individual needs of each child were emphasized, here the problems and traits of the children as a collective were the focus of the teachers' concerns. There was the construction of an image of a social type, whose characteristics were more encompassing and forceful than the individual needs so cherished by the teachers of the privileged. The same theory which casts this image of children as bearing an indistinguishable constellation of problems (misconduct, low motivation, poor achievement), tends to attribute the cause to the supposedly deteriorating material and moral conditions of living of these children's families — poor housing, poor health, violence, broken families (p. 282).

A last criticism of the public school system concerns the role of the community and family in the students' academic life. Parents' involvement in schools depends to a great extent on teachers' and administrators' attitudes toward them, and the attitudes of most public school staff members are not conducive to such involvement (Brandao *et al.*, 1984). An ethnographic study in an urban *favela* found that when the parents of lower-class students are called to school, it is usually to hear teachers' complaints about their children (Leonardos, 1986). As a consequence, the majority of low-income parents feel intimidated and alienated by public schools.

In sum, all these factors point to a deep insensitivity of the public educational system to the needs of lower-class students. By imposing on disadvantaged students an academic curriculum that is simply a diluted version of mainstream culture, public schools promote educational failure rather than educational equality. Furthermore, fragmentation and lack of integration among subjects, together with pedagogical practices characterized by rote memorization and drills, make it difficult for students to see underlying concepts among the seemingly disconnected bodies of knowledge. Teachers' inadequate curriculum adaptations, as well as their negative belief and attitudes about disadvantaged students, suggest that they are unconsciously collaborating in the role of schooling in maintaining the status quo. This complex of interrelated problems plaguing the Brazilian public education system has been addressed by a model known as the Integrated Centers of Public Education (CIEPs), which was initiated in 1982.

The CIEPS: Background

During the first democratically elected State administration of Rio de Janeiro from 1982–1986, the Integrated Centers of Public Education, or CIEPs, were created to bring about much needed change in public elementary education. This educational project was devised by Darcy Ribeiro, the Vice-Governor, who, together with the Governor and the Democratic Labor Party Leader, Leonel Brizola, made the construction of these new schools possible. These new elementary public schools were built throughout the State and the capital of Rio de Janeiro and were specifically aimed at enrolling economically disadvantaged children. CIEPs are easily identifiable by their standardized architecture of prefabricated cement modules, conceived by Niemeyer, the famous Brazilian architect who conceived the capital city of Brasilia, and by their strategic and visible location along freeways, highways, in the middle of city squares, or in elevated positions such as mountainsides.

Large, visible, and distinctive in construction, the CIEP schools immediately became widely popular but also the target of much criticism. Their construction exhausted the education budget of the State, and the middle class criticized this heavy spending; they argued that funds should have been used in remodeling the existing public schools. Low-income families were initially suspicious of the CIEPs, doubting that the large and beautiful schools had been built for their children. Although the governor's ambitious project included the renovation of existing public schools, almost all the energies and resources of the administration were concentrated on the construction of CIEPs and on the educational debates over the CIEPs; little was left over for the old public schools.

The party's program goal was to build 500 CIEP schools by the end of the governor's mandate, but the four-year term was not sufficient for achieving this goal. By the end of 1986, only between fifty and sixty CIEPs were fully functional. The remaining schools were left under construction or in the planning stage. Seeking to provide continuity to the CIEP project for another mandate, Brizola backed the candidacy of his Vice-Governor, Darcy Ribeiro, in the next elections but without success. Moreira Franco (1986–1990) from another political party (PMDB) was elected instead and did not provide the same continuity for the CIEP school project. More CIEP school buildings have been inaugurated under this last State government, but they all have been returned to the regular public school system. Today there are no schools at the State level following the CIEP's program philosophy.

The situation at the municipal level is somewhat different from that of the State of Rio de Janeiro. Brizola's party lost support in the municipality of Rio de Janeiro in 1987–88, leaving many CIEPs without guidance and resources. However, a city mayor from this party was elected in the end of 1988, and the CIEP schools were rescued. Since then these schools have gained renewed support and attention. Today there are sixty CIEP schools functioning under the jurisdiction of the municipality of Rio de Janeiro. A recent report gives a conservative estimate that twenty out of these sixty schools are following the original educational philosophy, and the remaining ones are gradually being brought back to the original program guidelines. Clearly, the changes in political parties in power at the State and municipal levels have affected the maintenance and support of the CIEPs' original project.

In creating the CIEPs the Democratic Labor Party was taking action on behalf of the impoverished population rather than favoring the middle-class interests. The CIEPs offer an alternative educational program that differs from the one usually offered in the traditional public schools. In the original concept, these schools were just new buildings where old ways of educating children would continue unchanged. Rather they constituted a radical change in strategy for teaching disadvantaged students. The CIEPs' philosophy stemmed from a widely held conviction that the existing public schools were failing in their mission of teaching basic academic skills to the majority of their students' population; they were failing to serve the children from the lowest strata of society.

CIEP Implementation, Conceptual Approach and Pedagogy

Program Implementation

During the implementation of the CIEPs project there was a general concern that these new schools would constitute a parallel system for public education, with no links with the State and municipal Secretaries of Education (Paro *et al.*, 1988). Such a system would create logistical problems in such activities as hiring and payment of teachers. The short-term solution of the CIEP project leader was to devise a school system that was not fully regulated by the Secretaries of Education, but was not totally disengaged from them. Instead of being managed through the bureaucratic structures of the Secretaries of Education, the CIEP program would be coordinated by the 'Coordinating Committee of Education' (Comissao Coordenadora de Educaçao, or CCE) consisting of only three members — the Secretary of Education, the Dean of Universidade do Estado do Rio de Janeiro (UERJ), and the Vice-Governor. This small and cohesive group, it was reasoned, could introduce pedagogic reforms at a faster pace than could a large, unwieldy bureaucracy (Paro *et al.*, 1988). This committee laid out the main objectives of the new educational project called the 'Special Program of Education' (Programa Especial de Eduaçao, or PEE); the CIEP project was part of this larger educational program.

After this initial organizational step, all public elementary school teachers of Rio de Janeiro were summoned and consulted about the public educational crisis. The teachers were then asked to elect representatives to attend the Congress of Mendes (Encontro de Mendes). Two hundred teachers, school administrators and union leaders were present at this Congress and together they worked toward a common set of beliefs that came to constitute the major educational guidelines of the CIEPs.

A Committee for Pedagogical Training (Consultoria Pedagógica de Treinamento, or CPT) was created at this time with the objective of training and assisting CIEP staff members in the project guidelines. The links established with the Secretary of Education were evident in the fact that these two committees (CCE and CPT) also undertook the reform of some old public schools and sought to provide support to public school teachers through training and distribution of academic material. The major function of the Committee for Pedagogical Training, however, was the training of CIEP personnel. Toward this purpose, the pedagogical coordinators of all CIEPs would first receive formal training in the literacy method adopted by the school and in the main pedagogical guidelines of the CIEP philosophy. Later these coordinators would pass on their knowledge of the educational program and literacy method to CIEP teachers on a weekly basis at the school site.

Finally, the CCE was responsible for the creation of a school council made up of school and community members in order to have students and their communities represented in the school's administrative process. These school boards were granted only a consulting role rather than decision-making power in the schools' administrative process.

Conceptual Approach and Pedagogy

This section summarizes the major educational issues that were aired in the Congress of Mendes. One of the most important conclusions drawn from this Congress is reflected in the following statement (Governo Brizola, 1985):

> Our public schools are geared toward an ideal child. One who does not need to struggle for survival; who is well fed; who speaks the school's language; who knows how to handle a pencil and is capable of interpreting symbols, and who is stimulated by parents through all sorts of means. As this is not the reality of the majority of the Brazilian families, the schools do not have the right to impose these criteria, which are valid for the middle class, upon its students' majority. Its task is to educate Brazilian children as they actually are. . . . This means that our school should adapt itself to the poor child with the conviction that the school is the one which fails when it does not succeed in educating the majority of its students.

This last sentence was translated into lines of action according to the different school levels. School organization, instruction, school–community relationships and participants' views and attitudes were reviewed in light of the problems identified in the existing public schools.

Organization. The CIEP schools reflect a different organization from the one found in the conventional public schools. The students are supposed to spend the entire day at the CIEP. The day is divided into four hours of instruction and four hours of extracurricular activities. This full-time program was created to assist working parents and to give students a comprehensive curriculum that provides opportunities to develop many abilities other than literacy skills. Additional subjects include art, music, physical education and dance. Second, organization of the school staff is different as well. The CIEP's administrative staff is structured to offer constant guidance and support to the teachers and other school employees. Frequent training, staff meetings and other activities are important as staff members move from traditional schools to a new type of school quite different in philosophy and practice.

Instruction. Three aspects of instruction in the CIEPs are different from traditional public schools: curriculum structure, classroom pedagogy/feedback, and curriculum content. With respect to the first, the CIEPs replaced the traditional assortment of separate subjects with an integrated curriculum. To achieve this integration, CIEP teachers meet frequently to plan across subject matter areas. Activities are designed to encourage students to make connections across subject matter areas and promote logical thinking. The following passage reflects this concern:

> It is important to offer the child means through which he/she can develop logical reasoning. . . . Logical thinking is not only useful to communication but also to learn math, science, etc. Very often these subject-matters are taught with no attention at all to their logical relationships. This is why the child does not have any other options but to memorize them. . . . It is common to talk about 'the capacity to transfer or generalize knowledge'. In fact, it means that the student should be allowed to discover those relationships that are the key to all types of knowledge. It is not through repetition that the student achieves a good command of knowledge (Governo Brizola, 1985).

In this approach subjects are not taught independently of one another; relationships and connections are pointed out whenever possible. Extracurricular activities also are designed to be closely integrated with the main curriculum, with continual exchange between classroom and activity teachers. The intention is to convey to students higher order concepts that pervade all lessons and activities.

At the CIEPs, classroom pedagogy is designed to motivate students to engage in dialogues and express their own viewpoints. Teachers are expected to share the stage with students and value students' opinions and past experiences. Students have more opportunity to express their ideas orally, which in turn enhances their self-esteem and confidence in class. Teachers' feedback should be positive and constructive in order to reinforce students' self-esteem.

With respect to the curriculum content, the CIEPs propose to establish the missing link between the students' culture and the dominant culture necessary for future success. The CIEP guidelines include the following statement describing the major pedagogical goal of the CIEP system:

> Poor children know how to do and actually do a lot of things to guarantee their survival. However, if left by themselves they should not have the means to learn what is necessary to function in a literate society. The school's task is then to introduce the child into the city's culture. By recognizing and valuing the child's background and experience, the school has to be a bridge between the child's practical knowledge and the literate society's formal knowledge (Governo Brizola, 1985).

This new school system aims at using the students' culture and knowledge as resources and means for teaching those skills and knowledge rewarded in the larger society. At the CIEPs it is still important for students to acquire formal knowledge; however, this knowledge is presented not as absolute truth but rather as conventions that need to be learned in order to succeed in life.

Towards these ends, the curriculum is designed to acknowledge students' culture, folklore and traditions; topics are usually presented in a critical form. History, for instance, is taught from a critical and dynamic viewpoint, encouraging students to be agents of their own history. Furthermore, every school has a group of 'cultural animators' whose purpose is to bring to the school the dance, music, and other artistic expressions from the student community. In this way, economically disadvantaged students' culture is being accepted, incorporated into the school setting, and used as a stepping stone to the teaching of higher order skills that allow students to function in a literate society.

School-community relationships. The CIEPs stress a greater integration between students' communities and the schools. This is clear in the presence of the 'culture animators' from the students' community and in the incorporation of the community's culture into the curriculum and school activities. Since the program depends on the student community's cultural resources, the school has to maintain a good rapport with the community.

Parental and community involvement is promoted through enjoyable activities held during weekends at the CIEPs. Parents, school staff, students, and community members participate in these extracurricular events, which are usually linked to a cultural celebration or activity. Besides these weekend events in which the community comes to the school, teachers are advised to go out in the community to become more familiar with the students' reality and more sensitive to it.

CIEP vs. Conventional Public School: A Critical Evaluation

A Comparative Case Study

A detailed picture of the implementation of the CIEP philosophy can be observed from a comparison of a conventional public school and a CIEP that were serving the same economically disadvantaged community in Rio de Janeiro (Leonardos, 1990). The conventional school selected was considered to be typical with respect to such features as high repetition rates, e.g., repetition of first grade was around 50 percent. The CIEP school selected was considered to be representative of the CIEPs' educational program's philosophy. An in-depth ethnographic study, which included site observations and semi-structured interviews in the two primary schools, was designed to assess the differences between their educational programs and program participants' views and functions. After observations were conducted in several school activities and meetings, two first-grade classrooms were selected for the investigation of educational activities at the two schools. Administrative staff members, teachers, parents and students were interviewed at both settings.

It is important to note that this study was conducted in 1987–88 when the CIEPs had just lost the political party support they had in 1982–1986. The political situation was reflected in the lack of material resources in the school, in the teacher's skepticism about the long-term future of the CIEP project, and in the fact that the CIEPs were starting to lose autonomy and be absorbed by the state and municipal education bureaucracies.

Furthermore, the city of Rio de Janeiro was going through a serious economic crisis which was reflected in the low salaries of all public school teachers. As a result, teachers from both school systems were frequently participating in prolonged strikes, not only to demand raises but also to fight for more resources for the schools. As examples of the difficulties being encountered in the city of Rio de Janeiro, the conventional public school selected for the study had just stopped receiving municipal funds for covering expenses for janitorial services and basic cleaning products, and the CIEP under observation spent almost two weeks requesting repair of water pipes in order to be able to initiate the school session. The two schools studied cannot be analyzed independently of this context — Rio de Janeiro's economic crisis that was affecting all individuals and institutions in numerous ways.

Description of the Schools

Conventional school. The conventional elementary school that was selected included preschool to eighth grade and had a total of 487 students and an average of twenty-two students per class. The number of classrooms per grade level was the following: four preschool classrooms, six first grades, three second grades, two third grades, two fourth grades, two fifth grades, one sixth grade, one seventh grade, and one eighth grade. Students came from a nearby low-income community.

The school staff consisted of one principal, one vice-principal, two pedagogical supervisors, an educational counselor, one teacher per class, and semi-skilled and unskilled personnel responsible for secretarial functions and facilities. The administrative staff members had not known one another or worked together before they started working in this school.

The school had two independent part-time sessions, one in the morning and one in the afternoon, and students usually had one meal a day at school. The curriculum implemented at this public school followed the regular primary school curriculum mandated by law. Some extracurricular activity teachers assigned to this school by the District were not actually performing their functions at the school. The school did not provide any special teacher training in literacy methods or pedagogical approaches. Teachers usually had to rely on what they had previously learned in their teacher training courses, which in Brazil correspond to the three high school years.

CIEP school. The CIEP school that was studied had been inaugurated in 1987. With the grades from preschool to fourth, the school had a total of 477 students and an average of twenty-five students per class. There were five preschool classrooms, six first grades, three second grades, three third grades, and two fourth grades. Although this specific CIEP only had the first five primary grades, there were other CIEPs that offered the full range of elementary grade levels. The CIEP school served the same low-income community traditionally served by the conventional public school.

The school staff at this CIEP consisted of one principal, three vice-principals for different functions, two pedagogical coordinators (one for the first three grade levels and another for the last two grade levels), one educational counselor, two part-time teachers or one full-time teacher for every class, a team of three cultural animators, physical education teachers, a music teacher, a library teacher, semi-skilled personnel to take care of the clerical work of the school, and unskilled employees such as cooks and janitors. The members of the administrative team had worked together at another public school and shared the same ideas about economically disadvantaged students' education.

Since the CIEP provided a full-day program, CIEP students were at school for more hours a day than students at the conventional public school, which offered only part-time school sessions. In the CIEP, some teachers remained with the same students for the entire day and were paid for two school sessions. In other cases, the students were assigned different teachers for the morning and the afternoon. Students were usually given three meals a day at school, and time was allotted for a shower. The curriculum implemented at this school was considered by CIEP project founders to be following closely the CIEP program philosophy, including the idea of building on the low-income students' knowledge and cultural background.

In the first three primary grade levels, teachers received specific training in the literacy method adopted by the school (a method similar to Paulo Freire's but designed specifically for children) from the pedagogical coordinator. The last two primary grade teachers were guided by their pedagogical coordinator on how to devise lessons consistent with the program's educational philosophy. It was found that new teachers needed some time to feel comfortable with the CIEP's literacy method and philosophical guidelines. Teachers coming from the conventional public school system usually held strong and sometimes conflicting beliefs about disadvantaged students, and these only changed with time.

School Organization

This section discusses the organization of the conventional public school and the CIEP, that is, the ways in which each school's staff members were organized around the activities of that school. The hierarchy system of the schools and their educational program goals will also be addressed in this section.

At the conventional public school, staff members tended to work individually in their tasks and to maintain a hierarchical relationship. Teachers related to the pedagogical supervisor only on a one-to-one basis and tended to work individually on lesson plans. Teachers applied different literacy methods and only got together to devise the final exams. They did not seem accustomed to working in teams, to exchanging information and experience, or to giving each other support in dealing with problems. The principal in the conventional school seemed distant from the teachers and from the actual school instruction; she seldom talked directly to the teachers or showed curiosity about students' progress. The principal seemed to have exclusive decision-making power, since teachers and other staff members rarely had the opportunity and the freedom to express their views or wishes to her. However, the principal would limit her activities to bureaucratic matters. School staff members did not seem sure about what the school's goals were or about what the school was supposed to be transmitting to students.

By contrast, CIEP's staff members had a collegial approach to discussing problems. The school administrative members encouraged teamwork among all school staff members, rather than independent work. At least once a week after the training session, teachers planned their lessons together, with the aid of the pedagogical coordinator. The fact that only one literacy method was being applied in the school brought the teachers closer together. Interaction between the principal, pedagogical coordinators, counselors, and teachers was planned and occurred rather frequently. Although staff meetings were usually headed by the principal, a vice-principal, or a coordinator, all proposals and problems were discussed and strategies adopted by a vote of the teachers. School staff members had clear and similar perceptions about the CIEP's educational goals.

The main function of the principal in this school, other than general bureaucratic duties, was to make sure that the CIEP's major program guidelines were being followed by all other staff members in their specific functions. A special challenge for the principal was to inculcate new teachers with the CIEP's philosophy. It was observed that the more experienced teachers were able to work together more cohesively than the new teachers, who did not yet share the common orientation.

School Instruction

This section discusses the curriculum design, pedagogy, and curriculum content of the two observed schools and their respective first-grade classrooms.

The conventional public school curriculum was characterized by a fragmentation in the teaching of individual subjects and units within a subject at the classroom level. The classroom pedagogy was predominantly teacher-dominated, with very little dialogue between the teacher and students. Teachers' comments and feedback about student responses tended to focus on what was wrong rather than what was correct. Curriculum content was found to be abstract and disconnected from the students' cultural background and past experiences. Classroom activities were rarely introduced by a talk or any other activity that would motivate students to learn the subject. In this classroom students typically worked individually at their desks; drills, dictation, fill-in exercises, and other exercises demanding only superficial understanding were the predominant activities. Apparently lacking confidence in what they were doing, students often asked the teachers to check their work.

By contrast, the CIEP classroom was characterized by an integrated curriculum in which all subjects and topic areas were linked together by their common or complementary aspects. The classroom pedagogy was marked by dialogues and debates in which the teacher shared the stage with the students. The teacher's feedback to students was predominantly constructive; there was a constant concern with building students' self-esteem.

The CIEP's curriculum content was based on students' cultural background and knowledge and was designed to foster higher order thinking and analytic skills. Sometimes the school took a rather extreme position in insisting that all activities at the school be related to students' cultural background (e.g., judo classes were replaced by classes in *capoeira*, an Afro-Brazilian martial art). The classes varied a great deal one from the other, as students engaged in a wide variety of activities such as drawing, writing, discussing a topic, explaining to the teachers what they had done, singing, or exercising. Students knew how to work both independently and in groups; they seemed confident of their work and motivated by the topics presented by the teacher. At the CIEP, students were encouraged to take a critical perspective — to question the reason and the meaning of what they were learning.

School–Community Relationship

The interaction of the school staff members with the students' community was also observed at the conventional public school and the CIEP, and a number of differences between the schools were found.

The conventional public school's staff members had very restricted interaction with students' parents and with the community in general. Parents only came to the school to attend the official school meetings, which were held once or twice a year. On these occasions the principal would inform parents of new school policies or regulations. The school program did not require teachers to meet with parents. As a result, their meetings with parents occurred haphazardly and depended on the individual teacher's initiative.

By contrast, the CIEP's school members made continuous attempts to involve parents and the community in the school's activities and program. Parents seemed always welcome at the school to talk about any subject. The administration organized frequent meetings with parents to make them aware of the difficulties the school was facing and to inform them about the school's goals and major events. The CIEP's program called for at least two meetings per semester between teachers and their students' parents. Teachers took this opportunity to inform parents about the innovative educational program, request their support, and let them know about their children's progress.

At the CIEP, parents and the community as a whole were frequently invited to take part in events held on the weekends. On these occasions, the entire school community took part in the preparation of the school events. These parties or events usually celebrated an important date for the students, and they included the participation of the community's folkloric and artistic groups. Despite the many efforts on the staff members' part, many parents — around two-thirds of all the parents — remained uninvolved in the school's activities. Parental participation fell far below what had been established as a school goal, but it was considerably greater than in the conventional school.

Participants' Views

At the conventional public school, teachers tended to hold conservative views of the educational program, and they did not view the program as something that could be changed. School staff members, with only a few exceptions, also tended to hold negative views of students and their communities. In general, staff members tended to think that the students were not suited to the educational program rather than thinking that the program was not well designed to meet the children's needs. Moreover, staff members did not believe that the school would change students or make a great difference in their lives. As for parents, they were not satisfied with the school's program and with their child's teachers; however, they did not seem comfortable enough to convey their viewpoints in the school meetings. They seemed to keep their criticisms to themselves and to accept passively what was being offered to their children.

By contrast, the CIEP's staff members perceived the school's educational program in a very dynamic way — as a process that should be constantly evaluated and revised in order to serve the student clientele more effectively. Staff members also tended to view students and their community from a positive perspective. Teachers, for instance, tended to rationalize students' problems and explain their plight from a larger socio-economic and political viewpoint. Furthermore, the teachers who had been with the CIEP the longest tended to feel responsible for students' academic failure, while the newer teachers still held negative views of students and tended to blame them for their problems in school. The more experienced teachers with the CIEP's philosophy tended to be highly motivated and to believe that the school would make a difference in the way students viewed themselves and the world.

Parents who participated in the school's activities and events — around a third of all the parents — tended to support the school's program and staff members' efforts. They also seemed to understand the schools' human and material resource problems from a larger socio-economic and political perspective. Parents who did not participate in the program or rejected it altogether seemed to perceive the CIEP's program as being too lenient and liberal and giving students insufficient discipline in relation to their behavior or academic work. The perception of most staff members was that those parents who did not participate or recognize the value of the educational program were historically alienated from any type of decision-making process that aimed at increasing their awareness or changing their social roles.

Summary and Analysis of Findings

On virtually all comparisons of these two public schools, it was clear that they were quite different. The CIEP offered a program that differed from the conventional public school in organization, instruction, relationship with parents, and educators' views. In the following section, the strengths and weaknesses of the alternative educational program in relation to the conventional public school will be summarized.

First, the fact that the CIEP's administrators and teachers, with the exception of the new ones, worked cohesively around common goals reflects a much more focused and structured educational program than the one observed at the conventional public school. This difference could be attributed to the fact that the CIEP's administrative team members had worked together previously in another school and shared the same educational philosophy and views towards economically disadvantaged students. The fact that this cohesive team had chosen to work at a CIEP helped make program implementation easier and more harmonious at this specific school. Beyond this, however, it should be stressed that the CIEP teachers' motivation and idealism seem to be linked to their firm beliefs that their actions in the school could bring about some type of change in the long run. That is, it was observed that the CIEP teachers and other staff members believed that their work would have an impact on students' lives and eventually on society.

Second, this comparative case study indicates that an emphasis on students' resources and cultural background makes the CIEP's program markedly different from the traditional public school program. It seemed that the CIEP's program not only respected students' culture but also tried to enhance it in many different ways and forms. The fact that the CIEP studied sometimes took extreme positions about what to teach can be interpreted as a reaction to the conventional public schools' curriculum. Some topics were not taught because they were seen as not being useful to children outside the middle class, but the CIEP's students were taught higher level thinking skills through all the academic activities. In this sense, the CIEP's concept of literacy skills seemed to be a much more complex one than the concept in the conventional public school's program.

Third, staff efforts to involve parents in school activities, meetings and events were more vigorous in the CIEP than in the conventional public school observed. Nevertheless, the fact that the CIEP school had succeeded in involving only a third of all parents in this innovative school program indicates that staff members must revise or rethink their strategies for parental involvement. As previously discussed, the parents who did not participate in the program held strong negative views of the school.

Case Study Conclusions

There is a continuing challenge in implementing this innovative program because of its sharp departure from strongly held beliefs, views and behavior patterns that are traditionally found among educators and parents. One of the problems identified at this CIEP school was to redefine educators' roles and change their attitudes towards the education of economically disadvantaged students and towards their communities. This process requires both time and exposure to the program philosophy and training. It was observed that a period of time was required before new teachers could be considered well adapted to the CIEP program. In entering the CIEP, they needed to modify their behavior and views towards disadvantaged students and their usual way of teaching.

With respect to the parents' rejection of the program or lack of involvement in it, CIEP's members tended to attribute these problems to the fact that parents historically had been neglected and passive in relation to the societal and political decision-making process. In the view of the CIEP's members, parents have been left aside by the conventional public system, which made them feel inferior and passive. Changing this pattern of parental accommodation and passive acceptance of the status quo turned out to be a much more difficult task than was originally predicted by school staff. Finally, as many teachers and other staff members noted, it was necessary to go beyond the CIEP's efforts to promote the students' self-awareness and attempt to increase self-awareness in new teachers and parents as well.

The problem of the parents' rejection of the CIEP's project can be interpreted in a different way. It should be recalled that the CIEP project started out without the full participation of the communities and parents. In developing this innovative school project for economically disadvantaged students, it was principally teachers and other educators who were consulted. That is, the CIEP came as the end product of educators' ideas; these ideas were not necessarily shared by the communities. As a result, many parents still do not understand how the CIEPs operate and how they are different from the traditional public schools, aside from their architecture and full-time school program. Thus, many parents and community members may have rejected the program because it was imposed on them rather than planned with them as involved partners from the start.

Another factor that may have contributed to the problem is that the CIEP school is still very new and had not yet graduated a class. Until the school has proven itself, parents may be suspicious about this new program which they perceive as being very lenient in comparison to the conventional school's program. They may be fearful of enrolling their children in it without seeing the outcomes. If this is the case, the CIEP's staff members need to recognize that parents and community members have a valid concern about the effectiveness of the program; they need to organize meetings with parents and community members to listen to what they have to say. Such communication is as important as clarifying to parents the CIEP's educational program and philosophy. In sum, it seems that CIEP's staff should make a point not only to inform parents but to listen to them as well.

The degree of the CIEP's program acceptance in the community and the society has implications for the survival of this alternative public school project. Although the leadership of the principal and the cohesion of the school staff are extremely important in the implementation and maintenance of the school's philosophy, without community support this program faces many obstacles for survival. The CIEP's project needs the involvement of the students' communities in order not to lose its basic characteristics in the face of limited political and financial support.

The CIEP program was a more open and collaborative program than the conventional public school; however, strictly speaking, it was a top-down educational program designed for, rather than with, the disadvantaged community. The results of this study suggest that future attempts at making the schooling process a more democratic experience should involve close interaction and collaboration between community and educators.

Outcomes: CIEP vs. Conventional Public School

No systematic evaluation of outcomes, such as students' achievement, retention and attendance rates at the CIEP schools, has yet been undertaken. The study that has been described here aimed at investigating the program features of a CIEP school in practice, rather than assessing students' outcomes or students' responses to this alternative educational program. In 1987 it was reported by the newspaper *Folha de Sao Paulo* that the CIEP schools had a higher student promotion rate — 82.74 percent — from first to second grade than conventional public schools — 62.33 percent. However, the reporting of these rates was premature, and a comparison of the rates is not easy to interpret. Since the CIEP schools are based on a totally different philosophy and educational strategy from the conventional public schools, it seems reasonable that the criteria for promoting or retaining students also differ in some respects.

It is important to assess the types of skills actually being acquired by students. The findings of the case study reported here suggest that CIEP students may be acquiring different skills from students of conventional public schools. It could be hypothesized that CIEP students are being trained to undertake more creative tasks while students in conventional schools are being trained for more routinized activities. This dimension, however, remains to be carefully and systematically examined.

It should be noted that the working climate for both staff and students seemed to be much better at the CIEP school than at the conventional public school. The CIEP staff's idealism, commitment to the common program goals, and belief that their work is going to have a positive impact on students could be responsible for the constructive climate observed among teachers and administrators. With respect to the students, the CIEP's integrated educational program that makes use of the students' own knowledge, culture, and experiences could be the primary factor in enhancing students' self-confidence and self-reliance.

CIEP's Philosophy: Lower Cost Alternatives

The Municipal Secretary of Education claims that the construction of a CIEP building costs around US$1.3 million and that its maintenance costs twice as much as the maintenance of conventional schools. Although it seems clear that the full-time school program of the CIEP is ideal for low-income working parents, there are many CIEP features that could be extended to the part-time conventional public school network at lower costs. Among them are all the CIEP's strategies that aim at creating a more integrated school program and at unifying school members around common goals. The adoption of a unique literacy method and educational philosophy at each school, the in-service teacher training program, the development of an integrated curriculum sensitive to the students' cultural background, the adoption of teacher–student interactive pedagogical practices, and the involvement of students' parents in the schooling process seem to be effective strategies for bringing all school participants closer to one another and facilitating the pursuit of common goals.

In the case of the CIEP studied, the fact that the school administrators had worked together before was considered crucial in holding the other staff members together around the main program goals. If guaranteeing an effective and committed school administration is not always easy, the idea and practice of teamwork can be passed on to all school staff members through systematic training. A potentially useful strategy for improving staff cohesiveness and effectiveness is an effective system of in-service training for public school teachers and administrators. This training should be based on essential principles and goals as defined by the Secretary of Education, and each school should have the choice of adopting them in order to guarantee participants' coherence of actions.

Finally, as previously mentioned, parents and communities should be informed of changes the school will undergo and invited to participate in the difficult enterprise of school restructuring. They should be brought into the process early enough so that they will feel part of it and be ready to offer the needed support for schools' initiatives and projects. All public schools, it appears, will benefit from regaining parents' support and belief in them.

References

ARNS, O., *et al.* (1978) *A Communicacao Linguistica Paranaense: Evasao e Retencao Escolar no 1² Grau*, Curitiba, Universidade Federal do Parana (UFPR)/Instituto Nacional de Estudos e Pesquisa (INEP).

BOURDIEU, P. and PASSERON, J-C. (1977) *Reproduction in Education, Society and Culture*, London, Sage.

BRANDAO, Z., *et al.* (1974) 'Evasao e Repetência no Brasil', in PAIVA, V. (Ed.) *Perspectivas e Dilemas da Educacao Popular*, Graal Editora.

BRASIL: SENADO FEDERAL. COMISSAO DE EDUCACO E CULTURA (1979) *Projeto Educacao*, Tomo III Brasilia, Universidade de Brasilia.

CASTRO, C.M., SANGUINETTI, J.A., *et al.* (1980) *Determinantes de la Educaion em América Latina: Acceso. Desempeno y Equidad*, Rio de Janeiro, Programa ECIEL.

COSTA, D. (1978) *Aprendizado Nao-Cognitivo como Resultado da Escolaridade*, master's thesis, Fundaçao Gutúlio Vargas, Rio de Janeiro.

COSTA, M. (1984) 'A Educacao e Suas Potencialidades', in LEVIN, H.M., COSTA, M., SOLARI, C.L.B., LEAL, M.A., MIRANDA, G.V. and VELLOSO, J.R. (Eds) *Educacao e Desigualdade no Brasil*, Petropolis, Rio de Janeiro, Editora Vozes.

DA SILVA, T. (1984) *Pedagogy and Social Class in a Brazilian Urban Setting*, doctoral dissertation, Stanford University, Stanford, California.

DIAS, M.T.R. (1979) *Desigualdades Sociais e Oportunidade Educaional: a Producao do Fracasso*, master's thesis, IUPERJ, Rio de Janeiro.

'EDUCACAO E CIENCIA' (14 June 1987) *Folha de sao Paulo*, p. A-30, Sao Paulo, Brazil.

FREIRE, P. (1983) *Pedagogy of the Oppressed*, New York, Seabury.

FRIGOTTO, G. (1977) *Efeitos Cognitivos de Escolaridade do SENAI e da Escola Academica Convencional. Uma Pedagogia para Cada Classe Social?*, master's thesis, Fundaçao Getúlio Vargas, Rio de Janeiro.

GATTI, B., *et al.* (1981) *A Reprovacao na 1² Série do 1² Grau*, Sao Paulo, Universidade de Sai Oayki (USP).

GOVERNO BRIZOLA, L. (1985) *Falas ao Professor*, Rio de Janeiro, Programa Especial de Educacao (PEE).

JAGUARIBE, H., *et al.* (1989) *BRASIL: Reforma ou Caos?*, Rio de Janeiro, Editora Paz et Terra.

LEONARDOS, A.C. (1986) *St. Jeronimus: The Facets of Cultural Oppression*, Stanford University (processed).

LEONARDOS, A.C. (1990) *Opportunities to Learn Academic Skills in the Brazilian Public Schools: A Comparative Case Study*, doctoral dissertation, Stanford University, Stanford, California.

LEVIN, H.M. (1984) 'Educaçao e Desigualdade no Brasil: Uma Visao Geral', in LEVIN, H.M., COSTA, M., SOLARI, C.L.D., LEAL, M.A., MIRANDA, G.V. and VELLOSO, J.R. (Eds) *Educacao e Desigualdade no Brasil*, Petropolis, Rio de Janeiro, Editora VOZES.

PARO, V.H., FERRETI, C.J., VIANNA, C.P. and SOUZA, D.T. (1988) *Escola de Tempo Integral. Desafio para o Ension Público*, Sao Paulo, Cortez Editora.

RASCHE, V.M.M. (1979) *The Discarded Children: the Creation of a Class of Misfits Amongst the Poor in Brazilian Schools. A Case Study of First Grade*, doctoral dissertation, Michigan University.

RIBEIRO, D. (1986) *O livro dos CIEPs*, Rio de Janeiro, Bloch Editores.

ROSENBERG, L. (1981) *Relacoes entre Origem Social. Condicoes da Escola e Rendimento Escolar de Criancas no Ensino Publico Estadual de 1² Grau*, Sao Paulo, S.P. Fundaçao Carlos Chagas/FINEP.

SARAIVA, T. (1984) *Educacao: Temas Para Debate*, Rio de Janeiro, Bloch Editores.

Chapter 6

Improving Educational Effectiveness in a Plantation School: The Case of the Gonakelle School in Sri Lanka*

Angela Little and R. Sivasithambaram

Gonakelle Tamil Vidyalayam (School) nestles high in the Namunakelle Mountains in the Passara district to the east of the central highlands of Sri Lanka. Tea bushes, draped like velvet over the lower peaks, surround the school and stretch into the far distance. Today is 28 March 1989, and 644 children out of the 811 enrolled are in attendance. Of the total number of students enrolled, 467 are boys and 344 girls. Thirteen of the fifteen teachers are present. The children, whose ages range from 5 to 17 years, begin arriving at the school around 7.15 a.m. They are all Tamils and all live inside the Gonakelle estate or on neighbouring tea plantations, which are owned by the government and managed by the Janatha Estates Development Board. The primary cycle children in years 1 to 5 are drawn entirely from the Gonakelle estate, itself divided into five divisions. All but two are the children of resident estate workers. The children living in the closest division arrive at the school singly or in pairs; those from the faraway division are shepherded in groups by *kanganis*, men employed by the estate to deliver and collect the children daily. Some of the older children, drawn from ten other feeder primary schools within a four-mile radius of Gonakelle, complete part of their daily journey by bus. This is the beginning of a typical day in the life of Gonakelle plantation school.

Historically, the living conditions of people on plantations have compared unfavorably with the rest of the Sri Lankan population, despite Sri Lanka's fine record of achievement in 'basic needs' satisfaction. Sri Lanka has achieved levels of literacy and health that compare very favorably with countries of similar per capita income. Its welfarist policies have been funded historically through revenues derived from an agricultural economy dominated by plantations. Paradoxically, while the economic activity of plantations has enjoyed a high degree of vertical integration into the national and international economy for over 150 years, the social structure that supports it has been, until quite recently, isolated from the national mainstream of social, political and educational activity.

* We would like to thank staff of the Badulla Integrated Rural Development Project, the principal of Gonakelle school, Mr Nadenesepapati, and the superintendent of the Gonakelle estate, Mr Atukorale, for assistance.

Plantations were self-contained 'total institutions' in which people were born, lived, worked and died (Jain, 1970; Beckford, 1972).

Although standards of welfare of plantation workers and their children have improved slowly since the mid-1970s when the tea estates were nationalized, they remain disadvantaged educationally in relation to the Sri Lankan population as a whole and even in comparison with the rural population in and around plantation areas. In 1981 the literacy rate for Indian Tamils was 67 percent, compared with a national average of 87 percent. The rate for female Indian Tamils was 55 percent. In 1984 there were 558 government-run plantation schools on tea and rubber estates and just over 63,000 students, of whom 46 percent were girls. Most of the schools are located in the up-country tea-growing areas around Nuwara-Eliya, Hatton, Bandarawela, Passara, and Kandy. Nearly all children of plantation workers attend Tamil-medium schools located inside plantations. Most of these schools offer the first five years of basic education. In the late 1970s plantation schools were integrated into the national system of education, and by 1984 about 78 percent of the teachers in the plantation schools were permanent government employees, and the remainder were individuals paid in cash or in kind by voluntary organizations and parents. Less than one-third of the government teachers were trained. The average pupil-teacher ratio in 1984 was 55:1, while the national average was 34:1 Dropout rates in the primary grades in plantation schools have been higher than national rates. Access to education beyond year 6 is limited, and university enrollment is rare (Little, 1987).

Total recurrent public expenditure on the Sri Lankan education system was Rs3.7 billion in 1987 (approximately US$125 million). While this represents real growth over the past decade (a remarkable achievement in view of the growth of defense expenditure over the same period), the real expenditure *per student* has declined from Rs1063 in 1977 to Rs874 in 1980, recovering by 1987 to Rs980 (in constant rupee prices) (World Bank, 1988). The period 1977–80 experienced the greatest decline in per student educational expenditure and coincided with the period when the majority of plantation schools were nationalized.

Yet despite the historical disadvantages of plantation children, despite the worsening financial climate for education, and despite the nationwide ethnic and political crisis, the Gonakelle school has flourished. This chapter examines the school's success and the reasons behind it.

We begin by presenting a glimpse of one day in the life of the school, its teachers and students. We describe the Badulla Integrated Rural Development Project, which supplemented normal government support for the school between 1984 and 1988. Project-level data on enrollment and achievement are presented to illustrate progress in all plantation schools included in the project between 1984 and 1988. Comparable data are presented for the Gonakelle school but extended and analyzed historically to illustrate the significance of recent enrollment expansion. We conclude with an exploratory account of change in Gonakelle school, looking at the interplay of human and material resources — of individuals, the school, the local community, the government, and foreign aid — and how these were influenced by events in the region.

The Gonakelle School

At Gonakelle Tamil Vidyalayam it is 7.30 a.m. The children assemble for prayers, school announcements, the national flag-raising ceremony, and the national anthem. The last two activities are a recent innovation in all Sri Lankan schools and were introduced by a former minister of education and youth affairs as part of a national effort to promote and reinforce national unity via education. Whether all schools in the war-torn North and East of the country, or in the increasingly troubled South, actually implement the government circular is unknown. But here in the hills of Passara, far away from the Regional Office of Education in Bandarawela and over 200 miles from the national capital of Colombo, the ceremony takes place daily. Although predominantly Tamil, the population of the Passara District has not been drawn directly into the broader ethnic crisis. The majority of the population here are members of the Indian Tamil rather than the Sri Lankan Tamil community. While Tamils comprise 18 percent of the total population, the Sri Lankan Tamils, whose ancestors arrived in the country more than 2,000 years ago and who now live mainly in the North and the East of Sri Lanka, make up two-thirds of the Tamil total. The Indian Tamils are of much more recent origin. Their ancestors arrived from Tamil Nadu in the south of India during the nineteenth century when they were recruited by Indian agents working on behalf of the British planters who established first the coffee and then the tea and rubber plantations that now cover a large area of the central hills of Sri Lanka.

The ethnic crisis over the past twelve years has involved mainly Sri Lankan Tamils in the North and the East of the country, the predominantly Sinhalese army, and the Sinhalese civilian population living in the North and the East. But the Indian Tamils in Passara were affected by the ethnic crises of 1977, 1979, and most dramatically in 1983. It was in 1983 that extreme groups from among the majority Sinhalese population in Colombo and in the major provincial towns, including Badulla and Bandarawela, took revenge against Tamils, whether Sri Lankan or Indian, in retaliation for a spate of killings of Sinhalese army personnel and Sinhalese civilians by Tamil terrorists in the North. More recently the ethnic crisis has developed into a national political crisis through the activity of the Sinhalese National Liberation Movement (the Janatha Vimukthi Peramuna [JVP]), which has called on the entire population to boycott presidential, general, and provincial government elections and has paralyzed the economy through hartals (strikes) and intimidation.

Gonakelle estate and its school are not untouched by these broad political forces. The school was closed for most of the term before the December 1988 vacation and for most of February 1989. Children who should have been promoted to new classes in January 1989 were not promoted until March. On *hartal* days, parents are asked over the early morning radio not to send their children to school; government buses do not run, preventing teachers and some of the children from the upper grades from reaching the school. Workers are asked to stay away from work, and plantation managers who encourage laborers to work face, at best, intimidation and, at worst, death.

Today there is no *hartal*. The children and teachers move from assembly to their first class of the day. Meanwhile, in the principal's office, an area separated by a cupboard from the main hall where eight classes are in session, a father sits patiently with his two daughters. He waits for over an hour until the school principal has time to attend to him. He had been working as a Hindu priest in Bandarawela until July 1983, but after the 'troubles' he fled to Jaffna with his wife and children, then babies. After six years he has returned to the Badulla district and wishes to admit his daughters to the Gonakelle school.

The bell rings at 8.35, the first lesson over. Class 6B children march outside to stand in the cool of the morning for a reading lesson. Class 5A children hand in their Tamil language exercise books for marking. Three boys stand at the back of the class. The teacher asks other children, already crowded together on chairs, to squeeze a little closer. The three boys edge their way on to the end of the lines of chairs. At 8.45 the student monitor collects some attendance registers and delivers others. The teacher hands out supplementary readers, but there are not quite enough to go around. The girls and boys, crammed together in separate rows, softly read their individual stories aloud. Two boys on the back row quietly discuss the text and the picture. The teacher uses this time to complete health checks on a few of the boys. One is called out, his shirt and then his teeth checked for cleanliness. Behind a movable partition forty students in Class 6A engage in an exercise from the environmental studies workbook. Seven children perch on a bench the same height as the bench that is their desk. Back in Class 5A the teacher calls out 'Vijay Kumar'. Vijay steps forward, hastily tucking his shirt into his trousers, hoping for a good score on the health chart. A gentle hum of activity pervades the building as the health chart is pinned up.

By 8.55 the teacher is ready to move on to the next part of the language lesson. She stands and calls the class to attention. She reminds them that on the previous day she had asked them to bring in some newspapers from home. She holds up a prepared teaching aid, a large card with the title of a daily newspaper written on it. She asks them which newspaper it is. The children reply in unison. She asks for a newspaper brought in by one of the children to be passed forward and explains a point about page layout and advertisements. She now turns her attention to another form of written communication, the greeting card. She holds up another of her teaching aids, a highly decorated festival greeting card. She opens it to display a plain paper inside and a series of handwritten greetings. The teacher sees that one of the children has brought in a card; she draws it to the attention of the others, and hands it back to the child.

At 9.02 the teacher asks the children to find their mathematics books. This request requires no more than a shuffling of books since the children keep all their text and exercise books with them, transporting this pile daily between home and school. The teacher begins to speak. Just at that moment, the children behind the adjacent partition respond loudly and in unison to another teacher's question. The bark is too much for the Class 5A teacher, a small woman with a high-pitched voice. She pauses, her efforts thwarted. She cleans the blackboard instead and writes out in Tamil 'seventeen thousand, nine hundred seventy-seven'. The children write out the words, translate them into digits, write out another set of words, another number, add the numbers and write out the answer in words. The teacher asks for the answer. The boys on the back row are keen to call out, but the teacher quiets them and asks a girl near the front to respond. They carry on working. Suddenly the English-language teacher walks in. The children scramble to their feet and call out in unison, 'Morning, teacher!' They stop their mathematics exercise and follow her outside for an English lesson under the trees.

In just forty minutes this class has read supplementary readers individually, received instruction in the composition and component parts of newspapers and greeting cards, matched and added words and numbers, and embarked on an English lesson — an extremely intense (possibly too intense) series of learning activities.

An engine roars! It is 9.30 and the Class 6B children rush to the window and peer out. Their teacher, another small young woman, shrieks in a high-pitched voice, trying in vain to maintain discipline. The Class 5A children, standing outside for their English lesson, break away from their reading circle and rush down the steps to the edge of the playground where a bulldozer has started work. The earthmover, operated by a local man from Passara, scoops the earth, moving it from one end of the playground to the other, picking up large boulders as though they were tennis balls. The children are excited. The year 1 children are shepherded outside for their language lesson but are much more interested in the activity of the earthmover. The teacher tolerates their excitement for a while, before urging them to congregate a little closer to the classroom, a little further from the edge of the earthmover. Some just cannot avert their eyes from the playground. The teacher tries her very best to distract the children with pretty pictures fixed to a felt display board. But the children steal every moment to witness the transformation of the playground from a rough area peppered with boulders to an area suitable for construction of a running track and other sports facilities. The transformation represents the realization of one of the principal's dreams for his school.

It is 11.00 a.m., and a teacher works with the children of both year 2 classes on a word-building exercise in Tamil. She writes a phoneme, calls it out, and the children repeat it in unison. Students in Class 3B are reading outside in the sun, while Class 3A children sing and clap in playing language games. It is nearly 11.30 and Classes 1A and 1B prepare to leave school. Meanwhile, one teacher struggles to be heard by about eighty children in Classes 4A and 4B. She moves swiftly between two blackboards, assigning work for both classes. The noise is deafening. In Class 7 no teacher is present, but all fifty-eight children engage in quiet self-study. The Class 8 students are engaged in a lesson on the importance of vitamins in nutrition. The teacher poses a question, and the class responds in unison. Today, only thirty-eight of the sixty-three enrolled students are present. One wonders where all sixty-three could possibly sit.

School finishes at 1.30 p.m., but today everyone is slow to leave. Children and teachers alike are fascinated with the earthmover. Those children obliged to return home with the *kanganis* move off first; those who live close by linger.

The Badulla Integrated Rural Development Project

Gonakelle Tamil Vidyalayam has developed rapidly over the past few years. Along with other plantation schools and remote rural Sinhala-medium schools, it has benefitted from its inclusion since 1984 in the Badulla District Integrated Rural Development Project (IRDP), a foreign-assisted program involving investment in several sectors: agriculture, irrigation, roads, health and education. The Badulla District was selected as the fifth district to benefit from foreign-funded rural development projects promoted by the United National Party government as one part of a three-pronged strategy for economic development. The education component of the Badulla project has been funded by the Swedish International Development Authority (SIDA).

A total of fifty-two Sinhala-medium schools in remote villages and forty-two Tamil-medium plantation schools were supported by the project over four years. This support consisted of physical resources (classroom materials, furniture, teacher accommodation and equipment) and other resources for the improvement of teaching and learning, including an increased number of teachers, as well as the training and curriculum support to improve educational effectiveness. In both the remote village areas and the estate schools support focused on the primary cycle of education. The decision to focus on the primary cycle was shaped by a concern for the contribution that education could make to the mass of young people most likely to remain *within* the district over the longer term. The implications of this decision included: (1) focusing on the lower end of the education system, (2) improving the material conditions in primary education under which children and teachers worked, and (3) improving the quality of teaching and learning (Little, 1989).

The international literature on education and rural development reflects two advocacies. The first maintains that the formal mainstream of education has worked ineffectively for rural populations and that radical, alternative, special and innovative structures of education are required (Evans, 1981). The second suggests that education designed for children in rural areas should be broadly similar to that provided for urban children, and that general formal education is superior in terms of equity and efficiency to education oriented to the specific content of rural life (Barber, 1981). The design of the Badulla Integrated Rural Development Project is consonant with the second line of argument. It was designed to supplement rather than substitute for current provisions for primary education in rural areas, to improve effectiveness and promote expansion simultaneously, and to direct investment to educationally and economically vulnerable groups.

The first phase of the program was aimed at schools in tea plantation areas where the medium of instruction in all but two of the forty-two schools was Tamil, and in fifty-two schools in a dry-zone area of the district where the medium of instruction was Sinhala. The program was organized from a project 'cell' located within the regional office of education, accountable vertically to the Ministry of Education through the Regional Director of Education and horizontally to the IRDP project office in Badulla; the IRDP project in turn was accountable vertically to the Ministry of Plan Implementation, which communicated with SIDA (Figure 6.1). The continuous and discontinuous lines in Figure 6.1 indicate formal and less formal lines of authority, respectively.

Improving Effectiveness in the Classroom

Within the Ministry of Education various departments were responsible for the development of individual aspects of the program to increase classroom effectiveness — curriculum development, textbook writing, in-service training, and teacher training. The Ministry of Educational Services, on the other hand, handled infrastructure inputs (e.g., buildings, furniture and equipment) for school development. This arrangement made the coordinated planning of inputs for any

Figure 6.1 Organizational structure of the education component of the Badulla Integrated Rural Development Project

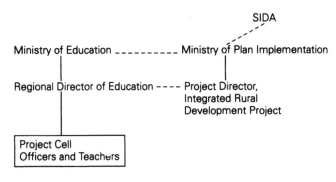

—— formal lines of authority
- - - - less formal lines of authority

given school difficult. A central thrust of the education sector program was the activity designed to improve effectiveness in the classroom, combined with an increase in teacher supply, buildings, furniture and equipment. The Badulla project was the first IRDP to include an education component with a strong orientation to improving educational effectiveness. Until 1984 the education components of Sri Lankan IRDPs had consisted of buildings, furniture and equipment. The *combination* of inputs designed to improve student learning and achievement as well as the physical conditions in which learning takes place (e.g., buildings, teacher accommodation, furniture, equipment) was a new departure for the IRDPs and the Ministry of Education.

The program for improving educational effectiveness was complex and consisted of four main elements (Figure 6.2). In the first, the production of

Figure 6.2 Program of activities for improving educational effectiveness

1/ Production of existing curriculum materials
   – Syllabi, remedial teaching guides, song/verse books
   – Production and distribution of learning kits (aesthetic, agricultural, primary learning)

2/ Design, production, and distribution of new material
   – Teachers' guides for integrated lesson units; health/nutrition/agriculture units; multigrade teaching; environmental studies; low-cost playgrounds
   – Supplementary readers
   – Minimum learning continuum and other teacher aids for assessment

3/ Training and Orientation
   – For untrained and inexperienced teachers
   – For trained teachers
   – For principals/deputy principals
   – For education support staff

4/ Support mechanisms for quality development
   – Classroom and school supervision
   – Newsletter, magazine
   – School Development Societies
   – Teacher visits

existing curriculum materials, an effort was made to ensure that basic materials such as the syllabi for years 1 to 5 were reproduced and placed in the hands of all teachers. In some schools syllabi were no longer to be found.

Some untrained teachers had never seen a syllabus. Others had never seen a teacher's guidebook. One might have expected such basic teaching materials to have been freely available at the National Curriculum Development Centre, but they were not. The project staff faced their first implementation problem. How were they to reproduce existing curriculum material in large quantities? The solution lay in two pieces of imported machinery — a scanner and a photocopier — and one piece of locally manufactured machinery — a duplicating machine. The production and distribution of learning kits posed implementation problems of a different kind. The kit designs were available already at the National Curriculum Development Centre, but they took some time to locate. Once found, they were modified slightly and tenders were invited — for scissors, colored paper, magnifying glasses, child-sized agricultural implements, and musical instruments. Because the project was part of a broader Integrated Rural Development Project with an emphasis on income generation, an effort was made to purchase items from within the district. The mass purchase of several small items from several small local shops posed a number of administrative headaches for the education office accountant, who took the initiative and organized not only the purchase of items but also their packaging and distribution.

The second aim of the program to improve educational effectiveness was the design, production, and distribution of new curriculum materials. These materials were not available anywhere in the country. Among the new materials developed were teachers' guides for environmental studies, integrated lesson units, multigrade teaching materials, and plans for the construction of low-cost playgrounds; storybooks to supplement the language textbooks; and items such as the 'minimum learning continuum' to assist teachers in the assessment of learning outcomes. The development of these materials involved small teams of teachers and resource persons from the regional education office and National Curriculum Development Centre. After their design, all materials were reproduced and distributed to schools.

The production and distribution of basic learning materials was accompanied by the third component, the training and orientation of key personnel. These included untrained and inexperienced teachers, trained teachers, principals and deputy principals, and education support staff (e.g., circuit education officers). This program built on existing in-service provisions in the district, but it was different in several respects. First, some of the untrained teachers followed a specially designed one-year teacher preparation course, the Plantation Sector Training Programme (PSTP), a course introduced nationwide in 1985 for General Certificate of Education (GCE) O-level qualified young persons from the plantation areas. Nationally, the teacher trainees followed a daily afternoon course. But the PSTP teachers under the Badulla IRDP program taught in school four days per week and followed the course on Fridays and during the weekend. This intensive program had the advantage of combining training with ongoing classroom experience. The in-service training courses for trained teachers also differed from the national courses. Courses were residential rather than non-residential and dual-medium (Tamil and Sinhala) rather than mono-medium; a special effort was made to make them as practical and non-theoretical as possible.

The residential nature of the courses doubled the amount of time available per day for workshop and seminar sessions as the teachers were prepared to work late into the night. Child care facilities enabled teachers with very young children to attend and stay overnight. The socio-cultural gain experienced by Sinhala and Tamil teachers who shared living arrangements while following separate language-medium seminars was considerable. Attendance at these courses was high. Of the 559 invitations issued for the fifteen courses held over four years, 95 percent were accepted.

The fourth strategy for improving educational effectiveness involved a variety of support mechanisms. The first, classroom and school supervision, was considered vital for the continued professional development of teachers. However, it was a system that was slow to develop. On the one hand, the project cell found it easier to bring large numbers of teachers together for short periods of time than to plan and organize supervision timetables for a small number of supervisors to visit a large number of schools over a long period of time. On the other hand, the system required a shift in the role of the supervisor from inspector and monitor to supporter and advisor. Under the prevailing system the circuit educator officers (many of whom had never themselves taught in a primary classroom) had multiple and complex roles. The number of schools for which they were responsible varied between thirty and seventy, and they were expected to inspect all aspects of school life from attendance and enrollment to classroom activity, equipment, and the condition of buildings. In practice they tended to spend more time monitoring enrollment and attendance figures in the principal's office than discussing with teachers their problems of pedagogy in the classroom.

As the project developed, two types of supervisor emerged. Teacher-supervisors became involved in the classroom work, while the officers of a higher status focused their supervisory attention on more general school-management matters. One of the officer-supervisors' more important roles turned out to be the meetings called with the School Development Societies (Parent-Teacher Associations). Many of these societies either did not exist at the beginning of the project or were inactive. An effort was made by project cell officers to meet with School Development Societies for half a day in all ninety-four project schools. One innovative support mechanism that proved especially popular among teachers was the program of teacher visits to schools where they observed and assisted with the work of other teachers, usually those with greater experience or skill. A monthly newsletter with short contributions from teachers also proved popular.

Costs

The annual project cost per student between 1984 and 1988 is shown in Table 6.1. Two types of cost are shown. The cost per student of total project expenses (furniture, buildings, equipment, materials development, in-service training, administration, etc.) averaged Rs364 or just over US$10 per annum. Excluding the furniture and buildings program, the annual cost per student was just US$2.50, approximately 7.5 percent of the unit recurrent cost of education in Sri Lanka in 1988 (Rs1137/US$33).

Angela Little and R. Sivasithambaram

Table 6.1   Project cost per annum, rupees/student

Year	All costs including furniture and buildings	All costs excluding furniture and buildings
1984	361	73
1985	329	80
1986	364	87
1987	326	87
1988 (6 months)	256	49
US$1 = 34 Rupees (1989)		

Project Impact

Enrollment.   During the project period 1984–88, enrollment in year 1–5 in the Tamil-medium plantation schools grew from 4,607 in 1984 to 6,278 in 1988. These figures represent an enrollment increase of 36 percent. During the same period the rate of increase in total enrollment across the national education system was just over 10 percent.

Achievement.   Baseline data on the year 4 primary students' achievement levels in math and language were collected in 1985 and 1987. The tests were constructed by experienced teachers based in the project management cell in the regional Office of Education and were designed to test achievement in the math and language objectives of the national primary year 4 curriculum. They were administered under examination conditions by teachers from neighbouring schools. No teacher administered tests to students in his/her own school. The teachers who administered the tests also marked them and sent the papers and marks sheets to the project cell for scrutiny. Table 6.2 presents the achievement data from thirty-three Tamil plantation schools that participated in both tests.

Table 6.2 indicates an increase in the mean scores of students in the year 4

Table 6.2   Year 4 student achievement in Tamil language and math, 1985 and 1987, (33 project plantation schools)

	1985	1987
Tamil Language		
Mean	16.70	27.76
S.D.	11.38	20.63
N	352	526
	$Z = 10.24$, $p \leq 0.001$	
Math		
Mean	20.50	33.76
S.D.	13.19	18.87
N	352	526
	$Z = 12.39$, $p \leq 0.001$	

classes between 1985 and 1987 in Tamil language from 16.70 to 27.76 (Z = 10.24, p ≤ 0.001) and in mathematics from 20.50 to 33.76 (Z = 12.39, p ≤ 0.001). The maximum score on both tests was 100. The dispersion of scores also increased from 1985 to 1987 in both subjects, as did the sample size, reflecting, no doubt, change on another of the impact indicators, enrollment. While this increase in achievement is apparent when the scores from the thirty-three plantation project schools are grouped together, not every school showed improvement. In fact, five of the thirty-three schools experienced a decline in mean achievement levels in both Tamil language and mathematics.

Achievement data were also collected from seven control plantation schools, i.e., schools outside the project area but geographically close, similar in terms of the socio-economic background of students, and identical in terms of curriculum and language of instruction. In these control schools, the mean achievement levels of year 4 students showed no change.

Impact in Gonakelle School

The Gonakelle school is regarded by many of those who manage and supervise the project and by many teachers in the Passara project area as a rapidly developing and successful school. Enrollment has been growing (from 261 students in 1984 to 811 students in 1989), and year-grades have expanded from year 6 in 1985 to year 10 in 1989. The number of teachers has grown from six in 1984 to fifteen in 1989, and achievement levels have increased.

Enrollment in Gonakelle School

The rate of enrollment growth over the last few years has been dramatic and is appreciated best in relation to the historical rate of growth. The Appendix to this chapter describes the historical and demographic context for understanding changes in the school enrollment and presents detailed enrollment data (Figures 1A, 2A, and 3A). Over the past thirty years the number of children resident on the estate has remained fairly stable; the total number of such children in 1986 was only thirty-nine more than in 1960. By contrast, school enrollment in 1986 was four times that of 1960.

The enrollment figures fall into four periods. The first period, 1943–68, had a remarkably stable enrollment of between 110 and 170 children; the second period, 1969–77, an increasing and then declining enrollment; the third period, 1978–84, an increasing and then levelling enrollment; and fourth period, 1984–90, a rapidly increasing enrollment.

Growth in Number of Teachers. During the project period there was some improvement in the numbers of teachers in the school. In 1984 there were four teachers. This number reached nine by 1985 but dropped to eight by 1988. Table 6.3 shows the change in the number of teachers and the pupil-teacher ratio since 1978. The overall situation has improved markedly since government takeover of the school in 1977 but is subject to considerable fluctuation as reflected in the 1988 figures. In 1988 a number of teachers left the school for training college. Current teacher-pupil ratios are still double the national average.

Table 6.3   Pupils, teachers, pupil–teacher ratios, Gonakelle School and national figures, 1978–90

Year	Gonakelle School			National pupil–teacher ratio
	Number enrolled	Number of teachers	Pupil teacher ratio	
1978	177	1	177:1	24:1
1979	225	2	112:1	23:1
1980	272	4	63:1	24:1
1981	270	2	135:1	26:1
1982	253	3	84:1	26:1
1983	273	4	63:1	27:1
1984	310	4	77:1	26:1
1985	382	9	42:1	26:1
1986	484	10	48:1	26:1
1987	552	10	55:1	27:1
1988	734	8	92:1	28:1
1989	823	15	55:1	n.a.
1990	950	19	50:1	n.a.

Achievement.   The achievement data from the Gonakelle school are presented in Table 6.4. The mean scores were above the average of all project plantation schools in both subjects in both years. The mean scores increased despite the near-doubling of the number of children taking the test. The achievement gain was greater in mathematics than in language, the former reaching acceptable levels of statistical significance. The dispersion of scores in math was similar in both years, but the dispersion in language increased. Table 6.5 presents the distribution of raw scores in the two years. The achievement gains have been enjoyed by both the highest and lowest achieving groups, though the gains of the highest achievers relative to the lowest achievers have been greater in language.

The achievement gains in this project-administered test are reflected in the fact that three children succeeded in passing the year 5 national scholarship

Table 6.4   Year 4 student achievement in Tamil and math (1985 and 1987), Gonakelle School, compared with 33 project plantation schools [in brackets]

	1985	1987
Tamil Language		
Mean	25.5 [16.70]	30.54 [27.76]
S.D.	14.28 [11.38]	22.03 [20.63]
N	38	71
	$Z = 1.43$, n.s.	
Math		
Mean	27.16 [20.50]	34.13 [33.76]
S.D.	14.35 [13.19]	14.25 [18.87]
N	38	71
	$Z = 2.40$, $p \leq 0.05$	

Table 6.5   Frequency distribution of raw scores, Tamil and mathematics, year 4, Gonakelle School (1985 and 1987)

	1985		1987	
	Freq.	%	Freq.	%
Language				
0– 24	22	58	35	49
25– 39	10	26	16	23
40– 59	6	16	8	11
60– 74	0	0	10	14
75–100	0	0	2	3
	38	100	71	100
Math				
0– 24	16	42	21	30
25– 39	14	37	25	35
40– 59	8	21	18	25
60– 74	0	0	6	9
75–100	0	0	1	1
	38	100	71	100

examination in 1989, resulting in financial assistance for their education. No other school in the Passara district achieved a single success in that exam.

Understanding Change in Gonakelle School

How then are we to understand the changes that have taken place in Gonakelle school? What have been the ingredients for success? There is not one simple answer. The complex answer lies in an interplay of human and material resources from the school, the local community, government, and an outside aid project, as well as in a number of fortuitous circumstances.

The Aid Project

The school's 'project' status explains part of its success. The project supplemented government provision in a variety of ways: an increase in the number of teachers in the school; a more intensive in-service training and supervision program; and inputs of extra classrooms, furniture, teacher accommodation, learning kits, teaching aids and books. The project status of the inputs meant that the school enjoyed additional external attention (the Hawthorne effect) from the local educational administration. Its location thirty miles from the regional office facilitated frequent visits by local and national education officers and foreign aid workers.

Fortuitous Timing of Project Intervention

Although planned during a period when national government support for plantation Tamil education was lukewarm, the inception of project implementation in February 1984 coincided with the aftermath of civilian Sinhalese attacks on civilian Tamils the previous year. Ironically, the master copy of the project plan was due to be completed on July 25, 1983, the day violence broke out in Colombo. But it lay dormant for some time at the bottom of the Colombo garden of a Sinhalese neighbour of the Tamil education officer who had worked on its final editing and who sought refuge for it as she fled. In the atonement that followed, the political climate changed. Aid projects that included Tamil areas were welcomed cautiously by a chastened government, anxious to maintain and increase foreign aid resources (Little, 1987). Moreover, the wise appointment of a trilingual Muslim as project director, in preference to either a Sinhala, or Tamil individual, increased the project's acceptability to Sinhalese, Tamil and Muslim teachers in the initial phase of implementation.

Building from a State-funded Base

But a fortuitously timed, foreign-aided project is not the only answer to Gonakelle's fortunes. In terms of material resources the project represented 'icing on the cake', the main ingredients of which were provided by government. Teacher salaries, the textbooks, the syllabus, the day-to-day administration, one new classroom block, and the salaries of project managers themselves were all paid for by government. The project merely supplemented what was already on the ground (a fact all too easily forgotten by many aid and lending bank workers). It built from a state-funded base.

Teachers from the Community

During the project period government introduced a new training and recruitment program for plantation area teachers that was to have an impact on teacher supply to plantation schools. The Plantation Sector Training Programme (PSTP) recruited teachers with six passes at the General Certificate of Education 'Ordinary' level ('O level') rather than the Advanced level passes required of other teacher recruitment schemes. The restriction of recruitment to persons from plantation areas was intended to change the profile of teachers in plantation schools. Many of the teachers in the plantation schools in the 1970s were Tamil speakers from the North and the East of Sri Lanka. Though linguistically similar to the local population, these teachers had the reputation of looking down on the plantation Tamil children they taught — their ancestry and, in particular, their dissimilar caste background. The new scheme was designed to encourage Tamil-speaking youth from plantation areas to secure the government jobs from which so many had been excluded for so long, and to ensure a flowback of educated persons to serve their own communities. In 1985 the Gonakelle school was to benefit from six new, young and enthusiastic teachers from this scheme in 1985. An added bonus derived from the fact that the school principal had been one of their PSTP lecturers.

Teacher Stability

The education officer responsible for the postings and transfers of Tamil teachers to schools in the Badulla District was also responsible part-time for project administration. This coincidence of function facilitated a decision to request the new teachers to serve for a minimum of three years in the project area. The implementation of this decision was facilitated by the fact that the transfers and 'welfare' of Tamil teachers were subject to considerably less political influence than those of Sinhalese teachers at that time.

The Leadership of the School

But if the success of a particular school in the project cannot be attributed solely to the foreign-aided status of the school and politically fortuitous timing, neither can it be attributed solely to government funding or to teacher supply. Many other schools had new and sometimes better qualified teachers posted to them. Other schools enjoyed closer links with the educational administration and with politicians. Others also received support from the fortuitously timed foreign aid project. And yet they have not succeeded like Gonakelle. Why?

The answer is rooted partly in the school itself and especially in the leadership of the school principal. The principal was posted to the school in April 1984, just two months after the inception of the project. Significantly, he was a former student of the Gonakelle school. Admitted to standard 3 in 1951 when his parents moved from a nearby estate, he was to stay in the school for two years before moving on to a larger school. At that time Gonakelle school was not designed for educational success. Of the thirty-one students admitted to the school in that year, only six completed six years of basic education in the Gonakelle school. Six left within the first year of their education, and of the remaining nineteen students, the majority completed three years or less. That an old boy of a plantation school could succeed in becoming a fully trained teacher and return to the school to serve and lead did not go unnoticed by parents. Within a month of his arrival he was compelled to seek special permission from the regional department to admit eighteen new students in the month of May (normally students are not admitted after March). He promptly set in motion his plan to transform the school from a six-year school to an eleven-year school preparing students for the GCE O level examination. In 1986 he introduced a seventh grade. His dream of an eleven-grade school preparing students for the GCE O level exam will come to fruition at the end of 1990, fulfilling one part of his commitment and plan for bettering his community.

Delegation of Responsibility

As the school has grown, so the principal has delegated responsibilities to teachers and students. Students are appointed as class monitors, as school prefects and as rotating leaders of the groups who maintain the school's sanitation facilities. Teachers are delegated to organize the literary association, the school feeding program, the library, cultural events, the attendance registers and other functions. The formation of a school identity has been forged through the symbols of the school flag, a school emblem, a school uniform and a school tie.

Horizontal Linkages with Nearby Schools

The principal's professional work extends beyond the confines of his school. As noted earlier, he serves as a lecturer in the plantation sector training program. He also acts frequently as a resource person for in-service training programs organized under the aid project. His school has been visited by teachers from other schools under the project's 'teacher visits' program. He has established a teachers' center for teachers from ten small schools in the vicinity. Together they discuss classroom practice and organize interschool events and student competitions. As a center they compete against other groups of schools within the district. Thus horizontal links and identities are forged between teachers and students across schools while vertical links between the school and the project have become reciprocal. The school receives and it gives; the project gives and it receives.

Community Support

The School Development Society has a membership of 400–500 parents. Each pays a membership subscription of Rs5 per annum. The principal has been able to build on the support of this organization, which had functioned well during his predecessors' time. Despite the fact that the school was closed for half the normal school days during 1989, the annual general meeting was held as usual, followed by two general parents' meetings and a series of committee meetings. Among the matters discussed were whether the school should remain open despite the communal and political disturbances in the district, how to organize the recently introduced government school feeding program, and the problems of transport faced by the older children travelling from distant estates.

The degree of parental support enjoyed by the school may have been affected by several factors. During the 1970s the effect of repatriation schemes was felt. A degree of insecurity over the future in Sri Lanka and uncertainty over life in India meant that some parents did not invest in their childrens' future through education. After the communal violence in 1983 and the difficulty of safe transport to the North and the sea crossing to India, repatriation slowed to a trickle. It began to be clear to most people, including those in government, that the individuals residing on the estates would live their lives in Sri Lanka — a Sri Lanka where opportunities for work outside the estates were opening up. Since access to such opportunities requires education, supporting the schools is important.

Another factor related to strong community support is the relatively homogeneous and leader-oriented characteristic of contemporary resident estate populations conditioned by more than a century of estate life. The residents are accustomed to a rigid authority structure controlled, on the one hand, by the superintendent, his assistants, field officers and *kanganis*, and, on the other, by the trade union leaders and officials. Seeing in the principal a strong leader who wished to meet their long-felt desire for improved educational opportunities for their children, parents have been unified and strong in their support.

Conclusion

The Gonakelle plantation school has flourished over the past decade experiencing a dramatic increase in enrollment and achievement over the past five years in particular. This change has occurred in a national social context characterized by the transfer of the immediate control of plantation schools from the plantation to the State; a change in status for plantation teachers from plantation employees to government employees; a history of social disadvantage of estate populations; declining government resources for education per child enrolled; and a growing ethnic and political crisis. The Gonakelle school benefitted from its inclusion in a district-based Integrated Rural Development Project aimed at the improved effectiveness of primary school education. Improvements during the project period were apparent in enrollment numbers, average achievement levels, and teacher-pupil ratios.

However, analysis of change in the Gonakelle school suggests that the aid project status of the school was not the sole reason for the school's development. A number of other factors have been important. The timing of the onset of the project was fortuitous, falling as it did just after the 1983 ethnic riots when government was anxious to appease foreign critics of its recent human rights record. The project built from a government-funded base, without which the project would have been extremely costly and vulnerable. The number of teachers available to the school increased greatly and made it possible to translate in-service training and provision of materials into improved classroom practice. The new teachers, mostly young and enthusiastic, were themselves members of the plantation community. Moreover, those trained by the project were required to serve in the school for at least three years before qualifying for transfer. In each of the two periods, 1978–1983 and 1984–1989, there was a school principal who played a significant role. The latter principal enjoyed the distinction of having been himself an 'old boy' of the school, a fact not lost on the plantation community, many of whom remembered him in his younger days. In his role as principal he delegated responsibilities for a range of activities to other teachers and projects. He also extended his professional work beyond the confines of his own school. He has been a lecturer in a variety of district training programs, and he established a teachers' center for teachers in the neighbouring small schools. His school receives aid. He gives of his time and expertise to train teachers in other project schools. The school has enjoyed the support of the parents whose children it serves.

The school is known in the local education community for its success. By national standards it would probably be judged as only of average success. Relative to its own starting point back in the seventies, however, change has been rapid, and the school faces the future with confidence but not complacency. As we left the school, the principal commented, 'How can we really say we have been successful? Our enrollment has increased, our teachers have increased, our results are better, but look at the cramped conditions in which the children are learning'.

It is true. Despite two new large buildings the children have less floor space in which to work now (5.4 square feet) than they did in 1984 (6.2 square feet). The nationally recommended figure is 10 square feet per pupil. The project planners never imagined that the enrollment increase could be so rapid — and the underlying government administration does not respond quickly to needs in faraway schools.

The principal continued, 'If we cannot increase our space, all our previous efforts will turn to failure. I'm trying to encourage the parents to help us build a temporary shelter. I'll be taking this up at our next meeting'.

Angela Little and R. Sivasithambaram

References

BARBER, E.G. (1981) 'General education versus special education for rural development', *Comparative Education Review*, 25, June, pp. 216–31.

BACKFORD, G. (1972) *Persistent Poverty: Underdevelopment in Plantation Economies in the
Third World*, New York, Oxford University Press.

EVANS, D.R. (1981) 'The educational policy dilemma for rural areas', *Comparative
Education Review*, 25, June, pp. 232–43.

GNANAMUTTU, G. (1976) *Education and the Indian Plantation Worker in Sri Lanka*,
Colombo, Sri Lanka, Council of Churches.

JAIN, R.K. (1970) *South Indians on the Plantation Frontier of Malaya*, Kuala Lumpur,
Malaya, University of Malaya Press.

LITTLE, A.W. (1987) 'Education and change in plantations: The case of Sri Lanka',
Institute of Development Studies Bulletin, 18, 2, pp. 31–7.

LITTLE, A.W. (1989) *The Badulla Integrated Rural Development Project: Education
Component*, paper presented at the Ministry of Education and Swedish
International Development Authority Seminar, Bandarawela, Sri Lanka.

MINISTRY OF EDUCATION AND SWEDISH INTERNATIONAL DEVELOPMENT AUTHORITY (1983)
Badulla Integrated Rural Development Project: Education Component, Main Report
and Technical Annexes, Colombo, Sri Lanka.

MINISTRY OF EDUCATION AND SWEDISH INTERNATIONAL DEVELOPMENT AUTHORITY (1986)
Plantation Schools Education Development Programme, 1987/1991.

WORLD BANK (1988) *Staff Appraisal Report: Sri Lanka General Education Report*,
Washington, DC, World Bank Population and Human Resources Division.

Appendix

The Appendix contains three figures presenting enrollment data for the Gonakelle school. Figure 1A presents enrollment data for the school as a whole from 1943–89, and Figure 2A presents data for the same period for years 1–6 only. Figure 3A presents the school enrollment data for 1960–89 alongside the number of laborers' children aged 0–14 resident on the estate. These figures, together with the following historical information, provide a picture of significant changes in the Gonakelle school over time.

Four Periods in the History of the Gonakelle School

The first period in the history of the Gonakelle school (1943–68) was characterized by private-sector ownership of the estate and government statutory frameworks for the provision of education. The Gonakelle estate was owned by the Ouvah Highlands Group of Companies. During this period estates were legally bound by conditions on estate education laid out in a 1939 ordinance (no. 31) and a 1956 revision of Chapter 185 of the Legislative Enactments of Ceylon. Under the 1939 ordinance on estates with more than twenty-five resident children aged 6–10 years, plantation superintendents were required 'to make such provision as may be prescribed for the education of the children on his estate' (Gnanamuttu, 1976, p. 38). The 1956 revision relaxed the compulsion implicit in the 1939 ordinance and acknowledged that neither the owner nor the superintendent of an estate was compelled to make provision for education. Where schools existed, superintendents were obliged to meet a number of conditions: a satisfactory building with 10 sq. ft. of floor space for each child on the school register, bench and desk space for each child, a competent teacher, and a minimum of two hours teaching per day for at least 180 days per year. Such schools were paid government grants based on examination results and attendance sanctioned by inspectors after an annual visit. An entry in the Gonakelle logbook dated October 25, 1943, sketches the inspector's concerns:

> Held the annual inspection today. 81/140 pupils were presented at the examination and the results were very satisfactory, the percentages of passes being 87. Progress has been maintained. Defects pointed out at last year's inspection have been remedied. Attention should be given to cleanliness of the children, a record of daily inspection in cleanliness should be kept. To higher classes verse literature should be taught in more detail. A taste for poetry should be evoked. Handwork and needlework of the girls were very satisfactory. . . . [The] school garden is in good condition. I am glad to note that the manager takes great interest in the education of the labourers' children. Furniture is rather old-fashioned and if they are replaced by new ones if possible it will be better (Gonakelle Logbook, 25.10.43).

The remarkably stable enrollment of the Gonakelle school between 1943 and 1968 may be attributed to a lack of incentive to increase it. Although government guidelines suggested that additional teachers be employed for larger numbers enrolled, pupil–teacher ratios of 140:1 were not uncommon in plantation schools generally. Although the estate received a government grant for running the school, based on a formula involving enrollment, rate of attendance, and percentage of passes, the grant only covered about 25–30 percent of actual expenditure. Plantation superintendents satisfied themselves that they had met their minimum obligation to provide a school building, furniture, equipment and a teacher. From time to time the government made recommendations about the integration of plantation schools into the national system of education, but these lacked the political commitment necessary to lead to action.

The enrollment pattern in the Gonakelle school during the period 1968–1977 is best understood in terms of a local change in population and three changes initiated at the national level. Between 1968 and 1971 the resident population aged 0–14 years increased from 1,150 to 1,280, an annual average increase of 5 percent. This is reflected in a growth of the school population from 152 to 183, an annual average increase of just over 5 percent. But between 1972 and 1977 enrollment fell. The 1970 election brought to power the Sri Lanka Freedom Party, which was committed to the nationalization of plantations. Companies began to run down their investments. Gonakelle estate was nationalized in 1975, and the school was taken over by the Ministry of Education in 1978. It is possible that the nationalization of the estate led to a degree of disruption in the school. Of more significance, however, was the 1972 national educational reform, which raised the school entry age from 5 to 6. Plantation schools that previously offered six grades of education now offered only five. The repatriation of children and their families to their Indian 'homeland' also contributed to the decline. An analysis of the 'admissions and withdrawals' register showed that more children were withdrawn from school for repatriation to India in 1973, 1974, and 1976 than at any other time between 1966 and 1988 (except for 1984 after the 1983 communal riots).

After government takeover of the school in 1978, enrollment began to rise (Figure 1A). Two factors are important here. In 1977 the United National Party returned to power and was quick to overturn many of the educational reforms introduced during the earlier regime. The Party returned to an earlier policy of admitting children to school at the age of 5 rather than 6. In 1978 a new teacher, a Jaffna man, was posted to the school. Faced with 177 children to teach alone, he succeeded in having another teacher posted to the school by 1979 and two more teachers in 1980.

Figure 1A   Gonakelle School total enrollment, 1943–89

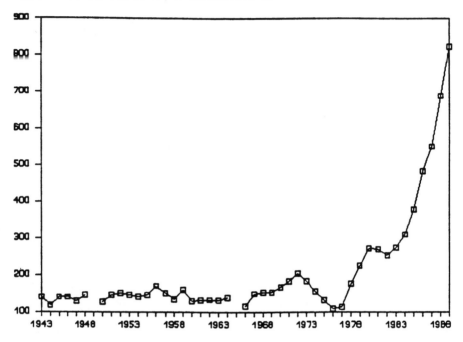

Source: Gonakelle School logbooks and attendance registers

He had the reputation of being an active teacher who succeeded in mobilizing support for the school from parents. Estate files from this period record the requests to the estate management by the school development society for various kinds of support for the school.

After 1984 enrollment rose in spectacular fashion — from 298 in 1984 to 427 in 1986, 700 in 1987, and 811 in 1989 — a 170 percent increase in just five years. This increase resulted partly from the principal's plan in 1985 to extend his six-grade school to an eleven-grade school year by year. But this is only a partial explanation. The enrollment in years 1–6 alone increased from 310 in 1984 to 612 in 1988 (Figure 2A). During the same period, the sex ratio also improved. In 1985 approximately 64 percent of the enrolled students were boys, and 36 percent were girls. By 1988 male and female students were in better balance — 59 percent boys and 41 percent girls. Figure 3A shows the Gonakelle school enrollment from 1960 to 1989 in relation to the number of children living on the plantation over those years.

Figure 2A   Gonakelle resident estate labour population 0–14 years and school enrollment, 1960–89

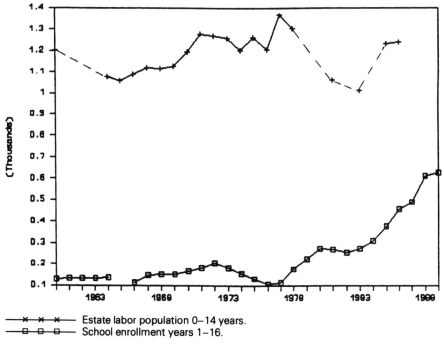

- ✕ ✕ ✕ Estate labor population 0–14 years.
- ▭ ▭ ▭ School enrollment years 1–16.

Source: Gonakelle school logbooks and attendance registers
Gonakelle estate food control files, 1960–79
Gonakelle estate labour return

Figure 3A   Gonakelle School enrollment, years 1–6, 1942–89

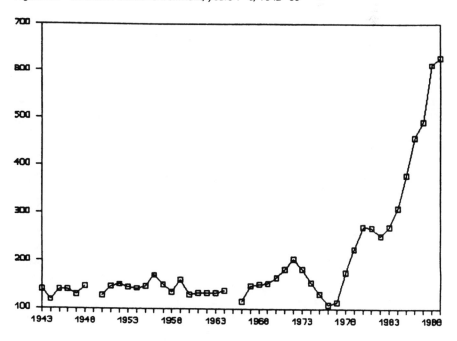

Source: Gonakelle School logbooks and attendance registers

Chapter 7

Local Initiatives and Their Implications for a Multi-Level Approach to School Improvement in Thailand*

Mun C. Tsang and Christopher Wheeler

Introduction

Given the crisis of resources and quality affecting schools in less developed countries, the policy challenges become how to expand available resources and how to raise quality within existing resource constraints. This chapter examines Thailand's response to these challenges.

In Thailand improvement in primary school quality has not kept pace with successful expansion of the primary school system (now encompassing 96 percent of every age cohort). For example, in 1985, the Office of the National Primary Education Commission (ONPEC, the agency that administers 85 percent of the primary schools in Thailand) found that mean test scores were lower than the 50 percent standard required by the government in almost all subjects (Bhumirat et al., 1987).

In Thailand, as in other less developed countries, the problems of school quality are especially severe for students from impoverished and economically disadvantaged backgrounds. For example, in rural areas of Thailand student malnutrition and high dropout rates between grades 4 and 5 continue to be severe problems, and there is an acute shortage of qualified teachers in areas like the Northeast region (Office of the National Education Commission, 1988). Tsang and Kidchanapanish (forthcoming) found that students from lower socio-economic backgrounds (such as less educated, lower income, and less wealthy families) often receive from their parents significantly less financial support for their schooling than students from higher socio-economic backgrounds.

Given this context, are there 'self-help' strategies that can mobilize additional

* This chapter is based on ongoing research conducted in Thailand as part of the Basic Research and Implementation in Developing Education Systems (BRIDGES) Project. The authors contributed equally to this chapter. They wish to acknowledge the helpful comments of Jack Schwille on a draft of the chapter.

local resources to the advantage of schools? Can existing resources be used more effectively to educate children from impoverished backgrounds? This paper provides two positive responses to these questions. First, it shows how additional economic resources for schools can be mobilized by strengthening the relationship between a school and its local community and by increasing parental involvement in school activities. It also examines the use of available educational resources through a management strategy of grouping schools in a district into school clusters. This strategy is designed to encourage sharing and better use of existing resources among schools, to promote cooperation among teachers and principals within schools belonging to the cluster, and to focus attention within schools on the academic purpose of schooling through various accountability measures.

Moreover, the paper shows that principal leadership is a common thread linking the two strategies. It argues that the school principal plays a critical, if not determining, role in mobilizing community resources and parental participation in school activities and in responding to school cluster policies.

In so doing, the paper shows how these strategies at the local level have implications for the policy roles that different levels of administration in Thailand can play in promoting the improvement of primary school quality. We argue that each level has a different role to play if school improvement efforts are to be effective. Specifically, we argue that strengthening the relationship between a school and its local community and increasing parental involvement in school activities can provide additional resources to schools.

School clusters may be especially useful in providing assistance to individual schools through staff development, the development of materials and increasing individual school access to materials and equipment in the cluster resource center. They can also assist the district office in promoting accountability through testing and other means. The district office, while assisting schools to develop their capacity to provide quality instruction and management, may be more suited to an accountability approach, given its distance from the school level and limitations on staff. Provincial and national levels, in turn, may contribute most to school improvement by maintaining a balance between capacity-building initiatives and accountability initiatives such that district and school cluster levels, while attempting to build capacity and maintain accountability, can emphasize one goal without giving up the other. Finally, provincial and national levels may play an important role in redressing inequalities in resources across lower levels.

The rest of the paper has five sections. The next section discusses the conceptual basis for the study of the two strategies of mobilizing additional resources through community involvement and using existing resources more effectively through the school cluster concept. The third and fourth sections describe and assess Thailand's experiences in strengthening community involvement in education and in implementing the school cluster concept. The important role of the school principal in determining the quality of either strategy is examined. The last section summarizes the findings of our study, draws lessons for improving the educational opportunities of students from impoverished or economically disadvantaged backgrounds in other countries, and suggests a multi-level approach for improving primary education in Thailand.

Mun C. Tsang and Christopher Wheeler

Figure 7.1 Model of school quality

(a) Macro-Level Model

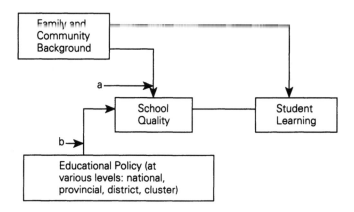

(b) Micro-Level Model: Components of School Quality

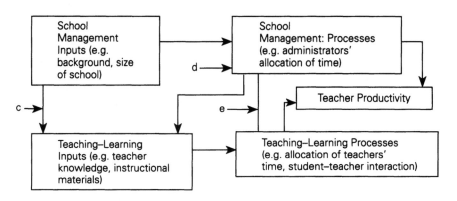

Source: Raudenbush and Bhumirat (1989)

Conceptual Framework

This paper draws from ongoing research on the quality of primary education in Thailand by the authors and their collaborators from the US and Thailand. This research is part of a cross-national study of primary education conducted by the BRIDGES (Basic Research and Implementation in Developing Education Systems) Project. The analysis of the paper can be understood by reference to the conceptual model on school quality developed in the current study in Thailand.

According to the model (see Figure 7.1), school quality needs to be understood at two levels. The first is a macro-level that specifies how educational policy, student family background, and community combine to influence school quality and, ultimately, student outcomes (such as learning). The second is a micro-level analysis of school quality. In this level of analysis, school quality is seen to be determined by *inputs or resources* available to a school and by the set of social relations or *processes* through which these resources are utilized to influence student outcomes. School processes can be further divided into teaching–learning processes and school management processes. The arrows in Figure 1 indicate the direction of influence among the various variables (for details, see Raudenbush and Bhumirat, 1989).

Promoting community support for schools can be a strategy for improving school quality. An important aspect of such support consists of household contributions, in cash or in kind. Household contributions can be used to increase the quantity or quality of inputs (such as instructional materials, teaching aids, equipment, and other school facilities) to the teaching–learning process (arrows a and c in Figure 7.1). Another aspect of community support is parental involvement in school activities, such as regular meetings between parents and the principal and teachers, both for discussing matters relating to student learning and for general social gatherings. Strengthening school–community relationships is a self-help strategy that can mobilize community resources to support the school. Such a strategy may play a significant role in complementing the otherwise meager public resources to schools in impoverished areas. In the section on school–community relations, we attempt to: (1) identify community and school organizations as well as practices that combine to channel community resources to school; (2) document the amount of household contributions to schools and the variation in household contributions among different social groups; and (3) assess the financial impact of such contributions on primary schools in Thailand. Information for this analysis comes from a 1988 national survey of schools and from interviews of school personnel and parents.

School clusters alter the management of schools and are aimed at achieving a variety of objectives. These objectives can be economic (sharing of resources among schools in a cluster), pedagogic (staff development and curriculum improvement through cooperation among school personnel), administrative (accountability through testing and monitoring, reporting information to administrative authorities) or political (raising awareness of government programs to deal with problems of economic and social development, and promoting community involvement in education). Thus, the formation of school clusters can affect school quality through its influence on inputs to the school, the teaching-learning process, and the school management process (arrows b, c, d, and e in Figure 7.1). It is a public educational policy that seeks to maximize the effectiveness of existing resources at the district or sub-district level. In this part of the paper, we attempt to describe the school cluster movement in Thailand and assess the effectiveness of school clusters as a management strategy for improving primary school quality. Information for this analysis comes from a field study of two school clusters in the Northeast region of Thailand.

Finally, we explore the implications of the findings on these two strategies for setting policy objectives at various levels of educational administration and how such objectives can be coordinated for improving primary school quality in Thailand.

Figure 7.2   *Community financing of primary schools in Thailand*

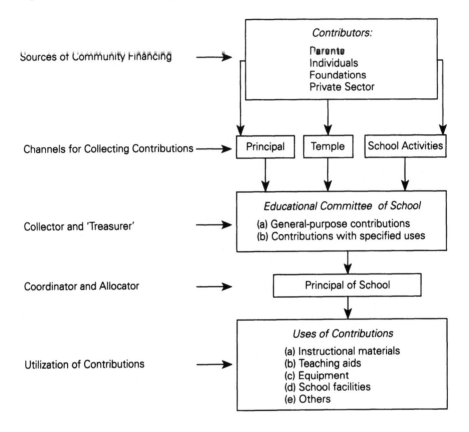

Community Support of Primary Education

This section discusses community support for primary education in Thailand. It describes how ties between a school and its community are developed and analyzes patterns of community contributions to schools. In particular, it examines the role of household contributions for financing quality improvement efforts in primary schools, especially for students in rural areas and students from lower income and less educated families.

Community Support for Education: Organization and Practice

While there may be some variation in different areas, Figure 7.2 presents the existing scheme for generating community resources for a school in Thailand. It involves community institutions, school organizations, individuals and households, as well as a set of practices for encouraging community support for education. In essence, contributions are collected through several channels by the educational committee of a school and are subsequently utilized by the principal of the school for educational purposes.

Individuals and parents are the most common contributors. In some areas, especially urban ones, foundations and the private sector also contribute resources to school. Such resources can be in cash or in kind. Most of the time, the cash contributions are for general educational purposes, although occasionally a donor may specify the use of such contributions. In each school, there is an educational committee that oversees the relationship of the school and its community. The committee usually has five to ten members, consisting of the school principal, community leaders, parents and teachers. It acts as a treasurer in collecting community contributions and monitoring their utilization.

Community contributions are usually channeled to the educational committee in three ways. The first is through the temple. In Thailand, the temple is the most important social and cultural institution in a local community. It is the center for religious and social activities; and traditionally it enjoys close ties to the educational system. Before the emergence of a public, compulsory primary education system in Thailand, education took place in the temple where Buddhist monks taught literacy to boys and young men through the teachings of Buddhism. As the public school system developed, many schools were built next to the temple, especially in rural areas, to draw upon the services of Buddhist monks. In many primary schools today, Buddhist monks play a key role in the moral development of Thai youth through direct instruction in ethics or by participating in religious holidays observed by the school. The temple, in other words, serves as an important link between a school and its community. In terms of financial support for the school, the temple collects contributions (mostly in cash) from the people for various purposes, and subsequently allocates part of these donations to the educational committee of a school. This is an indirect channel for a school utilizing a well established school–temple–community relationship.

Parental contributions from social gatherings held at the school represent a second channel for contributions. During certain occasions in the year (such as Sports Day, Thai New Year's Day, and Mothers' Day), the school organizes social activities for parents and students. Some communities use these festive occasions as an opportunity to raise funds directly from the community. Data on parental contributions to schools are presented in a subsequent section.

A third category consists of other direct contributions to the school from alumni, parents and community members, as well as direct contributions from foundations and the private sector. Some rural schools also receive contributions from individuals who reside in metropolitan areas but maintain ties with the village. Occasionally, parents may provide some contributions (especially in kind) to a teacher to show their appreciation for the teacher's work, but generally this is a minor part of a community's contribution to schools in Thailand.

The school principal plays an important role in stimulating community financing of education, especially the collection of community contributions and the allocation and utilization of such contributions for the school. A principal with good interpersonal and entrepreneurial skills can cultivate community support and thus encourage community contributions to school. The principal is also expected to provide leadership in organizing school activities for parents and in promoting parental participation in such activities. As will be shown below, the more parents participate in school life, the more likely they are to contribute to the school. The principal is also a key decision maker in how community contributions are utilized. Community contributions may be used in a number of ways, such as purchasing supplementary text materials, teaching aids, equipment (e.g., a slide tape projector or athletic equipment), and the repair or construction of school facilities. The principal will normally approach and persuade the educational committee to allocate funds for one or more of these uses. Finally, the principal is expected to play an active role in identifying the short- and long-term needs of the school in making plans for school activities, and in initiating contacts with community members to raise funds for meeting such needs.

Parental Contributions to Primary Schools

To determine quantitatively the pattern of community contributions to primary education in Thailand, data on parental contributions to primary schools were collected, as part of a national survey of parents, teachers, students and principals conducted by the BRIDGES Project in Thailand in 1988. Based on a multi-stage sampling strategy, 9,768 grade 6 students were first selected. The parents of a representative subsample of 2,305 students were then asked about their households' contributions to primary schools in 1987. The data provide information on household contributions (through all three channels) to various types of primary schools in different areas and from different socio-economic backgrounds. According to school administrators in Thailand, parents are the major source of community contributions to primary schools.

Among the 2,305 students, 83 percent attend government schools and 17 percent attend private schools. Private schools are almost entirely located in urban areas. Compared to government schools, private schools have a proportionally larger enrollment of students from families with higher incomes, greater wealth (in total assets), higher levels of education, and employment in white-collar occupations. Among government school students, most students (84 percent) are from schools administered by ONPEC, and most ONPEC schools are located in rural areas. The rest of the government schools are in the Bangkok metropolitan area (10 percent) and in other municipal areas (6 percent). The average household income of the students' families was 4,420 Baht (about US$175) per month in 1987. The average length of fathers' schooling was 6.7 years.

Table 7.1 presents information on the average amounts and distribution of household contributions to different types of primary schools in 1987. While it appears that parents of students in government schools and parents of private school students contributed about equally to primary education, large differences in contributions existed among parents of different types of government schools. Parents of Bangkok schools had the largest household contributions (174.7 Baht per year) and parents of municipal schools had the smallest contributions (86.3 Baht per year).

It is instructive to note that parents of students in ONPEC schools (schools in mostly poor and rural areas) made greater contributions in cash and in kind than did parents of private schools and municipal schools (both in urban areas). In fact, parents of ONPEC schools had the largest average contribution in kind (55.8 Baht) among parents of the four types of primary schools. Thus schools in impoverished areas received household contributions (157.3 Baht) that were above the average household contribution (152.9 Baht) for all schools in

Table 7.1   Household contributions to different types of primary schools in Thailand, 1987

	Amount				Distribution (%)		
	Government Schools						
	ONPEC Schools (1)	Municipal Schools (2)	Bangkok Schools (3)	All Govt. Schools (4)	Private Schools (5)	All Govt. Schools (6)	Private Schools (7)
Household Contribution (Bahts per household per year)							
To school in cash	93.6	39.8	121.4	92.2	89.1	59.9	60.2
To school in kind	55.8	38.9	46.9	54.0	42.7	35.1	28.9
To teachers in cash	2.4	2.1	3.7	2.5	1.5	1.6	1.0
To teachers in kind	5.5	5.5	2.7	5.2	14.7	3.3	9.9
TOTAL	157.3	86.3	174.7	153.9	148.0	100.0	100.0

Source: Adapted from Table 1 in Tsang and Kidchanapanish (forthcoming)

Thailand. This is consistent with the observation of the prominence of the temple and the strong school–temple–community relationship in rural areas in Thailand. The institutionalization of this community financing scheme (in Figure 7.2) in rural areas puts ONPEC schools on a par with schools in urban areas.

The distribution of total household contribution as shown in Table 7.1 indicates that 90–95 percent of household contributions were made to the school, while only 5–10 percent were made to individual teachers. This means that the utilization of nearly all the money from household contributions is under the discretion of the principal and the educational committee, for both government schools and private schools. Table 7.1 also indicates that household contributions in kind constitute a significant proportion (about 40 percent) of the total household contribution. In other words, studies that fail to consider non-cash contributions will significantly underestimate the total household contributions to primary schools in Thailand. And for the ONPEC schools in rural areas, parents contribute rather generously in kind to schools even though their incomes are generally meager compared to those of their urban counterparts.

Table 7.2 shows how total household contributions to government and private schools varies with the socio-economic backgrounds of students. Household contributions were generally higher for families with higher incomes, greater wealth (in total monetary value of family assets), and higher levels of education. This pattern holds true for both government schools and private schools. Total household contributions differed significantly among occupational groups. It was highest for top white-collar groups (executives and professionals); next for other white-collar groups (clerks), agriculturalists, and traders; and lowest for blue-collar workers (manual workers and craftsmen). Again, it is interesting to note that agricultural families were not at the bottom of occupational groups in terms of total household contributions. Finally regression analysis was conducted on household contributions and their determinants. It was found that household income, family wealth, father's occupation, religion, and parental participation in school activities were significant factors. In particular,

Table 7.2   Household contributions to primary education, Thailand, 1987 by family background and type of school

Socio-economic Background	Total Household Contribution (Baht per year)	
	Govt. Schools	Private Schools
Entire Sample	154	148
Household income		
(Baht per month)		
less than 650 (lowest 20)	57	**
651–1,600 (21–40%)	94	96
1,601–3,000 (41–60%)	83	53
3,001–6,000 (61–80%)	163	91
above 6,000 (top 20%)	1048	212
Father's education		
no education (4.5%)	43	72
some primary (10.5%)	86	34
primary graduate (63.8%)	148	89
lower secondary (9.2%)	187	169
upper secondary (6.3%)	263	156
diploma level (1.5%)	202	136
bachelor or higher (4.2%)	365	275
*Father's occupation*** *		
agriculturalist (56%)	173	58
trader (9.1%)	113	227
clerk (2.0%)	195	181
manual worker (12.1%)	55	37
govt. employee (5.1%)	85	90
craftsman (5.4%)	91	23
professional (4.2%)	316	102
executive (2.2%)	382	366
Family assets (Bahts)		
less than 25,000 (68%)	156	67
25,000–50,000 (13%)	104	38
50,001–100,000 (7%)	175	125
ABOVE 100,000 (12%)	216	298

Notes: *   Numbers in parentheses are percentage distributions
          **   Number of observations is less than 10
          *** Also include workers in other occupations (totalling 3.9%)
Source: Adapted and expanded from Table 2 in Tsang and Kidchanapanish (forthcoming)

the more parents participated in school activities, the more they contributed to school.

In summary, total household contributions differed significantly among different types of government schools. In general, it was higher for higher socio-economic groups. Nevertheless, families in rural areas were comparable to families in urban areas in contributions to primary schools. Finally, there appeared to be no significant differences in household contributions between government schools and private schools. This last result is in sharp contrast to the finding that for primary education the total direct private cost (DPC) of private schools was 3.5 times that of government schools (Tsang and Kidchanapanish, forthcoming).

Impact of Household Contributions on School Quality

Principals can use household contributions to schools for various purposes. The following illustrations show the potential impact of household contributions on improving school quality, and how important it is for the principal to recognize the opportunities for improvement these additional resources represent. In 1987, primary schools in Thailand had an average unit cost of 3,855 Baht, in terms of total recurrent and capital cost per student (based on school-level data collected in this study). Thus household contributions, which averaged 153 Baht in 1987, increased the school budget by 4.0 percent (assuming that there is an average of one primary school student per household). Recent research shows that school inputs such as textbooks and other instructional materials are effective in raising student learning (Heyneman *et al.*, 1981). Since an average of 65 Baht per student were spent by the school on these materials, household contributions would raise such expenditure by 235 percent if they were spent entirely on this item. Thus household contributions could have a significant impact on the amount of quality related inputs available to the school.

Consider the financial impact of these contributions for ONPEC schools in particular. Household contributions to ONPEC schools (averaging 157 Baht per household) increased unit expenditure (4,109 Baht) by 3.82 percent. If these contributions were spent entirely on instructional materials, they would increase the instructional materials expenditure (82 Baht) by 191 percent. While 94 of the 157 Baht per household were donated in the form of cash (the remainder was in kind), such cash donations alone would provide for an additional 115 percent in per student expenditure on instructional materials if all were spent entirely on this item. Similarly, schools with students from lower socio-economic backgrounds could also significantly increase their expenditure on quality-related educational inputs by utilizing household contributions solely for these purposes.

In short, this study shows that household contributions could play a significant role in financing educational inputs important for improving school quality, even for schools in impoverished areas and for students from lower socio-economic backgrounds. It should be pointed out, however, that household contributions are a source of educational inequality for students from different socio-economic backgrounds since higher socio-economic groups generally contribute more to primary schools than lower socio-economic groups. Finally, as will be discussed further below, strategies that successfully mobilize additional local contributions to schools may not be compatible with efforts to reduce educational inequalities unless accompanied by a national strategy of supplementary assistance to schools in economically impoverished areas.

School Clusters as a Management Strategy for
Improving Primary School Quality

While the previous section examined resource mobilization to a school from members of the community, this section investigates the utilization of existing resources among schools in a cluster. It describes the school cluster movement in Thailand and assesses its contributions to improving primary school quality. After providing a brief history of the cluster movement, the organization and functions of clusters are described. Drawing on field studies of two school clusters (a pilot study and an in-depth study) in the Northeastern region of Thailand, the scope and limits of cluster influence on schools and classroom learning are examined. Factors affecting cluster influence and proposals for increasing such influence are presented.

Both clusters studied were in adjacent provinces of the Northeast region of Thailand. This region was selected for study because of its reputation for school cluster activity. If clusters have an effect anywhere, it was reasoned, they ought to have an effect here. For some time, the Thai government has been trying to improve schools and other aspects of the quality of life in the Northeast because it is the poorest region in Thailand and politically it lies in a vulnerable area, bordering on Kampuchea and Laos. ONPEC has actively sought to stimulate cluster activity in the region and has recently completed a project that created new resource centers in each cluster in the region. We studied all seven primary schools in the in-depth case study and four of six schools in the pilot study.

Background on School Clusters in Thailand as a Strategy for
Improving Primary School Quality

The school cluster movement in Thailand originated in 1950 as a pilot project between the Ministry of Education and UNESCO in Chachoengsao province. In 1960 the project was expanded to all provinces in Thailand. By grouping primary schools that were near to one another in a voluntary administrative arrangement, it was hoped that staff at larger, better equipped and more academically effective schools would assist smaller schools, which often were less effective, to improve the quality of their instruction. In 1980 when the administration of most primary schools was transferred from the Ministry of Interior to ONPEC, which was then a new agency in the Ministry of Education, the previously voluntary cluster arrangement became mandatory. In addition to expanding the authority of school clusters to improve less effective schools through assistance, ONPEC also called on school clusters to play an accountability role, principally through monitoring the teaching/learning and management processes of primary schools. The school cluster as an organizational entity is deliberately designed to occupy an anomalous position in the administrative hierarchy. From Bangkok the administrative line of command goes from ONPEC to the province to the district to the school. Districts in Thailand, however, are large entities, typically with seventy to 100 schools. Having a limited number of staff members, the districts are constrained in their ability to monitor and improve schools; without some entity closer to schools, government policy would have a very limited effect. The school cluster is designed to be this entity.

Figure 7.3 School cluster as an organizational entity

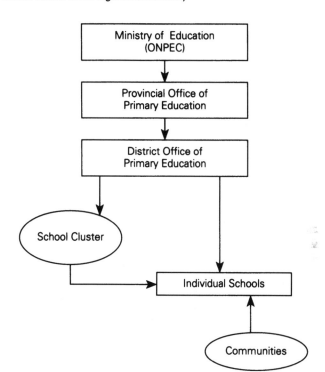

The cluster operates as a collective entity comprised of principals, elected teacher representatives and, since 1986, a central office staff reporting to the school cluster chairperson and cluster committee. The district office has final authority for approving promotions and school budgets; it plays an important role in monitoring school performance and provides some limited staff development. The school cluster's responsibilities (as defined in 1980 and revised in 1986) include recommending promotions for teachers and principals, evaluating principal performance, monitoring teacher performance, reviewing and recommending individual school budgets for district approval, and encouraging school improvement initiatives, staff development activities and school–community programs. As Figure 7.3 shows, in the conceptual model the school cluster is neither directly under the district office nor entirely separate from it.

A comprehensive study of cluster activity by Kunarak and Saranyajaya (1986) showed that while individual clusters had implemented these mandates with some degree of success, in practice cluster influence was largely symbolic and its scale of activity far less than hoped for by the government. Weak authority for the cluster chairperson and cluster committee, along with lack of office staff to develop and implement improvement policies across schools, had led most clusters to focus activities on only one area of responsibility: recommendations for promotion. In December 1986, a new reform strengthened cluster authority and created a cluster office with two to three staff persons to provide ongoing assistance to implement cluster policy.

Mun C. Tsang and Christopher Wheeler

The Effects of School Clusters on School Performance

Our in-depth study of one school cluster (where all seven schools were studied) and comparisons with findings from the pilot study (in which four of six schools were studied) show that some school clusters are able to make a difference; in these instances, they were found to influence both management processes within schools and teaching/learning processes within classrooms. Under certain conditions, clusters clearly contribute to improving the capacity of teachers and principals to perform their jobs well and to holding both accountable for the results of their efforts. The degree of influence, however, is much less than that of each individual school as an organization. School clusters, in other words, are not a panacea for educational ills; they represent one strategy for possible incremental improvement in school performance.

What seems to be at work in terms of school cluster influence is a threshold effect. That is, if all the internal organizational factors of the school cluster are working well, then maximum influence is possible. How much influence occurs is dependent on the degree of receptivity of each individual school; schools vary in accepting initiatives, modifying them, or even ignoring them. To illustrate these points, we turn to our case study and our pilot study.

Accountability vs. Capacity Building

By the late 1980s school clusters had emerged as an organizational means for ONPEC at the national level to pursue two approaches for improving primary school quality in Thailand: (1) the capacity-building approach, which emphasizes staff development, local improvement initiatives, and intrinsic rewards such as professional commitment to teaching; and (2) the accountability approach, emphasizing rules and regulations, testing and extrinsic rewards, such as double promotions. The cluster studied in depth, takes testing very seriously. Testing forms the cornerstone of the cluster's accountability approach to school improvement, an approach that dominates more limited efforts at capacity building (e.g., staff development). In response to a national focus on improving test scores, begun in 1985 with the first national sixth-grade examination, the province required districts to begin testing students, and districts began requiring school clusters to do the same. In the cluster studied, a 'working group' (consisting of cluster office staff and six 'academic cluster' teachers) develops first-term cluster tests for each grade and second-term cluster tests for grades 1, 3 and 5. The working group also assists the district office in developing second-term tests for grades 2, 4 and 6 and third-term tests for grades 1–5 (grade 6 students take a national examination that term). To motivate teachers to improve through competition, the cluster office tabulates results and publishes them by school and by grade so every teacher knows where he or she stands compared to other teachers in the cluster. Principals are encouraged to use test results as one criterion for teacher evaluation purposes in recommending merit or 'double promotions'. Classroom teachers are not involved in the construction of any tests; the working group develops all the items for the cluster test and submits suggested items to the district office for its tests.

All teachers are required to respond to the testing initiative, at least to the extent of giving the tests (while monitored by an academic cluster teacher).

Because of the emphasis on improving test scores, teachers across schools report a decline in interest in spending time on school-wide activities or volunteering for cluster responsibilities because these detract from time available to teach in their own classrooms.

In the area of testing, the school cluster as an organization operates at maximum effectiveness: the working group often spends up to two days a week just prior to a testing period developing items and then two days a week for several weeks after the test, tabulating results and preparing the report. Teachers are aware of the testing system and it affects what they do. But these effects vary by school. In one school the principal used the test results as a justification for changing the reward system from a rotation system whereby a different teacher each year was given an extra promotion regardless of student performance to a merit system where student performance became one of several important criteria for an extra promotion. In a second school the principal used the test results as a rationale for convincing parents to purchase supplementary textbooks (the next year this school's performance moved from sixth to second within the cluster). Two other principals used the test results as explicit justifications for their decisions several years earlier to move to a merit system of recommending extra promotions. Principals in three other schools simply ignored the test results, as did most of the teachers in these schools.

In contrast to the in-depth study, the pilot study showed that the cluster has the capacity to pursue effectively both the capacity-building and accountability approaches. Staff development and instructional materials development provide examples of the influence of the school cluster in the area of capacity building.

Staff in the pilot cluster took advantage of every opportunity to host staff development initiatives from the national, provincial and district offices. Academic cluster teachers, in contrast to most of their counterparts in the cluster studied in greater detail, were active in assisting colleagues in their respective schools to improve their pedagogy. The 'working group' was also more active in developing materials and in involving teachers from individual schools in materials development activities after hours and on Saturdays.

Such activities affected what teachers did in classrooms. Our researchers observed a greater variety of teaching styles and a greater use of materials in the schools in this cluster. But, again, the schools varied in their response to this level of cluster activity.

For example, principals in three schools encouraged their staff to take advantage of every opportunity for cluster-sponsored staff development. One principal went so far as to close the entire school whenever the cluster was sponsoring staff development activities so that all staff could participate and substituting school days on the weekend (with staff support) so students would not miss instructional time. A principal in another school was far less supportive and made no special arrangements to facilitate staff involvement; not surprisingly, a much smaller percent of his staff participated in these activities.

Why Does School Cluster Influence Vary by School?

Schools must respond to cluster initiatives. Teachers and principals are required to do the following: to allow academic cluster teachers to administer cluster-developed tests; to attend cluster-organized staff development sessions (such sessions are usually national, provincial or district-sponsored in origin); to listen to cluster office staff describe available materials when they visit their school; and to host supervisory visits by cluster committee officials to their school. But what is done in response to these initiatives is up to the school. The principal, as the examples above suggest, can influence the impact by affecting teacher participation in cluster-sponsored activities, by promoting building-level attention to issues raised by cluster interventions, and by encouraging the cluster to pursue policies congruent with teacher interests. The important role of the principal in shaping the scope of school response (i.e., teachers on an individual basis or a collective, school-wide response) proved to be related in very specific ways to performance in the schools studied in both the pilot and in-depth studies. (School performance was based on aggregated test scores on cluster and district tests over the year in each study and for the in-depth study rates of student/ teacher absenteeism as well). If the principal was trying to improve school performance, the school proved more receptive to cluster influence. If the principal was not interested in school improvement, the school was less receptive to cluster influence. If the principal was interested in maintaining the current level of performance, then cluster initiatives were used selectively to reinforce or legitimate policies already in place. Schools where the principals were not interested in improvement were the poorest in performance; schools where principals were interested in maintaining the current levels of performance were the highest achieving schools. Improving schools came from the low and moderate categories of performance. While some teachers in buildings where the principal was not interested in school improvement responded positively to cluster initiatives in an effort to improve their teaching, such responses were far fewer than in buildings where principals actively sought to use cluster initiatives to further such an internal policy agenda.

School Clusters and Educational Inequalities

We have seen that school clusters can encourage schools to improve through assistance (capacity-building strategies) and through sanctions and rewards (accountability measures). Our field studies, however, uncovered two contextual factors that seem to place limits on the overall influence school clusters can expect to have. The first factor is community wealth. In very poor communities, such as the one in the pilot study, cash contributions from surrounding communities were not likely to amount to much, although in-kind contributions to these schools were significant. The scarcity of cash contributions may explain the fact that all the schools in the cluster in a poor area made greater use of cluster resources, such as equipment from the cluster resource center or the opportunity to develop materials for teacher use at the cluster office, than did schools in the cluster studied in depth, which was in a somewhat more affluent community. In this cluster, schools seeking to maintain a good to excellent program tended to turn to their local communities for assistance in purchasing additional equipment or materials; other schools just coasted along in mediocrity with marginal community support. The schools in this cluster, on the whole, were less likely to use cluster resources. Of course, there was considerable variation among schools within each cluster as a function of whether or not the principal was interested in reform. Although only two clusters were studied and both were in one region, observations suggested the possibility that school clusters may play a particularly important role in economically impoverished areas. It also appeared that improving the efficiency of the school cluster office might increase use of cluster resources by all schools.

With respect to financial support for schools in Thailand, a second issue is the differences among individual schools within a community in the resources they receive. One major purpose of the school cluster is to reduce disparities in achievement across schools in the cluster; yet some schools have greater access to community resources than others, and, where the principal has developed good relations with the community, these resources can be tapped to the advantage of these individual schools. For example, in our in-depth study one school received 25,000 Baht (US$1,000) from the temple, another received 10,000 Baht (US$400) in interest from an endowment, and a third got 2,000 Baht (US$80) from the community, while other schools received little or nothing in the way of cash contributions. Principals spent these sums in various way: investing in programs to raise and sell buffaloes and chickens, repairing school grounds, and purchasing supplementary teaching materials. It is in the third area that implications for the cluster's role in reducing disparities becomes important. Over the last several years, four schools in the case study cluster received sufficient contributions from their local communities to purchase sets of supplementary text materials for the curriculum (including teachers' guides, exercises and practice quizzes [about 2,000 Baht or US$80 for each set]). On the whole, these schools ranked at the top in terms of student achievement (Wheeler *et al.*, 1988).

Such contributions represent both an opportunity for school clusters and a fundamental limitation on their scope of influence. Through staff development programs for principals, school clusters could provide principals knowledge in how to improve school–community–temple relations and in ways to involve parents more effectively in school life — two preconditions for increasing contributions to the school. School clusters, therefore, could expand the funding base available for all schools in their respective domains. Yet they lack the authority to redistribute funds across schools, and this is a fundamental limitation on the cluster's ability to equalize educational opportunities across schools. Moreover, clusters are unlikely ever to be given such authority for two reasons. First, national officials fear such authority would be likely to divide the cluster committee immediately into factions, threatening the ability of the committee to act at all. Second, national officials fear local contributions would be likely to decline drastically if portions were to be redistributed to schools other than the ones where the funds were raised. This dilemma is not unlike the limitation most states in the Unites States face as they wrestle with disparities in school finance between rich and poor school districts. Ironically, the more successful the Thai government is in encouraging local contributions to schools, the greater will be the disparities among schools within many clusters and across clusters, unless there is some national policy of providing supplementary assistance to poor schools and poor clusters.

In summary, the school clusters in our studies were found to play a role in improving the quality of primary schools in Thailand. This role is important, though limited in scope. It depends on the receptivity of the individual school, especially the principal, and on certain contextual factors over which the cluster has little control. Our results are based on findings in one region of Thailand. Further research on the role of school clusters in other regions is currently underway as a part of the BRIDGES project.

Principal Leadership: A Common Thread

The school principal plays a critical, if not determining, role in whether or not community resources and parental participation in school activities are mobilized and in how the school responds to school cluster policies. This role derives in part from cultural traditions that emphasize hierarchical decision making and deference towards leaders (elaborated in Wheeler *et al.*, forthcoming, b). It also results in part from the small size of Thai primary schools, which means that principals themselves often have some teaching responsibility as well as more collegial contact with teachers.

There is a danger in overemphasizing the role of the principal in school improvement. Learning occurs in classrooms through a complex relationship between teachers and students. But effective teaching can be facilitated or impeded by the role the principal plays. In a sense, he or she operates at the hub of a number of different responsibilities and the way these responsibilities are played out contributes to the operation of a number of other building-level factors that influence the conditions of teaching in powerful ways. Such factors include teacher collaboration in discussing pedagogical and content concerns, the development and use of materials, a school-wide climate focusing on academic instruction, and school–community–temple relations.[1]

By any reckoning, the role of the principal is important. In recent years, ONPEC has devoted considerable effort both to improving the capacity of principals to perform their responsibilities effectively and to holding them more accountable for the results of their efforts. For example, between 1985 and 1988 all principals in Thailand received intensive in-service training under a project funded by the World Bank. Following the in-service training, principals carried out projects in their schools based on the training and during the next year district and provincial supervisors used the content of the training sessions to design observation instruments for their site visits to schools. A 1987 evaluation of provinces and districts found that over 60 percent of principals ranked 'high' in terms of changed behavior as a result of the in-service (ONPEC, 1987a).

Concurrent with this initiative were a number of changes in the regulations governing the requirements to become a principal. Teachers can no longer simply move into the administrative ranks. Minimum qualifications are required, district and provincial approval is needed, and all candidates must complete a training program in educational administration. Rankings for available positions are determined on the basis of test scores upon completion of the training program and the quality of a 'mini thesis' research project on a theme or issue in educational administration.

Finally, principals' accountability has been increased through a national testing system developed in 1985 by ONPEC for a sample of sixth-grade students from every province in the country. This system, in turn, has spawned testing programs at the district and school cluster levels.

In terms of increasing principals' attention to the academic tasks of schooling, test results coupled with a national in-service training program for principals resulted in the resignation or voluntary reassignment to teaching of 2,000 principals. ONPEC officials view this result favorably as an indication that such principals got the message: administration requires leadership, hard work, and attention to academics (Wheeler *et al.*, 1989).

In terms of school improvement, the implication that a rigorous testing program coupled with some staff development represents an effective approach requires several important qualifications. First of all, tests as currently devised emphasize factual information and rote recall instead of analytical and problem solving skills. These may not be the skills of greatest benefit for Thai youth in the future. Moreover, the effect of the testing program has been to reinforce a teacher-centered form of classroom pedagogy that discourages student participation in classroom learning — a key goal of the 1978 curriculum reform. Finally, at least in the schools we studied, the emphasis on competition among teachers for extrinsic rewards, such as merit promotions ('double promotions' in the Thai context), has reduced teacher interest in certain building-level activities that would appear to be critical in creating a more effective work environment for teachers. For example, there is less teacher collaboration on issues of pedagogy and content, less interest in development and use of materials, and less teacher participation in the decision-making process of the school (elaborated in Wheeler *et al.*, 1988).

Policy Implications: A Multilevel Approach for School Improvement

This paper has shown that local initiatives such as strengthening community involvement in school life and responding in a receptive way to school cluster initiatives can lead to school improvement. However, we have suggested that strategies to increase resources to the school or to use existing resources more efficiently do not exist in a vacuum; these strategies are influenced by policies pursued at other administrative levels, and they influence these other levels in turn. The implication of these findings is that different administrative levels may have distinctly different roles to play in the educational process and that sustained school improvement may result from mobilizing and coordinating educational efforts at different administrative levels (see Figure 7.4).

The School Level

Local communities and school clusters are part of a school's immediate environment. Principals play a critical role in mediating the effects of both communities and clusters on what the school does *and* in mobilizing the resources from each for school improvement purposes. Skillful leadership can lead to significantly increased resources, which can be used for improving the quality of education, even in areas that are rural and/or poor. Improving school–community relations by involving parents, community members, and temple leaders in school life in meaningful ways appears to be a viable policy option for mobilizing additional resources to schools in Thailand. A relevant issue to consider is whether or

Mun C. Tsang and Christopher Wheeler

Figure 7.4   Administrative roles for school improvement

(1) School Level: The Principal
   * Mobilizing Community Resources
   * Internal Reform (Supervision and Staff Development)
   * Using School Cluster Resources for Internal Reform

(2) Different Roles for Different Levels of Administration
   * *Cluster*:
     Major Role: Capacity-Building
     Minor Role: Accountability
   * *District*:
     Major Role: Accountability
     Minor Role: Capacity-Building
   * *Provincial and National*:
     Redistribution
     Support for a Balance Between: Capacity-Building Policies
                                     Accountability Policies

not it is also a viable option for other countries, for example, countries with much lower per capita income than Thailand or countries in which the relationship between the school and religious institutions is not so strong. If a country is very poor, most families may have to spend a large proportion of their income on nondiscretionary items (such as food items for subsistence) and have little income available for contributions to their local school. In countries where there are not organizations or institutions that are supportive of the school, they may have to be created and developed for this strategy to work. Further research on community involvement in these other countries is desirable.

With respect to school clusters in Thailand, this paper has demonstrated their potential for improving primary school quality and has described some of their limitations. In particular, the effectiveness of school clusters seems to depend on principal response. The policy issue becomes how to get the principal, and thus the school, to be more receptive to school cluster influence. This is a difficult issue. How influential should the cluster be in what the school does? The answer depends in part on one's perspective on the policies the cluster ought to pursue as well as one's views on how to bring about meaningful change at the school and classroom levels. The 1978 curriculum in Thailand specifically calls for more student-centered instruction and several ONPEC sponsored national in-service initiatives have focused on building teacher capacity to delegate more authority to students. However, the balanced approach where capacity-building programs were given equal emphasis with accountability initiatives gave way by the late 1980s to an ever greater emphasis on accountability, which in turn has led to more and more school clusters pursuing policies similar to those of the cluster we studied in depth (Wheeler *et al.*, forthcoming, a). This poses a dilemma for some principals. Unless the balance between the two approaches is restored at the national level, increased school receptivity to cluster influence would mean increased pressure on principals to focus on accountability, which typically would mean teacher-centered classrooms emphasizing rote memorization of facts rather than the more student-centered instruction that principals might otherwise seek to promote (see Wheeler *et al.*, 1988, for examples). Moreover, unless the balance between the two approaches is restored, school clusters will no longer occupy an

126

organizational position that allows them to pursue both approaches; they will simply become another layer in the hierarchical chain of command from Bangkok through the provinces to the districts to the schools.

A second dilemma is that school cluster influence seems greatest with principals who want to improve the quality of education in their schools (regardless of how they define quality), but the cluster's emphasis on accountability over capacity building may inhibit the ability of some principals to accomplish the goal of school improvement. For example, in our studies the principals of improving schools viewed tests and test results as one of many tools, and not the most important one at that, for improving performance. The real tools for improvement were their own efforts: (1) to promote greater collaboration among teachers in developing and using materials and in discussing pedagogical and content concerns; (2) to promote shared decision making within the school; and (3) to promote good school–community relations. These principals knew — or learned — how to create such building-level processes for change, but many principals lack such knowledge. It is precisely in such areas that additional assistance at the cluster level could improve principals' knowledge and indirectly strengthen their position of leadership for improving educational effectiveness. Yet it is these areas where national and local policies currently are weakest because of the almost single-minded pursuit of increased test scores.

The District Level

The third dilemma is what to do when there is little interest in improvement on the part of certain principals and, thereby, certain schools. Cluster accountability policies as currently designed seem to have no effect on such schools. In other words, schools that need accountability the most seem to be the ones least affected by the current array of accountability policies. What may be needed is to vary the strategy depending on the situation of each school. It should be recognized that principals differ in their commitment to improvement and in their capacity to bring it about and that organizations such as school clusters and district offices may have different roles to perform. While the school cluster can give districts some assistance with accountability policies, its greatest contribution may lie in emphasizing the capacity-building approach. In contrast, the district office's greatest strength, given its distance from schools and limited personnel, may lie in focusing on the accountability approach and in supporting the cluster's capacity-building initiatives.

Provincial and National Levels

A fourth dilemma stems from the tension between unequal financial contributions to individual schools within a cluster and the cluster's mission of reducing disparities in educational opportunities across schools in the cluster. While the cluster could serve as a focal point for staff development initiatives for principals in how to improve school–community relations, thereby increasing the overall resource base of the cluster, it cannot reallocate funds from schools in wealthier communities to schools from more economically disadvantaged communities. Such a reallocation strategy raises the question of the role provincial and national administrative levels might play in a coordinated strategy for school improvement in Thailand. We have seen that efforts to promote greater community involvement can lead to increased mobilization of local resources on behalf of individual schools. This finding, when coupled with the inability of school clusters to redistribute resources across schools in their administrative domain, suggests an important redistributive role for provinces and the national government. In short, if resource mobilization and equalization are essentially incompatible strategies at the local level, as seen in the United States, one way to minimize the disequalizing effects of community contributions is for higher administrative levels to make adjustments in allocation of public funds to schools and school clusters. For example, while schools and clusters in all areas might get a standard amount of subsidies for non-personnel expenditures, schools and clusters in impoverished areas might receive additional governmental subsidies to compensate for base level differences in community wealth. Another possibility would be to explore fund raising through higher administrative levels, such as the district of provincial levels, while at the same time local fund raising initiatives are encouraged. These organizations may have access to funding sources such as businesses and foundations that individual schools may lack. Resources collected at higher levels could be shared among schools in an economically impoverished cluster or allocated to school clusters in impoverished areas of the province.

Finally, the role of the national level of administration may be uniquely suited to fostering, maintaining, and supporting a balance between the accountability and capacity-building strategies that currently characterize Thailand's approach to school improvement. Striking such a balance requires new and innovative ways of thinking about how to lessen the tensions that have emerged between the two approaches in recent years. In summary, while local initiatives in resource mobilization and utilization can be used to improve primary school quality, their effects will be limited without the coordinated efforts of other administrative levels.

Note

1 Wheeler *et al.* (1988) discuss how these factors contribute to classroom learning in the schools studied in these two clusters. Schwille *et al.* (1986) consider the role of these factors in Third World countries and the United States.

References

BHUMIRAT, C., KIDCHANAPANISH, S., ARUNRUNGRUENG, P. and SHINATRAKOOL, R. (with assistance of Sirigirakal, V.) (1987) *Research and Evaluation on the Quality of Primary Education in Thailand*, Bangkok, Office of the National Education Commission.

HEYNEMAN, S., FARRELL, J. and SEPULVEDA-STUARDO, M. (1981) 'Textbooks and achievement in developing countries: What we know', *Journal of Curriculum Studies*, **13**, 3, pp. 227–46.

KUNARAK, P. and SARANYAJAYA, A. (1986) *Project RECOMB: Remodeling the School Cluster's Organization and Management Boundary: A Synopsis Report* (research report submitted to UNICEF), Bangkok, Office of the National Primary Education Commission.

OFFICE OF THE NATIONAL PRIMARY EDUCATION COMMISSION (ONPEC), THAILAND (1987a) *The Use of Manuals for the Followup and Supervision of School Administrators* [In Thai], Bangkok, National Primary Education Commission.

OFFICE OF THE NATIONAL PRIMARY EDUCATION COMMISSION, THAILAND (1987b) *National Evaluation Results for Sixth Grade Students* [In Thai], Bangkok, Research and Development Section of ONPEC.

OFFICE OF THE NATIONAL EDUCATION COMMISSION, THAILAND (1988) *Determinants of Effective Schools: Thailand Country Review*, Bangkok.

RAUDENBUSH, S. and BHUMIRAT, C. (1989) *The Effects of Educational Policy on Student Achievement and the Practice of Teaching in Thailand, Preliminary Findings from a National Survey*, paper presented at the annual meeting of Project BRIDGES, Bangkok.

SCHWILLE, J., BEEFTU, A., NAVARRO, R., PROUTY, R., RAUDENBUSH, S., SCHMIDT, W., TSANG, M. and WHEELER, C. (1986) *Recognizing, Fostering and Modeling the Effectiveness of Schools as Organizations in Third World Countries*, Project BRIDGES, College of Education, Michigan State University, East Lansing, Michigan (Processed).

SOOKPOKAKIT, B. (1988) *Improving Primary School Quality in Thailand: A Case Study of a School Cluster*, College of Education, Michigan State University, East Lansing, Michigan.

TSANG, M. and KIDCHANAPANISH, S. (forthcoming) 'Private resources and quality of primary education in Thailand', *International Journal of Educational Research*.

WHEELER, C., CHUARATANAPLONG, J., BHUMIRAT, C., EAMSUKKAWAT, S., PUMSA-ARD, S., SHINATRAKOOL, R., SIRIGIRAKAL, V. and SOOKPOKAKIT, B. (forthcoming, a) 'School clusters in Thailand: A management strategy for improving primary school quality', *International Journal of Educational Research*.

WHEELER, C., RAUDENBUSH, S., KUNARAK, P. and PASIGNA, A. (forthcoming, b) 'Accountability, capacity-building and enduring dilemmas: Policy initiatives in Thailand from 1980–1988 to improve primary education', *International Journal of Educational Research*.

WHEELER, C., RAUDENBUSH, S. and PASIGNA, A. (1989) *Policy Initiatives to Improve Primary School Quality in Thailand: An Essay on Implementation, Constraints, and Opportunities for Educational Improvement* (BRIDGES Research Report Series), Cambridge, Mass., Harvard Institute for International Development.

WORLD BANK (1988) *World Development Report 1988*, New York, Oxford University Press.

WYATT, D. (1984) *Thailand: A Short History*, New Haven, Conn., Yale University Press.

Chapter 8

Providing Quality Education When Resources are Scarce: Strategies for Increasing Primary School Effectiveness in Burundi*

Thomas Owen Eisemon, John Schwille, Robert Prouty, Francis Ukobizoba, Deogratias Kana and Gilbert Manirabona

Introduction

While a great deal of attention has been given to documenting the poor quality of African primary schools and the need to improve them (World Bank, 1988), the supporting evidence is often drawn either from international studies of educational achievement or from national research which uses a metropolitan language to measure achievement. African students, it seems, have not learned very much at primary school or even in secondary schools which select students on the basis of rigorous national examinations that are generally administered in a metropolitan language.

What such results indicate is not entirely clear. The use of a metropolitan language to measure achievement is justified on the grounds that it is the medium of instruction for the upper stage of primary schooling and for secondary schooling in Burundi and other African countries (Eisemon and Schwille, 1991; Eisemon, Schwille, and Prouty, 1991a). But the use of a metropolitan language in assessment may strongly bias performance in most academic subjects, particularly those like science that are important to improving health status, to increasing agricultural productivity, and to a wide range of social and economic outcomes of educational investments. A better understanding of how language may affect

* The research reported in this paper was supported by the USAID BRIDGES Project administered by Harvard University (DPE 5824-A00-5076-00). The research was planned and carried out by the Centre de Perfectionnement et de Formation en Cours d'Emploi (CPF) in collaboration with Michigan State University and McGill University. Heather Usher and David Williams, graduate students at McGill, assisted in the data analysis. Many valuable suggestions and comments on particular aspects of the analysis were made in consultation with Drs Michael Abrahamowicz, Carl Frederiksen and Socrates Rapagna, McGill University; and William Schmidt and Richard Houang, Michigan State University. The authors take responsibility for any remaining shortcomings.

measurement of individual differences is central to the objectives that have guided the research reported in this paper.

We will be concerned as well with what contributes to effective instruction at the classroom level. Effective teaching is, of course, difficult to define for any educational system. But for countries that use national examinations to allocate educational opportunities, a teacher whose students have a record of success in examinations is viewed as successful. This formulation may ignore many things, though it captures what is significant for students and parents as well as many teachers and educational administrators. Teacher qualifications and experience may be as important for successful examination preparation as are in-service teacher training and inspection (Mwamwenda and Mwamwenda, 1989). Since these teacher characteristics and administrative practices can be manipulated by educational policies, they are of much interest to policymakers (Alexander and Simon, 1975). However, the effects of gross manipulations of policies affecting, for instance, years of teacher training on student achievement are uneven and often ambiguous (Heyneman and White, 1986, p. 49).

Not surprisingly, efforts to correlate achievement with more subtle indicators of instructional effectiveness, such as use of time, curriculum coverage, and monitoring of learning, suggest that 'some elements of effective teaching are common cross-culturally, while others may be culture specific' (Lockheed and Komenan, forthcoming, p. 15). For African countries with influential examinations systems, teacher understanding of assessment tasks, sources of student errors, and strategies for remediating them should also be considered important features of instructional effectiveness.

Finally, we will investigate the impact of student repetition on achievement. Depending on how internal efficiency is defined, repetition may either enhance or erode it. Repetition increases the number of years it takes a primary school to produce a graduate and, thus, wastes instructional resources. On the other hand, repetition may increase student achievement and, in doing so, bring more students up to a level of learning expected of primary school graduates. In Burundi, as in many other African countries, repetition is largely voluntary, that is, students repeat to improve their chances of educational success. Some authorities (cited in Schwille, Eisemon and Prouty, 1990b) assert that repetition simultaneously wastes resources and may have only a negligible impact on student achievement. That is the position of many African ministries of education and of donors to African education. According to a World Bank (1988) report, 16 percent of primary school students in sub-Saharan African countries were repeaters — 23 percent in the Francophone countries.

The Policy Context

Unlike most African countries, Burundi moved slowly to expand primary schooling. When the government did begin to expand primary schooling rapidly in 1982, it introduced double shifts. Double shifts were combined with a policy of collective promotion to increase educational attainment. In consequence, school enrollments grew dramatically: by 256 percent in the period 1980–81 to 1986–87 (Ministry of National Education, personal communication, 1988).

Another consequence was that the curricular changes proposed in the 1973 reform emphasizing 'Kirundization' and 'ruralization' of primary schooling, which continue to guide educational policy, could not be easily implemented (Ministry of National Education, 1988a; Ministry of National Education, 1988b). Kirundization and ruralization were predicated on two unrealistic assumptions. The first was that access to schooling could be increased without raising aspirations for academic rather than practical training, and for instruction in French, the language of secondary and higher education, instead of Kirundi, the mother tongue of most Burundians. Second, it was assumed that the curricular objectives of the 1973 reform would continue to guide instruction despite less instructional time, larger class sizes, and heavier teacher workloads that resulted from the introduction of double shifts and collective promotion. The scope of the school curricula had to be reduced. The teaching of agriculture was one casualty. The amount of agriculture instruction was cut to one period of 30 minutes per week (Eisemon, 1989).

In the 1973 reform Kirundi was intended to become the medium of instruction at the primary level and, eventually, of lower secondary schooling. However, French has been retained as the medium of instruction for grades 5 and 6 largely because of fears that students would be unable to cope with French in secondary school (Ministry of National Education, 1988b). In 1989 lack of student facility in French led the government to begin instruction in the metropolitan language in the first grade rather than in the third.

Educational effectiveness has been equated with achievement in academic subjects, which are assessed mainly in French in the rigorous *concours national*, the national secondary school entrance examination. The small proportion of students admitted to secondary schools on the basis of their examination results, less than 10 percent, has not increased since the introduction of double shifts, though the number of entrants has increased in absolute terms, The examination orients instruction at the upper stage of the primary cycle (Eisemon, Schwille and Prouty, 1989). Primary school teachers and school directors do not participate in the selection of examination questions or in the marking of answers, and until 1989 individual student scores were not announced. These measures have ensured that the examination is viewed as an almost lottery-like event.

The *concours national* consists of examinations in French, Kirundi, mathematics, and a combination of science and social studies (known as *étude du milieu*). Two hundred points are awarded. French and mathematics are the most important papers, accounting for 80 percent of the possible marks. The selectivity of the *concours national* contributes to the high reported rate of student repetition in grade 6: 51 percent in 1988–89 (Proceedings, 1989). Ministry policy has called on schools to limit repetition to an overall 10 percent average across all grades of primary school. But the overall national repetition rate for primary school in 1988–89 was 25.7 percent (Proceedings, 1989). As students are not given unique inscription numbers when registering for school, repetition cannot be easily monitored. Students wishing to repeat grade 6 can enroll in other schools. Collective promotion of students reduces wastage in the lower stage of the primary cycle but increases repetition in the final year. The absence of a strict control over repetition in grade 6 is curious in an educational system that is otherwise highly managed and well controlled. The explanation may have to do with the fact that the examination is the principal determinant of a student's economic future. No student is prevented from repeated failure, from experiences likely to convince parents and students that the causes of poor performance have to do with individual effort and ability rather than with a selection mechanism that does not afford sufficient opportunity to succeed.

The desire to expand enrollments prompted the government in the early 1980s to introduce double shifts, which decreased the amount of instruction students receive to three and a half hours a day. Double shifts increased efficiency in the utilization of staff and facilities but also increased requirements for other resources that support teaching, including instructional materials. School fees of about US$1.70 are assessed for purchase of student textbooks, which are available only for language arts subjects in French and Kirundi. Teachers' guides (*fichiers*) are used for other subjects even in the upper stage of the primary cycle.

Although all primary schools are given a common curriculum to follow and teaching is circumscribed by the teachers' guides, there is still opportunity for alteration of the program of studies, especially in sixth grade when students are preparing for the *concours national*. For example, teachers and principals may increase in several ways the amount of instruction students receive in the subjects tested in the *concours national*. They may reduce the number of lessons given in subjects like agriculture. Teachers may combine morning and afternoon shifts, teaching both groups together all day. Or they may increase the length of instruction by beginning classes earlier and/or ending later. Some of these measures deviate from the guidelines school directors and teachers are given to follow.

What emerges from the foregoing are many unreconciled objectives, policies and practices. Access to primary schooling has been expanded through double shifts and educational attainment raised by collective promotion. But this has not been accompanied by a proportionate increase in opportunities for secondary education. While primary school is the terminal stage of schooling for most children, instruction in the upper stage of the cycle is oriented to gaining admission to secondary school. Selection mechanisms and double shifts do not support the curricular objectives of the 1973 reform. Although emphasis is placed on efficient utilization of instructional resources, the selectivity of the *concours national* fosters grade repetition. Policies adopted to facilitate school expansion produce qualitative variations in instruction notwithstanding efforts to ensure uniformity.

Study Design

This study was planned and carried out in collaboration with the Centre de Perfectionnement et de Formation en Cours d'Emploi (CPF). A more detailed account of design, instrument development, and analyses can be found in the technical report by Eisemon, Schwille, Prouty, Ukobizoba, Kana and Manirabona (1990). Sixth-grade students and teachers in predominantly rural areas of the country were the focus of data collection. Of the thirty-one school cantons in the country, three were excluded as predominantly urban, two were excluded because they were still disrupted from recent (1988) ethnic violence, and five were excluded because they were judged to contain too many inaccessible schools to permit the execution of a probability sample. From the remaining twenty-one cantons a multi-stage, stratified cluster sample was drawn by probability methods. All students in the sampled classes were to be tested. The sample was executed virtually according to plan. Thus, a total of 1,946 students in forty-seven classes in twenty-four clusters were surveyed during a two-month period (mid-March through mid-May 1989) prior to administration of the *concours national*. The number of units drawn at each stage of sampling was a compromise between efforts to make the data collection manageable and our attempt to acquire all the data needed for the envisaged analyses. In the analyses of student data reported below, weights have been used to compensate for the fact that the sampling was not self-weighting in the final stage.

The sample ranged in age from 11 to 19 years. More than half (54 percent) of the students were 14 or 15 years of age. Only 10 percent started school at age 6 and progressed to the sixth grade without repeating. A majority (55 percent) were repeating the sixth grade, and 50 percent had repeated previous grades. The majority were male (59 percent).

All but one of the school directors and most (83 percent) of the grade 6 teachers were men. Given the lack of substitute teachers for staff on maternity leave, few women are assigned to teach the final year when students are preparing for the *concours national*. Nor were there any untrained teachers in the sample. But a large proportion (41 percent) had been teaching two years or less. And 40 percent of the teachers had finished only a one-year program of teacher training offered to students with four years of academic secondary schooling. This program was abolished in 1982 and teacher training lengthened to two years. As for the school directors in the sample, 49 percent had three or fewer years of experience in that position.

Tests were developed to assess student performance in the domains of reading comprehension, written composition, mathematics and science, the latter including elements of agriculture and health as well. The tests were initially prepared in English and then translated into French and from French into Kirundi. In the case of the French comprehension tests, two versions were developed. One employed standard French vocabulary, similar to the vocabulary contained in the teachers' guides prepared and distributed by the Bureau of Rural Education in the Ministry of Primary and Secondary Education. Included in the comprehension test were texts dealing with the filtration of water and how to construct a water filter from ordinary household materials. The Bureau of Rural Education has promoted such filters in its efforts to improve health instruction. The comprehension tasks elicited skills involving locating and recalling information as well as making inferences from text propositions or prior knowledge. The tasks were constructed in the multiple choice format used for the *concours national*.

The *concours national* examines knowledge of French and Kirundi production rules with tasks requiring students to select answers that are grammatically, syntactically or semantically correct. However, knowledge of production rules may have little to do with skills in applying them to composition tasks, particularly if the method of assessment discourages teaching of composition. Thus, a picture task was constructed to stimulate production of a narrative composition in French or Kirundi. Nine pictures were used for the story composition task in an effort to increase the amount of text students produced for subsequent analysis. Three scores (overall quality, coherency of narrative, and use of language) were derived, based on ratings by CPF researchers trained for this task.

A test of mathematics was developed measuring computational skills and problem solving. Four of the nineteen questions dealt either with computations or operations involving numerical transformations (for example, representing common fractions as decimals) and required little or no text processing for successful performance. Most were story problems with one-step or two-step solutions. They tested application of text processing and problem solving skills imbedded in practical tasks requiring numeracy and literacy, such as calculating correct application rates for an agricultural pesticide.

Still another 19-item test was developed for measuring learning in science, health and agriculture, which are covered in different parts of the school syllabus. Science and health are taught in *étude du milieu* which also deals with geography, history, and civics. *Etude du milieu* constitutes one of the four main parts of the national secondary school entrance examination. Other topics on the BRIDGES test are covered in the practical subjects of agriculture and home economics, which are not included in the secondary school entrance examination.

Most of the items on the test measured students' ability to make observations or process scientific information in such a way that inferences could be drawn consistent with a scientific principle. Some questions elicited knowledge of physical laws and their application: for example, determining how much force is needed to lever an object of known weight, given the distance to and from the fulcrum. About half of these items required integration of knowledge of academic and practical subjects that are usually taught and assessed separately.

Draft versions of the BRIDGES tests were pretested as well as reviewed for curriculum validity by the relevant curriculum development units of the Ministry of Primary and Secondary Education. In all, five versions of the tests were produced and administered to subsamples as follows; French comprehension and composition (with standard French text) administered to approximately one-eighth of the sample; French comprehension and composition (with simplified, colloquial French text), one-eighth; Kirundi comprehension and composition, one-fourth; French mathematics, science and agriculture, one-fourth; Kirundi mathematics, science and agriculture, one-fourth. Within the tested classes, these five versions were distributed in a predetermined order to avoid bias in the selection of the subsamples taking each version of the tests. Students were given two hours to finish one of the five versions.

School Director and Teacher Instruments

The school director and teacher instruments provide most of the information used to analyze the effects of school and teacher characteristics on student achievement. The school director instrument, which was administered as a questionnaire, elicited information with respect to: (a) the number, qualifications, experience, and supervision of staff as well as size of instructional groups and incidence of repetition in the sixth year; (b) variation in implementation of double shifts, coverage of the school curricula, and application of the policy of using French as the medium of instruction for most subjects in the upper stage of the primary school; and (c) practices involving preparation of students for the *concours national*, such as lengthening the number of hours of instruction.

The teacher instrument, also administered as a questionnaire, consisted of three parts. One, using an adaptation of IEA (International Association for the Evaluation of Educational Achievement) opportunity-to-learn ratings, required

Table 8.1   Student performance in reading comprehension, written composition, mathematics and science/agriculture: French vs. Kirundi as language of assessment

Test	Mean Scores			F value
	Standard French	Simplified French	Kirundi	
Reading comprehension total test (15 items)	6.04	6.53	8.05	F = 44.6 ***
Narrative text subtest (8 items)	3.02	3.36	4.27	F = 47.86***
Procedural text subtest (7 items)	3.01	3.18	3.78	F = 21.48***

	French	Kirundi	F value
Composition test (ratings 0–10)			
Overall quality	2.27	4.11	F = 137.32***
Coherency of narrative	1.96	3.06	F = 60.28***
Use of language	2.14	4.01	F = 147.11***
Mathematics (19 items)	8.65	8.19	F = 2.56
Science/agriculture (19 items)	7.16	9.31	F = 168.67***

*** p < .001

the teacher to review each question in the mathematics and science-agriculture tests given to students and determine if the information needed to answer the question had been taught. Another section of the instrument obtained information on how much of the prescribed curricula teachers had been able to cover and on their examination preparation strategies. The third section contained six types of questions measuring teachers' understanding of the knowledge and skills elicited in assessment tasks similar to those in the student instruments. Teachers' responses to these questions were rated through comparison to a scoring scheme for analyzing how well the responses articulated what the specific questions were intended to elicit. These six ratings were intended to measure the insights teachers have into what is expected of students for successful performance or difficult assessment tasks, why students make mistakes, and what can be done to correct them.

Results of Analyses

Effects of Language on Test Performance

Language of assessment, French or Kirundi, profoundly influenced the measurement of achievement in most of the subjects tested, as Table 8.1 indicates. The mean number of correct answers was significantly higher for the Kirundi versions of the language comprehension, composition, and science/agriculture tests. The variations in performance under the different language conditions were greatest for scores on the science/agriculture test and the three ratings of the student compositions. Only in mathematics were the results for the French and Kirundi tests similar. The lowest scores were obtained for the student compositions. For instance, the mean score (M = 2.27) for the overall quality of the French compositions represents an evaluation of 'poor'. The Kirundi compositions received higher scores, but the mean scores were also low (M = 4.11 for overall quality), suggesting that students have little practice with such tasks.

The comprehension test mean score for standard French (M = 6.04) was only slightly lower than that for colloquial French (M = 6.53). Both were well below the score for Kirundi (M = 8.05, or about 53 percent of the maximum score). Interestingly, the differences in total scores for the French and Kirundi tests result more from answers concerning the *narrative* text on water filtration than from those concerning the *procedural* text. Student responses to questions pertaining to the procedural text on how to construct a water filter differed significantly by language of assessment, but the absolute differences were small. Procedural texts are less often used for instruction and are more difficult for children to comprehend. Unfortunately, comprehension of procedural texts is perhaps a better measure of functional literacy.

The variations in the mean scores for the French and Kirundi tests of knowledge of science and agriculture were the largest for the four sets of tests. Still, the mean score for Kirundi, M = 9.31, was less than half (49 percent) of the highest possible score. For the French test of science/agriculture, studies selected about a third (38 percent, M = 7.16) of the correct answers. These poor results may have to do with the fact that, although the knowledge tested in this examination is supposed to be taught in the integrated science and social studies class or in the practical subjects of agriculture and home economics, the students' teachers reported that only half (53 percent) of the questions had been covered in class. Questions that had not been covered generally dealt with agricultural topics. Nevertheless, most (68 percent) of the teachers claimed that the questions on this test were identical or very similar to the kinds of question items selected for the *concours national*.

The results for the mathematics tests in French and Kirundi were nearly identical. Mathematics was the only subject in which students scored slightly higher in French. Most teachers had covered the topics examined in class (89 percent of the questions), and most felt that the test items were similar to those appearing in the *concours national* (95 percent of the questions). Nevertheless, the mean scores for the French and Kirundi versions of the mathematics test were only 46 percent and 43 percent of the highest possible score, respectively. Though the mathematics test had the highest instructional validity and the lowest differences in performance under the two language conditions, these favorable factors did not lead to much better results.

Responses to the question items included in the reading comprehension, mathematics, and science/agriculture tests were examined using monotone regression splines analysis to determine how language of assessment affects performance for students of different ability. This approach was developed by Ramsay and Abrahamowicz (1989), who carried out this analysis as an exploratory application. For this analysis, ability was estimated from the student's response pattern for each test, and the estimate compared to the student's response to individual questions. No independent estimates of student ability were obtained, such as scores on related tests administered in the student's mother tongue. Since test difficulty affected the ability estimate, the developers

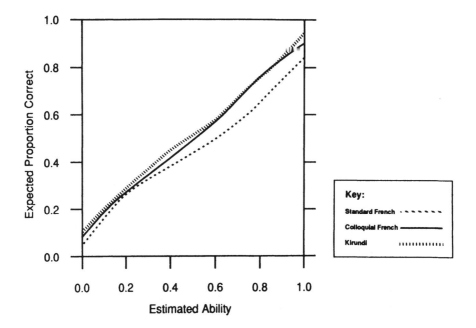

Figure 8.1   Comprehension test scores

of this methodology have suggested that these initial results could *understate* language effects (Ramsay and Abrahamowicz, personal communication).

Figures 8.1–3 present aggregate results for the three tests. The vertical axis represents the probability of success expressed as the expected proportion of correct answers (corresponding to the probability of answering the individual item correctly in the case of the individual item graphs). Ability is estimated along the horizontal axis. The aggregate results sum the item analyses, which used a one-knot spline function to produce the item characteristic curves. A question that is highly discriminating for students of varying levels of ability should have a curve that rises steeply with higher estimated ability and probability of successfully answering the question.

The curves representing the French and Kirundi results for each item and total test scores indicate how well they measured the students' knowledge and skills. Different curves for French and Kirundi reveal underlying differences in measurement. An important feature of monotone regression splines analysis for this study is that it permits identification of which kinds of students are most affected by being tested in their mother tongue or in a second language.

In Figure 8.1 these curves are represented for the expected scores on the standard French, simplified or colloquial French, and Kirundi comprehension tests. At the lowest levels of estimated ability, the curves follow a similar trajectory and then begin to diverge. At the highest levels of ability, the curves for the Kirundi and colloquial French tests are close together. The curve for the standard French test is much lower and flattens out at the high end of the ability range, meaning that the results for this test give lower estimates of the proportion of correct

Figure 8.2   Science test scores

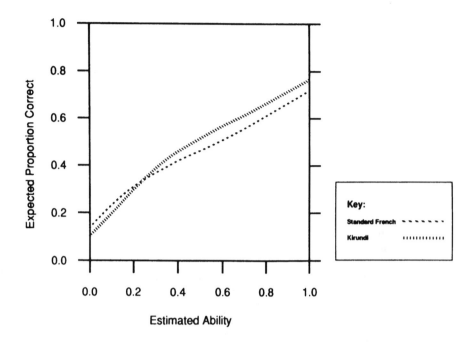

Figure 8.3   Mathematics test scores

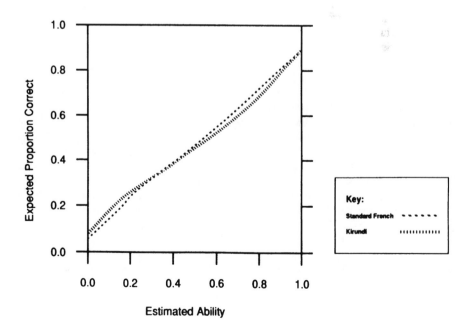

Figure 8.4   Comprehension test item 15: What is the best title for this text?

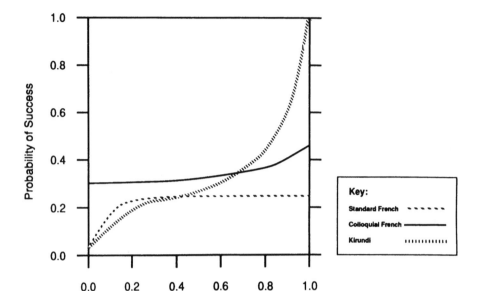

answers among the most able students, and Kirundi science tests, which were not nearly as successful in.

Because Figures 8.1–3 represent the summation of item results, they necessarily conceal wide variations in responses to individual items and tend to suppress language effects. The item analyses revealed that several items on the French science test were not well translated into Kirundi. Such difficulties could have either increased or decreased the mean differences in student performance between the two language conditions. For instance, the second question asked students to select the most desirable rotation of food crops in order to control soil-borne plant diseases. The correct answer to this question required an inference from a complex set of premises regarding the vulnerability of crops to particular diseases. This was a good question in the French version of the test. In the Kirundi test, student responses peaked at a low level of estimated ability and levelled off. The most able students were not more likely to get the correct answer in Kirundi, probably because they did not understand the question.

On the other hand, in numerous other instances the Kirundi curves were substantially higher than the French ones. This was particularly true of the questions in the comprehension tests requiring high level inferences. An example is a question requiring students to select an appropriate title for the procedural text (see item 15 in Figure 8.4). For this question, the curve for standard French peaked at the level of a 30 percent probability of successfully answering the question and then flattened out. The curve for colloquial French reached 45 percent. The Kirundi curve was near perfect, reaching 100 percent probability of success for students at the highest level of ability.

The principal finding derived from the analyses presented in Figures 8.1 and 8.2 is that comprehension skills and knowledge of science and agriculture are more poorly measured in French than in Kirundi. Of particular importance is the fact that the performance of the most able students was the most affected by being tested in French. Conversely, testing in the mother tongue did not increase the performance of less able students who had great difficulty with the tests in either language. And, to reiterate, an independent Kirundi measure of student ability would probably magnify the language effects for these tests.

Figure 8.3 presents a very different finding. There were no language effects for mathematics. The French and Kirundi curves follow the same paths, indicating that the two tests performed similarly in discriminating among students. Since most of the test questions were story problems, the similarity in the French and Kirundi results cannot be explained simply in terms of the fact that the items required little language comprehension for correct solution. Linguistically demanding problems, such as one requiring students to solve an ordering problem using a set of 'bigger/smaller than' premises, sometimes produced differences — in favor of Kirundi. But many problems of comparable difficulty requiring students to process a great deal of textual information for accurate problem representation (such as area problems necessitating multi-step solutions) did not.

Certain kinds of computation and mathematical problem solving may involve little cognitive interference when carried out in French because equivalent symbols, structures, or concepts now exist in Kirundi, having been imported from French. The base ten number system is an illustration. It has no traditional equivalent in Kirundi (Zaslavsky, 1973) or in many indigenous African languages, which use a base five system (Gay and Cole, 1967; Reed and Lave, 1979). Consequently, complex computations are often performed in Kirundi with a number system and operations for manipulating numbers that are derived from French and taught in Kirundi in the lower stage of primary school. This method may facilitate mathematical thinking in French and in part explain differences between performance in mathematics and the other domains.

Finally, it should be noted that test scores for the BRIDGES tests in both languages were correlated with the scores students in these schools received on the 1989 *concours national* examination. For instance, the school mean scores in BRIDGES for comprehension of standard French and Kirundi were correlated with mean school level results for the French and Kirundi papers from the *concours national* ($r = .37$, $p < .01$; and $r = .32$, $p < .01$, respectively). The correlation between results on the *concours national* mathematics paper and the scores for the BRIDGES French test of mathematics was somewhat higher ($r = .48$, $p < .001$).

Effects of Grade Repetition on Student Performance

Measures of factors affecting school effectiveness in preparing students for the tests developed for this study were grouped according to whether they related to (a) student social and educational background; (b) school management and teacher supervision; (c) implementation of the national curricula and instructional practices that influence opportunity to learn; and (d) teacher experience and skills. Of all the variables examined, the one with the greatest impact on test scores was whether a student had repeated grade 6. The differences between the mean scores

Table 8.2   Mean test score differences by test: repeaters versus nonrepeaters at sixth grade

	Mean test scores		
Test	Repeaters	Nonrepeaters	F value
French mathematics (19 items, n = 469)	10.46	6.06	136.80***
Kirundi mathematics (19 items, n = 486)	9.69	6.40	81.03***
French reading, comprehension of standard text (15 items, n = 269)	6.94	4.99	34.49***
French reading, comprehension of simplified text (15 items, n = 241)	7.78	5.19	57.51***
Kirundi reading comprehension (15 items, n = 481)	9.09	6.79	74.01***
French composition: general quality (ratings 0–10, n = 474)	3.33	1.10	154.64***
Kirundi composition: general quality (ratings 0–10, n = 451)	4.83	3.24	49.71***
French composition: coherence (ratings 0–10, n = 474)	2.80	1.02	116.17***
Kirundi composition: coherence (ratings 0–10, n = 451)	3.64	2.36	37.20***
French composition: use of language (ratings 0–10, n = 474)	3.14	1.03	144.45***
Kirundi composition: use of language (ratings 1–10, n = 451)	4.71	3.17	47.35***
French science/agriculture (19 items, n = 469)	7.82	6.20	51.94***
Kirundi science/agriculture (19 items, n = 486)	9.74	8.79	16.57**

* $p < .05$
** $p < .01$
*** $p < .001$

of repeaters and nonrepeaters were both large and highly significant. Repeaters scored higher on all tests, especially in mathematics (Table 8.2).

In general, the differences were greatest for the French tests. In the French version of the mathematics test, for instance, the repeaters got 55 percent of the questions correct and the nonrepeaters only 32 percent. Nevertheless, the language effect appears in large part to compensate for the repetition effect. In other words, on certain tests the nonrepeaters did as well, or almost as well, on the Kirundi version as the repeaters did on the French version. This pattern can be seen in the comprehension test (nonrepeaters 6.79 in Kirundi vs. repeaters 6.94 in standard French), the general quality of composition (nonrepeaters 3.24 in Kirundi vs. repeaters 3.33 in French), and especially in the science/agriculture test (nonrepeaters 8.79 in Kirundi vs. repeaters 7.82 in French). In addition, whereas the repeaters did better on the French version of the mathematics test than on the Kirundi version (10.46 vs. 9.69), the nonrepeaters did slightly better in Kirundi than in French (6.40 vs. 6.06).

In Burundi, decisions of whether or not students repeat are subject to teacher and school director influence as well as to student and parent wishes. In grades 1–5 school directors are authorized to allow repetition for students whose end-of-year grades do not exceed a certain minimum (40 percent), whereas at the end of sixth grade repetition is authorized for better students who are thought deserving of additional tries at the secondary school entrance examination. Normally, permission to repeat sixth grade is contingent on the student's passing the examination given in the final semester (which is different from the *concours national*). Teachers and school directors may adopt a permissive policy toward student repetition if they feel that it increases the proportion of students who succeed in the *concours national* examination. Many (61 percent) of the school directors reported that *concours national* success rates strongly influenced how their work was evaluated by the Ministry of Primary and Secondary Education. Fewer (39 percent) felt that controlling student repetition was very important in affecting evaluations.

The fact that in Burundi sixth-grade repeaters did better than nonrepeaters runs against the grain of much that has been written (see Schwille, Eisemon and Prouty, 1990, for references), and hence it is tempting to discount such findings on methodological grounds. For example, one argument is that the comparisons are inappropriate because repeaters and nonrepeaters are drawn from such different populations. But in our view, the reason for making these comparisons is precisely to raise questions such as these: How do these repeaters differ from nonrepeaters at the same grade level and from those who get promoted to the next grade level? What is the variation in the nature and effects of repetition across schools and countries?

Our Burundi data do not completely answer these questions, but they do suggest that the social meanings and consequences of grade repetition may differ greatly across settings. Many Burundi repeaters at the sixth-grade level are well motivated and scholastically capable children who are taking extra time to prepare for additional attempts to pass the very selective secondary school entrance examination. This situation contrasts sharply with those in which repeaters tend to be students who are doing very poorly at school and who are held back because they are judged not to have learned enough to meet minimum standards for promotion.

In considering the selectivity of repeaters versus nonrepeaters, we examined several background factors to the extent possible with data that are limited in these respects. The proportion of repeaters who were male was nearly the same as the overall proportion of males in grade 6. The fathers of repeaters had, on the average, a little more schooling than the fathers of nonrepeaters (M = 4.26 years vs. M = 3.82 years, F = 8.779, p < .05). There was no such difference in mothers' education. A more important difference derives from the fact that nonrepeaters were the first class to go through the double shift system which was adopted progressively one grade at a time beginning in 1982. Since this system reduces instructional time, repeaters had more advantaged school conditions in their earlier years.

Use of Instructional Supervision to Increase Student Performance

School management and teacher supervision comprise many activities associated with monitoring instruction to ensure compliance with Ministry of Education policies. An important responsibility of school directors is to visit teachers, observe their classes, and provide guidance to them. School directors are required to make 150 classroom visits a year. Information was obtained from the school directors as to the number of times they had visited the schools of teachers whose students were tested. Information was obtained as well from cantonal school inspectors on the number of classroom visit reports received from school directors for the first and second trimesters of the 1988 89 school year. There was a great deal of variation among school directors in the number of class visits they reported. In one of the cantons sampled, for instance, one director had made ninety visits and another only fifty-one, or half the number of visits required. School directors generally have a cluster of schools (with core and satellite schools) under their supervision. Distance between schools and lack of transportation sometimes make it difficult for directors to visit satellite schools as often as core schools.

When school directors visit classes, they are supposed to evaluate many aspects of a teacher's performance: punctuality, whether the lesson is being taught at the time specified in the calendar given for each academic subject, how well the teacher follows the teachers' guide, and so on. In addition, the school directors observes the language of instruction and provides advice to teachers in the upper stage of the primary cycle on the use of French and Kirundi. Ministry policies call for all subjects except Kirundi, even agriculture and home economics, to be taught in French in the fifth and sixth year. Unfortunately, many students cannot follow instruction in French. Teachers estimated that less than a third (30 percent) of their students understood French well enough to be taught in that language without frequent recourse to Kirundi. School directors were asked what advice they gave to the teachers on the use of French and Kirundi in the fifth grade when the transition to French occurs. Such information constitutes a useful measure of the extent to which teachers are encouraged to use French exclusively.

Instructional Practices that Increase Opportunity to Learn

Instructional practices that may be effective in increasing learning outcomes include some that involve adherence to ministry policies and others that require deviations from them. Successful implementation of the school curricula is predicated on fidelity to the teachers' guides provided for academic subjects and to the schedule for teaching lessons. Teachers cannot easily accelerate coverage of the curricula through, for instance, selecting some topics for independent study. There are no student textbooks for most academic subjects. Moreover, double shifts have reduced instructional time, necessitating adherence to the teaching schedule to cover what may be examined in the *concours national*. Only two to three weeks are provided for review for the examination. This period cannot be increased without skipping topics. Many topics of examination questions are introduced in the lesson schedule in the period immediately preceding testing. The highly variable syllabus coverage of the *concours national*, together with the factual content of many examination questions, discourages teachers from being very selective, especially in teaching academic subjects.

However, as noted above, teachers can increase the amount of instruction students receive on important topics in other ways. A majority (55 percent) of the teachers admitted to often combining morning and afternoon shifts during the school year, and almost all (88 percent) had done so for the teaching of French in the two weeks preceding the questionnaire. This deviates from the double shift policy that schools are expected to follow. Teachers also combined different grade levels for instruction in practical subjects. Most (60 percent) did this for teaching practical agriculture. A fourth (25 percent) of the teachers said that they skipped teaching practical agriculture often or occasionally, and about the same proportion (27 percent) reported skipping home economics. In the two weeks prior to the time when the teachers were interviewed, most teachers had skipped one or more lessons in agriculture (61 percent) and home economics (57 percent), usually using the period to teach French or mathematics instead. Another strategy to increase instruction is to lengthen the school day.

Measures of Teacher Skills and Experience

In highly selective educational systems in which teaching in the upper stage of the primary cycle is oriented to preparing students for a national secondary school entrance examination, one way to measure effective teaching is in terms of student results and the skills implicated in examination success. Teachers' previous experience in grade 6 and their success in preparing students for the *concours national* may also be considered indicators of teacher skill. Still another indicator could be the frequency with which the teacher has given demonstration lessons to colleagues during in-service training.

Further measures of teacher skills were obtained from the instrument measuring teachers' understanding of student assessment tasks, sources of student errors, and strategies for remediating them. For example, teachers were given the following examples of errors students often make in spoken and written French:

1 *Je ne vois lien* (The word *rien* is often mispronounced by Kirundi speakers, becoming *lien* and transforming its meaning: 'I don't see link' for 'I don't see anything').
2 *Je vais venir hier* (I will come yesterday).

Asked about the source of these errors, one of the teachers said: 'It's phonetics and [semantics] that are the problems, as well as translation from the mother tongue to a foreign language which creates interference. For example, *ejo* in Kirundi means at the same time yesterday and tomorrow in French. This distinction between the past and the future is not the same as in French'. In order to assist students to correct these kinds of errors, the teacher described several oral exercises to improve pronunciation and increase students' awareness of tense structures in French.

Ratings for the language arts and mathematics/science items in the teacher skills instrument were correlated with years of teaching experience in grade 6 ($r = .33$, $p < .01$; and $r = .36$, $p < .05$, respectively). They were also correlated with demonstration teaching ($r = .26$, $p < .05$; and $r = .29$, $p < .05$). Unexpectedly, level of teacher training was negatively related to the two measures of teacher skills ($r = -.25$, $p < .05$; $r = -.23$, $p < .05$). This anomaly may be explained by the fact that level of teacher training is negatively confounded with teaching experience in grade 6. Graduates of the older teacher education program, which provided only one year of training after four years of academic secondary education, have more experience at this grade level.

Of the instructional and school characteristics discussed above, the number of class visits in the past two weeks to sixth-grade classes (as reported by the school director) had the closest relationship to test scores. The correlation was large and significant for all of the tests (for example, r = .47, p < .001, for the combined mathematics/science/agriculture test in Kirundi). The number of times the teachers studied were supervised ranged from two to twelve. Two-thirds (65 percent) of the teachers received four or fewer visits from the school director. Reported teacher punctuality was significantly correlated with three of the mean test scores, most highly for the mathematics/science/agriculture test given in Kirundi (r = .46, p < .001). Correlations of other instructional and teacher characteristics with student scores (not shown) were usually much weaker. Application of the language policy was correlated with the two language arts tests.

Most measures of opportunity to learn (such as the number of combined shift classes given in the past two weeks) were not significantly related to class scores. Among the teacher characteristics and measures of teaching skills, teacher experience in grade 6 and demonstration teaching were related to the Kirundi test of mathematics and science; previous success in preparing students for the *concours national* was related to the Kirundi language arts and French mathematics and science tests; and teacher assessment skills in mathematics and science were related to the associated Kirundi test.

A Model of School Effectiveness

The relationships among the supervisory and instructional characteristics mentioned above and their contribution to variations in student performance for the classes sampled were investigated using a model for examining linear structural relations among variables (as estimated by LISREL, see Joreskog, 1978; Joreskog and Sorbom, 1986). This method allows investigation of the relationship of variables to underlying theoretical constructs, as well as among variables whose causal relationships are specified *a priori*. The latter feature is of more importance for this analysis, which tests a structural model of how school and instructional characteristics might influence student achievement.

A path analysis model was developed to describe relationships among variables that theoretically affect student performance in language arts and mathematics/science assessed in French. For exploratory purposes, student level variables such as fathers' schooling and grade 6 repetition were excluded and class mean scores used for the data analyses. That is, information about supervisory and instructional characteristics pertains to classes rather than to individual students. This has several implications. Using mean scores for the achievement tests obscures variations in performance within classes. The effects of student background characteristics are ignored. In addition, the number of observations is reduced substantially, potentially inflating correlations and controverting some assumptions of the LISREL method that normally require large sample sizes to satisfy. Our intentions are, however, modest. We wish to explore whether a general model of the impact of supervisory and instructional characteristics on student achievement at the primary school level is consistent with the data for the French tests in language arts, mathematics, and science.

The general model contained four exogenous variables: the number of class visits to sixth-grade classes in the past two weeks as reported by the school director (NUMVIS), the advice given by the school director on the extent to which French should be used exclusively (LGADVD), the number of extra teaching hours added to the class schedule in the past two weeks (NUMHRS), and the number of years the teacher has taught in grade 6 (YRSIN6). Endogenous variables included reported teacher punctuality (PUNCT), the number of times shifts have been combined for instruction in the past two weeks (MIXTOT), the number of lessons skipped in the less important subjects over the past two weeks (TOTSKP), the average predicted number of days required to finish the school syllabus in various subjects (TOTEND), the number of demonstration lessons given by the teacher in the past two years (DEMTCH), the teacher's success in preparing children for the *concours national* examination the previous year (EST7SC), the teacher's assessment skill ratings in language arts (SET123), and the French test scores for language arts (LARTSF), the latter being the sum of individual comprehension and composition scores. This model is shown in Figure 8.5.

Arrows indicate the direction of relationships. For example, teacher supervision, i.e., the number of visits made by the school director (NUMVIS), was considered to 'cause' teacher punctuality (PUNCT) which, in turn, was viewed as 'causing' higher student achievement (LARTSF). Similarly, number of director visits (NUMVIS) was expected to have a negative relationship to skipping lessons (TOTSKP), and through it, a positive relationship to achievement (LARTSF).

In the general model, several instructional practices were regarded as being affected by teacher supervision in different ways. Closer teacher supervision might be expected to foster greater adherence to ministry policies, resulting in less lesson skipping, fewer instances of combining shifts, and fidelity to subject-matter syllabi that call for completion of subjects not earlier than two to three weeks before the administration of the *concours national* examination.

Teacher characteristics and skills constitute a submodel within the general model. Years of teaching experience in grade 6, an exogenous variable, was represented as influencing teacher skills, demonstration teaching, and previous success in examination preparation. It is shown in Figure 8.5 as indirectly influencing student achievement. Teacher characteristics and skills were not connected to particular instructional practices in the model; they were regarded as being conceptually independent. For the same reason, most instructional practices were not linked to teacher supervision in the model. Closer supervision, for instance, was not predicted to directly affect demonstration teaching, though it was thought to influence teacher success in preparing students for the *concours national*. The number of extra hours of instruction was not seen as a policy variable affected by teacher supervision, an outcome of teaching experience, or necessarily an indicator of teacher skill, but instead was thought to be related directly to student performance.

Results of the Path Model

The LISREL method requires testing of the assumptions of a model through chi-square tests or other indices of fit. Using the measure of student achievement in French language arts, the full model was tested as depicted in Figure 8.5. It

Thomas Owen Eisemon, John Schwille, Robert Prouty, Francis Ukobizoba

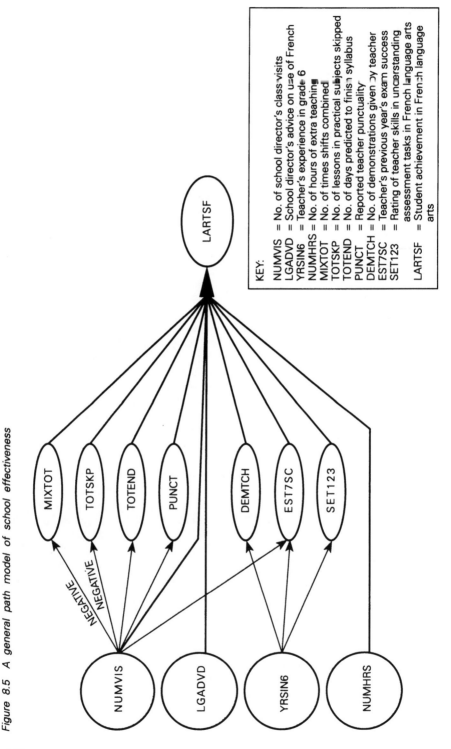

Figure 8.5 A general path model of school effectiveness

148

yielded a chi-square of 38.32, with 40 degrees of freedom (p = .546), a moderate fit to the data indicating that the model cannot be rejected. The model was also estimated after removing the direct path linking number of extra hours of instruction (NUMHRS) to the outcome measure. This second model produced a chi-square of 35.57 with 33 degrees of freedom (p = .348).

Figure 8.6 presents the results of the latter model for the French language arts scores. Among exogenous variables, the number of director visits has the highest coefficients, particularly for the paths to teacher punctuality and previous teacher success in examination preparation, and the one leading directly to scores on the French language arts test. The connection between teacher supervision, teacher punctuality, and achievement was the strongest indirect relationship. Instructional practices that were predicted to be related to teacher supervision, such as combining shifts and skipping lessons, had relatively weak relationships to supervision. However, the signs of these relationships are of interest. Combining classes and skipping lessons were positively influenced by director supervision. Moreover, these practices were positively related to student performance. It seems that teachers that are supervised more closely and, presumably, held most accountable for the performance of their students, are those that in certain respects exhibit less, not greater, adherence to ministry policies. While the path coefficient for the link between director visits and combining classes is weak, the coefficient connecting combining shifts to student scores is more substantial. Combining shifts did seem to increase achievement.

The number of director visits is strongly related to the measure of previous teacher success in examination preparation. But we cannot conclude that closer teacher supervision necessarily causes successful teaching, as the coefficient for the path leading from external examination success to the BRIDGES outcome measure is relatively low. Moreover, our measure of supervision was collected *after* not *prior* to the measure of teacher examination success. Nevertheless, the direct effect of teacher supervision on teaching success is noteworthy.

Among the variables in the submodel, the relationships between years of teaching experience and demonstration teaching, and especially the measure of teaching skill in language arts, are for the most part stronger than the connections between these variables and achievement. The endogenous variables seem to 'absorb' the effects of teaching experience and do not themselves consistently and strongly influence student achievement. Demonstration teaching is the one variable linked to teaching experience that has considerable impact on achievement. The effect of the teacher skill measure is disappointingly small.

In brief, the most powerful features of this model of school effectiveness have to do with school director visits, the direct impact of visits on learning outcomes as well as the indirect impact through teacher punctuality. Similar results (not shown) were obtained from testing the revised model with the French mathematics scores.

Discussion

Five conclusions are supported by the various data analyses. First, students exhibited low levels of achievement in all of the subject domains tested. Although testing in the mother tongue improves the measurement of learning outcomes,

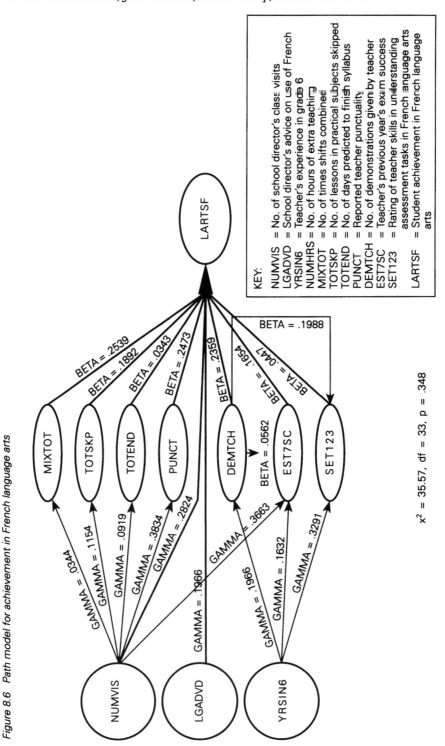

Figure 8.6 Path model for achievement in French language arts

KEY:

NUMVIS = No. of school director's class visits
LGADVD = School director's advice on use of French
YRSIN6 = Teacher's experience in grade 6
NUMHRS = No. of hours of extra teaching
MIXTOT = No. of times shifts combined
TOTSKP = No. of lessons in practical subjects skipped
TOTEND = No. of days predicted to finish syllabus
PUNCT = Reported teacher punctuality
DEMTCH = No. of demonstrations given by teacher
EST7SC = Teacher's previous year's exam success
SET123 = Rating of teacher skills in understanding assessment tasks in French language arts

LARTSF = Student achievement in French language arts

$x^2 = 35.57$, df = 33, p = .348

it mainly enables a more precise estimate of levels of performance for better students. Although few students performed well under either language condition, the mean level of performance by repeaters in Kirundi was high enough to give one the sense of how much the Burundi system could accomplish under better conditions.

The low levels of performance in the language arts tests should be of particular concern to policymakers. Most students, for instance, had difficulty comprehending the kinds of procedural texts in French and Kirundi that they are likely to encounter in daily life. Students' skills in written communication were even poorer, particularly in French. That, of course, has serious implications for secondary schooling.

The performance of students was relatively strong in the test of knowledge of science and agriculture when the examination was in Kirundi. This finding might be seen as consistent with the objectives of the 1973 reform, which stressed practical studies and mother tongue teaching. Unfortunately for this explanation, practical studies currently have an inconsequential place in the primary school curricula, largely separated from science and other cognate academic subjects, and they are to be taught in French and not in Kirundi. Moreover, the content of the science and agriculture test was generally not covered by the students' teachers.

Second, the policy of switching to French as the medium of instruction in grade 5 profoundly influences how much students learn. Even in grade 6, according to the teachers interviewed, only a small proportion of students can follow instruction in French. This depresses test performance in both languages, because French is used as the medium of instruction for most subjects taught in grades 5 and 6. The exception is mathematics. Although the mean scores in mathematics were a little below 50 percent of possible marks, some students obtained perfect scores. Student performance in mathematics was least affected by the use of French as the language of assessment. Moreover, an experiment we did to compare the teaching of mathematics in French and Kirundi, which is described elsewhere (Eisemon *et al.*, 1990), indicated that teaching mathematics in Kirundi without extensive preparation poses many problems for both students and teachers. The implication is that language policy should be more sensitive to the subject domains that are to be taught in French and the mother tongue.

Third, some instructional practices that increase opportunity to learn, such as providing extra hours of instruction, have a relatively weak impact on learning outcomes, both directly and indirectly as estimated in the path models. That may be because the BRIDGES tests measure cognitive skills that are less sensitive to practices that many teachers feel are useful for preparing students for the *concours national*. Examination 'cramming', though it may increase the likelihood of *concours national* success, may not be particularly effective in developing high-level cognitive skills.

Fourth, school management has a strong direct and indirect influence on instruction and learning. Teacher supervision is an important means through which the amount and effectiveness of instruction are influenced. School directors also do substitute teaching, organize in-service training, and have other responsibilities such as liaison with school committees and ministry and party officials. As a result, many may have too little time and too few resources to carry out their primary responsibility, which is to supervise instruction in several schools.

Fifth, repetition has more effect on student performance than any other social background, school or instructional characteristic measured. A threshold effect cannot be established from this study, because we did not collect information on the number of times a student repeated. Nor, more pointedly, do we know how repetition affects success in the *concours national*. Nevertheless, students who repeat grade 6 do benefit from the additional opportunity to learn. High repetition rates are often represented as an indicator of low educational effectiveness; 'poor quality teachers, too few textbooks and other relevant learning materials, inadequate guidelines for assessing learning, too few national examination(s), and too few well-qualified educational managers and school directors' (Heyneman and White, 1986, p. 48). High repetition rates may, as well, be an indicator of limited opportunity to learn what is expected of students for entry into secondary school.

Conclusion: Strengthening Basic Education

Strategies for Change

The findings summarized above suggest many strategies for raising levels of achievement, improving monitoring of learning, and reinforcing school management, as well as for increasing the internal efficiency of primary schooling.

Increasing opportunity to learn: The double shift policy has reduced the school day to little more than three hours in order to expand school participation. Many teachers combine shifts and classes to increase the amount of teaching and curriculum coverage of academic subjects during the school year, and especially prior to the administration of the *concours national*. Combining classes at different grade levels for practical instruction, for example, allows teachers to spend more time on lesson preparation and marking, while combining shifts increases the number of periods of instruction in mathematics and other subjects examined in the *concours national*.

Combining classes in different grade levels for *practical* instruction is not likely to have an adverse effect on learning or seriously strain school facilities and resources, at least not as such instruction is presently conceived and organized. Much of this practical teaching takes place outside school buildings in school gardens and involves no formal instruction or use of equipment apart from the tools students bring with them to school.

However, combining shifts for instruction in *academic* subjects has more serious implications for learning, though not the same implications for all subjects. In the upper stage of the primary cycle, student textbooks are available only for language arts subjects, French and Kirundi. Doubling class sizes for these subjects make it difficult to teach reading and written communications skills, which are best developed through study and exposition of printed texts. On the other hand, the teachers' guides (*fichiers*) are the only instructional materials for mathematics and *étude du milieu*. This lack of student materials may not be desirable for teaching independent study skills, but it affords opportunities for increasing class sizes without a proportionate reduction in the amount of learning material that a teacher can cover.

Changing the curricula and language of instruction. The difficulty and scope of the primary school curriculum in Burundi probably go well beyond what is expected of sixth-grade students in many other countries, both developed and developing. Faced with this curriculum, teachers reduce the scope of instruction by neglecting the teaching of practical subjects. One way to address the problem would be to integrate instruction in certain scientifically oriented subjects and to cover all of them in the secondary school entrance examination. Such a change would involve biology, health, nutrition, and agriculture that now are largely taught as separate subjects. They could be profitably combined into a single subject, integrated science. The separation of scientific from practical instruction in the program of studies is reinforced by the use of French to teach *étude du milieu*, while Kirundi is used for most practical subjects. Though practical subjects are officially to be taught in French in grades 5 and 6, they are in fact usually taught in Kirundi since they are not examined in the *concours national* (Schwille, Eisemon and Prouty, 1989). On the BRIDGES test, students exhibited little understanding of the scientific information that the question items elicited in French, but great improvement when Kirundi was used. This contrasts with the results of the mathematics tests where language effects were less pronounced. Much French mathematical vocabulary has been absorbed into Kirundi, perhaps because it is used for instruction in mathematics prior to grade 5. The use of French for teaching most science in primary schools may inhibit the development of Kirundi as a language of ordinary scientific discourse and, in consequence, the dissemination of modern science.

Progress toward Kirundization, an important objective of the 1973 educational reform, has been impeded by concern for the French language skills of students who are admitted to secondary schools and who have experienced the double shift system. Whether today's graduates have less facility in French than earlier students is the subject of much controversy. Our study indicates that most students have poor French language skills, particularly in composition. Whether double shifts have adversely affected the quality of entrants into secondary schools cannot be determined from our data. That many students are unable to benefit fully from instruction in French has been well established.

Elsewhere (Eisemon and Schwille, 1991) we have proposed improvement and expansion of the teaching of French in the lower stage of the primary cycle while at the same time expanding the use of Kirundi in grades 5 and 6 for teaching science and practical subjects. This change would bring about a balance between the two languages throughout primary school. The government took an important step in this direction in 1989 by deciding to introduce French as a subject in grade 1 instead of grade 3.

Improving assessment of student learning. To improve the effectiveness of primary schooling in Burundi will require changes in the *concours national.* As long as secondary schooling remains highly selective, the secondary school entrance examination will greatly influence the instruction of all primary school students whether or not they go on to secondary school. If those who are not going on to secondary school are to benefit from primary school, the design of the *concours national* must take them into account, too.

Therefore, in our view, the examination should be designed for three purposes: (1) to select students for secondary school as is presently done; (2) to certify satisfactory completion of primary school; and (3) to provide feedback to parents, students, teachers, principals and policymakers on what all students are learning. To implement the different purposes of the examination, different pass rates could be used. The highest cutoff score might be used to identify students going on to secondary school; it could continue to be based on the number of places available in secondary school. Another level might be used to signify successful completion of primary school. This cutoff should be domain-referenced in the sense of representing as nearly as possible that minimum level of knowledge and skills that students need in order to benefit from primary schooling. The examination should cover all those domains judged important for primary school students to learn, including those elements of health, nutrition, and agriculture-related science that are particularly needed by students who will not be going on to secondary school.

Strengthening teacher supervision and improving in-service training. We have drawn attention to the importance of teacher supervision. Now that universal primary education is close to being achieved, it may be useful to consider whether present school clusters permit effective supervision. The number of satellite schools, their size, and the distance from core schools all influence the amount of attention they receive from school directors. In comparison to school headmasters in several other East African countries, school directors in Burundi have greater administrative responsibilities, both in scope and substance. The number of school directors might be increased; if this is not possible, other ways of improving supervision in satellite schools need to be explored (such as giving directors bicycles or motorcycles for transportation).

Improving the effectiveness of teaching is fundamental to increasing school effectiveness and reducing variability in student achievement. Conventional approaches to in-service training focus on improving teacher knowledge of subject matter and/or demonstrating 'effective' methods of lesson presentation. Nevertheless, good teaching involves more than understanding the teachers' guides and being able to present them. It also involves an understanding of what is expected of students, why students make errors, and how to improve their performance. Involving teachers in the examination process in suggesting items and marking papers can be important in fostering a better understanding of assessment tasks and the difficulties students have in performing them. The knowledge gained from these activities is excellent in-service education and will help teachers improve their instruction. That is the experience of many countries where this is practiced (Eisemon and Schwille, 1988).

Achieving appropriate rates of repetition. The high repetition rates at the grade 6 level in primary schools are an outcome of policies intended to increase educational participation and attainment in primary schools but without greater opportunity for secondary education. The rigor of the *concours national* and, until 1989, the lack of feedback to students on their results, encourages the belief that the likelihood of success is increased with subsequent trials. We have no way of confirming or refuting this belief with the data collected in the present study. Nevertheless, for students who repeat, it is clear that retention raised their levels of performance in the domains that we examined and that are also tested in the *concours national.*

Repetition probably increases students' ability to learn in French and, in doing so, to perform better on examinations. Apparently, the shift from Kirundi to French as the medium of instruction in grade 5 is too abrupt for many students for whom repetition may be a strategy for catching up. The retention of French as the medium of instruction in grades 5 and 6 and for examination for admission to secondary school favors the persistence of high repetition rates. Because students are not given unique national inscription numbers in the first grade, repetition cannot be easily monitored. The introduction of national inscription numbers would facilitate further research on the effects of repetition, which in turn could suggest appropriate measures of control.

In 1989 more than 73,000 students sat for the *concours national* and only about 7,000 received places in secondary schools. Between 30,000 and 40,000 students would be expected to repeat the sixth grade. It will require considerable expenditure of scarce resources to educate them. Therefore, a limit on the number of times a student is allowed to repeat might be established, based on a minimum score on the secondary school entrance examination. Or, the proportion of secondary school admissions awarded to students who retake the entrance examination might be limited to further discourage repetition. But reductions in repetition make sense only if considered in conjunction with other changes designed to increase learning or at least to ensure the same level of learning outcomes at less cost.

Needed Experimentation

In part, these findings are a vindication of conventional thinking about what makes for effective primary schooling in Burundi, such as the value of principals making frequent classroom visits and the positive effects of repetition. However, given the shortage of resources in Burundi and the difficult conditions under which many teachers and principals work, just doing more of the same is not likely to be effective in strengthening primary schooling. The variables found to have a positive impact may be nonlinear in their effects, resulting in diminishing returns. Moreover, in some respects our findings deviate from conventional thinking. For example, conventional wisdom might suggest that weak students suffer most from assessment in French. But our results indicate that testing in French may have a still more negative effect on evaluating the ability of the most able students.

It is important to proceed with careful experimentation in pilot projects to see how levels of student performance might be increased and variation reduced. Teachers and principals should play an important role in developing projects to answer questions such as the following: Which students should be allowed to repeat, at what grade level and how often? What modifications of the double shift system should be encouraged? How can one get principals who do not make enough classroom visits to make more of these visits and to monitor teaching more effectively? What changes in incentives are needed and feasible to increase teacher engagement, reducing absenteeism and lateness? And what combinations of French and Kirundi across subject-matters and grades would bring about the best balance of the two languages so that the foundations of literacy are established as much as possible in both languages?

Thomas Owen Eisemon, John Schwille, Robert Prouty, Francis Ukobizoba

References

ALEXANDER, L. and SIMON, J. (1975) *The Determinants of School Achievement in Developing Countries: The Educational Production Function*, Washington, DC, World Bank.

EISEMON, T.O. (1989) 'Becoming a modern farmer: The impact of primary schooling in Kenya and Burundi', in WARREN, D.M., SLIKKERVEER, L.J. and TITILOA, S.O. (Eds) *Indigenous Knowledge Systems: Implications for Agriculture and International Development*, Ames, Iowa, Iowa State University.

EISEMON, T.O. and SCHWILLE, J. (1988) *Examinations Policies to Strengthen Primary Schooling in African Countries*, paper prepared for World Bank Seminar on Using Examinations and Standardized Testing to Improve Educational Quality, Lusaka, Zambia.

EISEMON, T.O. and SCHWILLE, J. (1991) 'Should schools prepare students for secondary education or for self-employment? Addressing a dilemma of primary schooling in Burundi and Kenya', *Elementary School Journal*, **92**, pp. 23–39.

EISEMON, T.O., SCHWILLE, J. and PROUTY, R. (1989) *Does Schooling Make a Better Farmer?: Schooling and Agricultural Productivity in Burundi*, paper presented at the annual meeting of the BRIDGES Project, Bangkok.

EISEMON, T.O., SCHWILLE, J. and PROUTY, R. (1990a) 'What language should be used for teaching?: Language policy and school reform in Burundi', *Journal of Multilingual and Multicultural Development*, **10**, pp. 473–497.

EISEMON, T.O., SCHWILLE, J., PROUTY, R., UKOBIZOBA, F., KANA, D. and MANIRABONA, G. (1990b) *Empirical results and conventional wisdom: Primary school effectiveness in Burundi*, Project BRIDGES, Michigan State University, East Lansing, Michigan (processed).

GAY, J. and COLE, M. (1967) *The New Mathematics and an Old Culture*, New York, Holt, Rinehart and Winston.

HEYNEMAN, S.P. and WHITE, D.S. (1986) *The Quality of Education and Economic Development*, Washington, DC, World Bank.

JORESKOG, K.G. (1978) 'Structural analysis of covariance and correlation matrices', *Psychometrika*, **42**, pp. 443–77.

JORESKOG, K.G. and SORBOM, D. (1986) *LISREL VI: Analysis of Linear Structural Relationships by Maximum Likelihood, Instrumental Variables, and Least Squares Methods* [computer program], Mooresville, Ind., Scientific Software, Inc.

LOCKHEED, M.E. and KOMENAN, A. (1989) 'Teaching quality and student achievement in Africa: The case of Nigeria and Swaziland', *Teaching and Teacher Education*, **5**, 2, pp. 93–111.

MINISTRY OF NATIONAL EDUCATION, REPUBLIC OF BURUNDI (1988a) *Politique et stratégies pour améliorer la qualité de l'éducation de base* [Policies and strategies for improving the quality of basic education], Bujumbura, Burundi (processed).

MINISTRY OF NATIONAL EDUCATION, REPUBLIC OF BURUNDI (1988b) *Rapport final: Séminaire national de réflection sur l'évaluation systématique de l'enseignement primaire, 16–21 Mai 1988* [Final report: National seminar of deliberation on the systematic evaluation of primary education, May 16–21, 1988], Bujumbura, Burundi.

MWAMWENDA, T.S. and MWAMWENDA, B.B. (1989) 'Teacher characteristics and pupils' achievement in Botswana primary education', *International Journal of Educational Development*, **9**, pp. 31–42.

PROCEEDINGS OF THE SEMINAR OF DELIBERATION ON IMPROVING THE INTERNAL AND EXTERNAL EFFECTIVENESS OF PRIMARY EDUCATION (1989) East Lansing, Mich., Michigan State University, USAID BRIDGES Project, in collaboration with the Ministry of Primary and Secondary Education, Bujumbura, Burundi and the Centre de Perfectionnement et de Formation en Cours d'Emploi (CPF), Bujumbura, Burundi.

RAMSAY, J.O. and ABRAHAMOWICZ, M. (1989) *Binomial Regression with Monotone Splines: A Psychometric Application*, Department of Psychology, McGill University, Montreal (processed).

REED, H.J. and LAVE, J. (1979) 'Arithmetic as a tool for investigating relations between culture and cognition', *American Ethnologist*, **6**, pp. 568–82.

SCHWILLE, J., EISEMON, T.O. and PROUTY, R. (1990) *Between Policy and Students: The Reach of Implementation in Burundian Primary Schools*, paper presented at the annual meeting of the Comparative and International Education Society, Boston, Massachusetts.

SCHWILLE, J., EISEMON, T.O. and PROUTY, R. (1990, March) *How Wasteful Is Grade Repetition? Unanswered Questions Posed by the Test Scores of Rural Sixth Grade Repeaters in Burundi*, paper presented at the annual meeting of the Comparative and International Education Society, Anaheim, California.

WORLD BANK (1988) *Education in Sub-Saharan Africa: Policies for Adjustment, Revitalization, and Expansion*, Washington, DC.

ZASLAVSKY, C. (1973) *Africa Counts*, Boston, Prindle, Weber and Schmidt.

Chapter 9

Accelerated Schools in the United States: Do They Have Relevance for Developing Countries?

Henry M. Levin

Introduction

A majority of the developing countries of the world are facing serious challenges in advancing the education of their populations. The standard model of educational development assumed that as the nations developed, enrollments as a proportion of each age group would expand; educational resources for each student would increase; and the quality of education would rise. To a certain degree this was the pattern of the sixties and seventies for many countries. However, by the eighties it was clear that a new trend had emerged. While enrollments as a proportion of each age group continued to increase, expenditures for each pupil declined, and the quality and effectiveness of schooling were seen to deteriorate. As a result, in the poorest countries, completion rates began to decline. Dramatic evidence of these trends are reported in two recent World Bank publications, *Education in Sub-Saharan Africa* (1988) and *Primary Education* (1990).

Up to this point the search for efficiency and effectiveness has focused on low-cost and cost-effective means of expanding schools and raising their quality. It was assumed that the basic model of schooling as practiced in the developing countries was a sound one, but that incremental changes in practices and added resources were necessary to increase available spaces and raise quality. However, for some observers it has become obvious that there is simply no way that a quality education can be provided to all primary-age children within existing resource constraints. These observers (e.g., Nicholas Bennett) argue that in the absence of radical school reform, little headway will be made against the present trend of educational deterioration.

In the United States, a similar debate has emerged over the crisis of disadvantaged students or, to use the current parlance, at-risk students. These are students who lack the family and community resources to succeed in schools as schools are currently constituted (Levin, 1986). They enter schools unprepared to take advantage of the standard curriculum and fall farther and farther behind in academic achievement. Their test scores indicate that they are two years behind other students by grade 6 and four years behind at the end of grade 12 , if they reach that level. About half do not graduate from high school, which is a minimum requirement for productive entry into the US labor force.

The purpose of this paper is to describe a strategy that has been effective in educating at-risk students in the US and may be useful in addressing the needs of students in developing societies. This strategy, known as the Accelerated School approach, is aimed at: (1) accelerating the academic progress of at-risk'students, especially those in poverty; and (2) accomplishing acceleration largely within existing resource levels by transforming the fundamental organizational, curricular and instructional dimensions of schooling. It builds on the notion of shifting both students and teachers from their roles as *objects* of the educational process to the *subjects* in that process.

Educationally At-Risk Students in the United States

As in developing societies, US students who are most at risk in the educational system are those who are drawn from poverty populations. Currently about one of five US students — and a large majority of students in the typical developing countries — are living in poverty and thus are considered to be educationally at risk. In the US students from minority groups, immigrant and non-English speaking populations, and single-parent families are also considered to be educationally at risk. When all risk factors are taken into account, it is estimated that about one third of all students in US elementary and secondary schools are educationally at risk (Levin, 1986; Pallas, Natriello and McDill, 1989). This proportion is rising rapidly because of the substantial immigrations from impoverished and rural areas of Asia and Latin America and because of high birth rates among at-risk populations.

Unless we are able to intervene successfully, there are dire economic consequences for higher education, the labor force, and the cost of public services. Larger and larger numbers of educationally disadvantaged students will mean that public institutions of higher education either will have to become more restrictive in their admissions criteria or will have to commit more resources to remedial academic work. Restrictive admissions policies would be politically controversial at a time of increasing population growth and political power of disadvantaged populations. Further, such policies might restrict the supply of college-educated workers below the number needed by the economy. Alternatively, increasing numbers of remedial courses and students will cause substantial cost increases to both the colleges and universities and to the students who must forego earnings for a longer period to get a college education.

A further consequence of the expansion of disadvantaged student populations will be a serious deterioration of the future labor force. As increasing numbers of disadvantaged students continue to experience low achievement and high dropout rates, a larger and larger portion of the labor force will be unprepared for available jobs. Even clerical workers, cashiers and salespeople need basic skills in oral and written communication, computation and reasoning, and these skills are not acquired by many educationally disadvantaged students. A national assessment found that while only 13 percent of all 17-year-olds in the United States were classified as functionally illiterate, about half of the educationally disadvantaged were illiterate (National Assessment of Educational Progress, 1976). Without successful interventions to improve the plight of the educationally disadvantaged, employers and the economy will suffer lagging productivity, higher training costs, and competitive disadvantages as well as lost tax revenues. This will be especially true in those states and localities most affected by disadvantaged labor forces, but there will be a national impact as well.

These economic losses will come at a time of rising costs for public services for persons disadvantaged by inadequate educational attainments. More and more citizens will need to rely on public assistance for survival, and increasing numbers of undereducated adolescents and adults will pursue illegal activities to fill idle time and obtain the income that is not available through legal pursuits (Berlin and Sum, 1988). Further, economic analyses suggest that educational investments on behalf of at-risk students yield financial benefits to society that are far greater than the social costs (Levin, 1989).

Are We on the Right Track?

What is clear is that we are not on the right track to meet the challenges of educationally at-risk students, despite recent educational reforms for the general population (e.g., National Commission on Excellence in Education, 1983; US Department of Education, 1984). These reforms have not really addressed the specific needs of educationally at-risk students. The reforms stress raising standards at the secondary level, without providing additional resources or new strategies to assist the disadvantaged in meeting these higher standards (National Coalition of Advocates for Students, 1985).

Consequently, it is not surprising that the status of at-risk students has not improved with the latest reforms. Any strategy for improving the educational plight of at-risk children must begin at least at the elementary level and must be dedicated to preparing children to do good work in secondary school. Simply raising secondary school standards without making it possible for at-risk students to meet the new standards is likely to increase the dropout rate (McDill, Natriello and Pallas, 1985). This outcome is at least as likely in developing societies as in the US.

How to Produce Educational Failure

Students from poverty backgrounds begin school with a learning gap in those areas valued by schools and mainstream economic and social institutions. The existing model of intervention assumes that they will not be able to maintain a normal instructional pace without prerequisite knowledge and learning skills. Thus, such students are placed in less demanding instructional settings — either by being pulled out of their regular classrooms or by adapting the regular classroom to their 'needs' — to provide remedial or compensatory educational services (Evertson, 1982; Knapp and Turnbull, 1990; Oakes, 1985, 1990; Peterson, 1986; Romberg, 1986; Slavin, 1987). Many of the characteristics of remedial programs in the US are found in schools serving disadvantaged populations in the developing world as well. While the remedial or compensatory approach appears to be both rational and compassionate, it typically produces effects that are quite different from the intended outcomes.

First, this approach reduces the learning expectations of the children and the educators who teach them. Moreover, it stigmatizes both groups with a label of inferiority, undermining social support for the educational activity, denoting low social status to the participants, and giving all participants negative self-images. The combination of low social status and low expectations is tantamount to treating the students as discards who are marginal to the mainstream educational agenda. Thus, the model creates conditions under which significant educational progress is unlikely to occur. In contrast, an effective approach must focus on creating learning activities that are characterized by high expectations and high status for the participants.

Second, the usual approach to teaching the educationally disadvantaged is not designed to bring students to the point where they can benefit from mainstream instruction and perform at grade level. There are no timetables for doing so, and there are rarely incentives, or even provisions, for students to move from remedial instruction into the mainstream. In fact, since students in compensatory or remedial situations are expected to progress at a slower than 'normal' pace, a self-fulfilling prophecy is realized as they fall farther and farther behind their non-disadvantaged counterparts. The result is that once a disadvantaged student is relegated to remedial or compensatory interventions, that student will be expected to learn at a slower rate, and the achievement gap between advantaged and disadvantaged students will grow. A successful program must set a deadline for closing the achievement gap so that educationally disadvantaged children ultimately will be able to benefit from mainstream instruction.

Third, conventional approaches deliberately slow the pace of instruction to a crawl, placing a heavy emphasis on endless repetition of material through drill and practice. The result is that the school experience of the disadvantaged lacks intrinsic vitality, omits crucial learning skills and reinforcement, and moves at a plodding pace that reinforces low expectations. Exposure to concepts, analysis, problem solving and interesting applications is largely proscribed in favor of decoding skills in reading and arithmetic operations in the primary grades on the premise that these fundamentals must be learned before anything more challenging can be attempted. Mechanics are stressed over content. Such a joyless experience further contributes to the child's negative feelings about school and diminishes the possibility that the child will view the school as an environment in which learning progress can be made. An effective curriculum for the disadvantaged must be fast-paced and must actively engage children's interests to enhance their motivation: it must include concept development, analysis, problem solving, and interesting applications.

Another important aspect of the Accelerated School approach is involvement of parents and other community members. Most compensatory educational programs do not involve parents sufficiently or draw adequately upon available community resources. Parents are not viewed as a potentially positive influence in their children's learning. Although parental involvement has been an integral part of the Head Start pre-school program for disadvantaged youngsters, it is not a prominent feature in many Head Start schools and is found only rarely in elementary and secondary schools attended by disadvantaged children. There is considerable evidence on how different parental involvement strategies are connected with student success in (Epstein and Scott-Jones, 1990). Furthermore, the professional staff at the school level are usually left out of the process of making important educational decisions that they must ultimately implement.

Such an omission means that teachers are expected to dedicate themselves to the implementation of programs that do not necessarily reflect their professional judgement, a condition which is not likely to spur great enthusiasm. The design and implementation of successful educational programs to address the needs of the educationally disadvantaged require the involvement of parents, the use of community resources, and the extensive participation of teachers in formulating the interventions that will be provided.

An effective approach to educating disadvantaged students is characterized by high expectations; specified deadlines by which such children will be performing at grade level; stimulating instructional programs; involvement of the educational staff in planning the program they will implement and use of all available resources, including students' parents. In addition, an effective approach uses instructional strategies that are particularly appropriate for disadvantaged students and make better use of time. It incorporates a comprehensive set of strategies that reinforce each other to create an organizational thrust towards raising students' achievement to grade level.

Accelerated Schools for At-Risk Students

The Accelerated School Program at Stanford University, designed as an alternative to present practice, builds on the knowledge base that argues in favor of a different set of assumptions for achieving school success for at-risk students (Edmonds, 1979; Levin, 1987, 1988; Madden *et al.*, 1989). At the heart of the program is the attempt to do for at-risk students what we presently attempt to do for gifted and talented students, striving to accelerate their progress rather than slowing it down (Chase, 1990). The goal of the Accelerated School Program is to accelerate the learning of at-risk students so that they are able to *perform at grade level by the end of elementary school.*

To accomplish this goal, schools must be restructured completely. The restructured schools must be characterized by high expectations on the part of teachers, parents and students; specified deadlines by which students are expected to meet particular educational requirements; stimulating instructional programs, planning by the educational staff who offer the programs, and the use of all available resources in the community, including parents, senior citizens, and social agencies. Over the last two and a half years, some forty of these schools have been established in the US, most of them within the last year (1990–91).

Such schools are designed to enable at-risk students to take advantage of mainstream or accelerated middle school or secondary school instruction by effectively closing the achievement gap in elementary school. The approach is also expected to reduce dropouts, drug use, and teenage pregnancies by creating a strong sense of self-worth and educational accomplishment for students who now feel rejected by schools and frustrated about their own abilities. Specific dimensions of the accelerated school are outlined below.

Organization

In the accelerated school approach, the entire organization of the school focuses on the goal of having students achieve at or above grade level by the time they leave sixth grade. A key characteristic is placing curriculum and instructional decisions in the hands of the instructional staff of the school. Classroom teachers know the students best. They understand students' learning needs, styles and capabilities in ways most administrators and program specialists cannot. If desired changes in student achievement are to be realized, teachers must have the authority and responsibility to design curriculum and instructional programs that are compatible with their unique classroom perspective.

To facilitate this process, each accelerated school has an overall steering committee and task forces composed of the principal, teachers, other staff, and parents. The principal serves a central function as instructional leader in coordinating and guiding this activity and in addressing the logistical needs for translating decisions into reality. School staff members work together to design a program that is consonant with student needs and the strengths of the district and school staff. Information, technical assistance and training are provided by district personnel. In this way, the reform is a 'bottom-up' approach; those who are providing the instruction make the decisions that they will implement and evaluate.

These broad features of the accelerated school are designed to make it a total institution for accelerating the educational progress of the disadvantaged, rather than just grafting on compensatory or remedial classes to schools with a conventional agenda.

We believe that this approach has a high probability of ultimate success because of its emphasis on the instrumental goal of bringing students to grade level or above by the end of sixth grade; its stress on acceleration of learning, critical thinking, and high expectations; its reliance on a professional model of school governance that is attractive to educators; its use of instructional strategies that have shown good results for the disadvantaged in existing models of compensatory education; and its emphasis on mobilizing the resources available in the community, including parents and senior citizens.

In the accelerated school the stress is on the school as a whole rather than on a particular grade, curriculum, approach to teacher training, or other more limited strategy. The organizational approach assumes that the strategy must do three things: (1) develop a unity of purpose among all of the participants; (2) 'empower' all of the major participants and raise their feelings of efficacy and responsibility for the outcomes of the school; and (3) build on the considerable strengths of the participants rather than decrying their weaknesses.

Unity of purpose refers to agreement among parents, teachers and students with respect to a common set of goals for the school that will be the focal point of everyone's efforts. Clearly, these goals should focus on bringing children into the educational mainstream so that they can fully benefit from their further schooling experiences and adult opportunities.

Empowerment refers to the ability of the key participants to make important decisions at the school level and in the home to improve the education of students. It is based upon breaking the present stalemate among administrators, teachers, parents and students in which the participants tend to blame each other, as well as factors 'beyond their control', for the poor educational outcomes of disadvantaged students. Unless all of the major actors are empowered to seek a common set of goals and influence the educational and social processes that can achieve those goals, it is unlikely that the desired improvements will take place or be sustained.

An accelerated school must build upon an expanded role for all groups to participate in and take responsibility for the educational process and results. Such an approach requires a shift to school-based decision making with heavy involvement of teachers and parents and new administrative roles.

Building on strengths refers to employing all the learning resources that students, parents, school staff and communities can bring to the educational endeavor. In the quest to place blame for the schools' lack of efficacy in improving the education of disadvantaged students, it is easy to exaggerate weaknesses of the various participants and ignore strengths. Parents have considerable strengths in serving as positive influences for the education of their children, not the least of which are a deep love for their children and a desire for their children to succeed. Teachers are capable of insights, intuition, and teaching and organizational acumen that are lost when schools exclude teachers from participating in the decisions they must implement. Both parents and teachers are largely underutilized sources of talent in the schools.

The strengths of disadvantaged students are often overlooked because they are perceived as lacking the learning behaviors associated with middle-class students. Yet they have a number of assets that can be used to accelerate their learning (Cummins, 1986). Many disadvantaged students have curiosity and interest in oral and artistic expression. They are able to learn through the manipulation of appropriate learning materials, and they become engrossed in intrinsically interesting tasks. Many are able to learn to write before attaining competence in decoding skills that are prerequisite to reading (Graves, 1983). In addition, disadvantaged students can serve as enthusiastic and effective learning resources for other students through peer tutoring and cooperative learning approaches (Slavin, 1983).

School-based administrators are also underutilized when they are placed in 'command' roles to meet the directives and standard operating procedures of districts rather than being allowed to work creatively with parents, staff and students. And communities have considerable resources, including youth organizations, senior citizens, businesses and religious groups, which should be viewed as major assets for the schools and the children of the community. The strengths of these participants can be viewed as significant resources for creating accelerated schools.

Curriculum and Instructional Strategies

The instructional program is based on an accelerated curriculum that is designed to bring all children to grade level or higher in core curricular areas (e.g., scoring at the 50th percentile or above on norm-referenced standardized achievement tests in reading comprehension, language, mathematical computation and applications) and to perform well on a variety of other assessment criteria that are more qualitative. A major curriculum feature is a strong emphasis on language across the curriculum, even in mathematics; writing and reading are introduced early in the program. Interesting applications of new tools to everyday problems and events stress the usefulness of what is being learned and introduce a problem-solving orientation.

Other features include the implementation of an extended-day program that provides periods for rest, physical activity and the arts, as well as for working on independent assignments or homework. During this period, college students and senior citizen volunteers work with individual students to provide learning assistance. Since many of the students are 'latch-key' children, the extension of the school day is attractive to parents. Instructional strategies also include peer tutoring and cooperative learning, both of which have been shown to be especially effective with disadvantaged students (Slavin and Madden, 1989).

Parent Involvement

Parent involvement is an essential feature of the accelerated school approach. Research on parental and family involvement supports the important role that families can have in raising the educational accomplishments of their students (Epstein, 1987). The accelerated school builds on parental involvement in several ways.

Parents or guardians are expected to affirm an agreement that clarifies the goals of the Accelerated School Program and the respective obligations of parents, students and school staff. The agreement is explained to parents and translated, if necessary. Parental obligations include such supportive roles as ensuring that children go to bed at a reasonable hour and attend school regularly and punctually. Parents are asked to set high educational expectations for their children, to talk to them regularly about the importance of school, and to take an interest in the children's activities and the materials that they bring home.

Parents are expected to encourage children to read on a daily basis and to ensure that they complete their independent assignments. They are also expected to respond to queries from the school. The importance of the parental role is emphasized through the dignity of an agreement that is affirmed by all parties. Students and school staff also have appropriate obligations regarding their roles, with the understanding that the accelerated school will succeed only if all parties work together.

Parents participate in the governance structure of the school through membership on task forces and the steering committee. They also are given opportunities to interact with the school program and school staff through an 'open door' policy and a parent lounge, as well as to receive training for providing active assistance to their children. Such training includes not only the skills for working with a child, but also many of the academic skills necessary to understand what the child is doing. In this respect, it may be necessary to work closely with agencies offering adult basic education to provide the educational foundation. The parental dimension can improve the capacity and effort of the child, increase the time devoted to academic learning, and provide additional instructional resources in the home.

Evaluation

Progress is evaluated by an assessment system that monitors student performance to assure that children are on the appropriate learning trajectory. Periodic evaluations on wide-spectrum, standardized achievement tests, as well as on tailored assessments created by school staff for each strand of the curriculum, are essential ingredients. These evaluations emphasize the students' acquisition of higher order thinking and reasoning skills in core curricular areas. Unfortunately, assessment instruments that are presently available are not suitable for these purposes. Accordingly, this dimension is the focus of a major developmental effort.

Accelerated Schools in Action

At the heart of the accelerated school model is the emphasis on site responsibility for the educational process and outcomes. This responsibility implies that there must be an appropriate decision-making structure built around the school's unity of purpose, and there must be an appropriate process for developing the school's capacity to identify challenges, to create an inquiry process for understanding the challenges and potential solutions, and to implement and evaluate solutions.

Governance Structures

We have found that three levels of participation are necessary to encompass the range of issues that must be addressed in a democratic but productive way: the School as a Whole; the Steering Committee; and Task Forces or Policy Committees.

The School as a Whole (SAW) refers to the principal, teachers, teachers' aides, other instructional and non-instructional staff, and parent representatives as well as student representatives. The SAW is required to approve all major decisions on curriculum, instruction, and resource allocation that have implications for the entire school. At the opposite extreme in terms of group size are the task and policy committees or cadres. These are small groups organized around particular areas of concern for the school, such as various subject matter areas, personnel, or particular school challenges. Where the concern is a continuing one, such as personnel selection and evaluation, assessment, or parent participation, a cadre is formed. In cases where there is a need of limited duration, such as the planning of new facilities, an *ad hoc* committee is formed for the duration of the task. The major guideline for forming committees is to create as few as possible, always looking for ways to combine related responsibilities and to dissolve committees that are no longer needed in order to avoid overburdening staff.

The cadres do most of the analytic and preparatory work, such as defining specific problems that the school faces and searching for and implementing solutions. The cadres build on the camaraderie, ease of communication, and strong motivation associated with small teams working together on a regular basis.

Before implementation begins, the recommendations of cadres must be approved by the Steering Committee and, in some cases, by the School as a Whole. The Steering Committee consists of the principal and representative teachers, aides, other school staff, and parents. Its purpose is to appoint the cadres, to monitor their progress, and to develop a set of recommendations for consideration by the school as a whole. Steering committee members can be elected or they can be drawn from the committees, with rotating membership over time to give all persons a chance to serve. Committees are expected to meet on a weekly basis, the steering committee on a bi-weekly basis, and the school as a whole on a quarterly basis or as needed. Meetings of all entities require a public display of agendas at least 24 hours in advance and minutes of meetings within 48 hours following the meeting.

Clearly, the principal in the school has a different role than in a traditional school. The principal is responsible for coordinating and facilitating the activities of decision-making bodies and for obtaining the logistical support that is necessary in such areas as information, staff development, assessment, implementation, and instructional resources. A good principal in an accelerated school is an active listener and participant who can identify and cultivate talents among staff, keep the school focused on its mission, work effectively with parents and community, motivate the various participants, and marshal the necessary resources. The principal of an accelerated school is dedicated to the students and their success and is 'the keeper of the dream'. In the last role, the principal is the person who must remind participants of the 'dream' — the school's aspirations for students, staff and parents — especially during periods of temporary disappointments or setbacks.

With this approach school districts need to play a more service-oriented role with respect to individual schools than districts normally do. Instead of relating to schools primarily as regulators with rules, mandates and policies to ensure compliance with a centralized plan, the school district must provide support services to help the accelerated school succeed in its mission. Central office staff can assist task committees and the steering committee in identification of challenges, obtaining information on alternatives, implementation, staff development, and evaluation. District staff can also assist the schools in working with parents and helping families sponsor activities in the home that support the educational progress of their children.

While schools for at-risk students need considerable additional resources (Levin, 1989), the transformation to an accelerated school is one of qualitative change that can be accomplished largely within existing resources. The major resource need is providing additional released time of staff to be involved in meetings, staff development, discussion, reflection, planning and exploration of alternatives. Pilot schools have been successful in using various school district resources, grants from foundations, and changes in school organization to accommodate some of these time requirements. In addition, expertise is needed from the district central office or through outside consultants to assist the school in building the capacity to accelerate the education of its students.

Building School Capacity

Existing schools can be transformed structurally through devolution of decision making to school sites, but they will not function as accelerated schools unless they have developed the capacity to establish a unity of purpose, to make responsible decisions, and to build on strengths. Certainly school staff have not been trained to function in this way, nor have they been expected to function this way in traditional schools. This challenge is as true in the developing societies as in the United States. Institutions must be developed that will build schools' capacity to accelerate the students' education and that will support the needs of these schools.

This is tyically a matter of refocusing existing resources at national and regional levels rather than requiring additional resources.

Ultimately much of the capability to become an accelerated school evolves directly from the implementation of new practices, that is, through learning by doing. School staff and community members become expert at the new practices by using them. But in order to get the process started, there are a number of steps that must be taken.

It is usually necessary to provide some training in making decisions within groups. Rarely do principals, teachers and school staff have this experience. Meetings in traditional schools tend to be highly structured and run in a routine and often authoritarian fashion. Teachers, in particular, consider meetings a waste of time. School staff rarely view meetings as having the potential to be productive and to accomplish major goals on behalf of the school. Accordingly, school staff members need experience in working together with special attention to group process and participation, sharing of information, and working towards decisions. In addition, they need exposure to inquiry-oriented processes that help to identify and define challenges, to look for alternative solutions, and to implement those solutions.

These needs can be met through special training in the identified areas. But, direct involvement in the accelerated school process is also a critical part of building capacity. This process is initiated in four steps. At the first phase, the school is asked to establish baseline information on itself. All school staff participate in assembling a report for discussion among all site participants. The report includes a history of the school; data on students, staff, and school facilities; information on the community and cultures of the parents; identification of particular strengths of the school; data on attendance, test scores, and other measures of student performance; and a preliminary identification of the major challenges faced by the school. Some of this information is quantitative, while much of it is descriptive. The purpose of this exercise is to begin the accelerated school process through a self-examination. The preparation of a written record of the school's status at the outset serves as a comparison point for assessing progress. The process of collecting, reporting and discussing the baseline information goes on for several weeks.

The second part of the initial process is to develop for the school the vision that will be the focus of change. In a series of meetings of the school as a whole and smaller components of staff, the participants focus on building a description of a school that works for students, staff, and community. Since the accelerated school transitional process is expected to take about six years, that is the time period for which the participants project a new vision of their school. Out of this process emerges a vision for the future, which will be the focus of accelerated school implementation. This phase of the process can be carried out in a one-day meeting, if staff members prepare for the meeting by discussing the vision and informally exploring possibilities.

The third phase involves the comparison of the vision articulated for the school and the baseline report. Clearly, there will be a large gap in almost every aspect between the vision and the existing situation. School staff are asked to work on specifying all the things that must be done in order to move from the present situation to the future vision. Of course, they amass a very large number of changes that must be made, often forty to fifty major alterations.

In the fourth step the list of things that need to be accomplished is reduced to a small number of initial priorities that will become the immediate focus of the school. No organization can work effectively on more than three or four major priorities at a time; the staff now must select those three or four major priorities. This process can generate very animated discussions that get to the heart of staff concerns. The discourse dynamics themselves are useful as staff members come to realize that they are responsible for change and for choosing those areas where they must begin. The agreement on priorities is followed by the establishment of the first cadres — the small groups that will work on these priorities and — assignment of staff to each group, usually through self-selection. The final stage is deciding how to construct the steering committee and its functions.

At this point the school is ready to adopt the full accelerated process. However, this process must be supported by the principal, steering committee, and school district as well as by training staff in an inquiry process. Cadres need training in how to take an overall challenge, such as students' poor mathematics performance, and to refine the focus to understand the specific concerns. They must be able to translate these concerns into specific hypotheses for further exploration. Once they narrow the problem to a specific cause or causes, they need to seek out alternatives for addressing it. Finally, they need to choose a solution or strategy, implement it, and evaluate the results. In this respect, it is necessary to provide training and guidance to all task groups on problem solving and implementation of decisions.

Present Status of Accelerated Schools

The Accelerated School Program at Stanford University began its implementation of the accelerated school process in 1987–88 with the selection of two pilot schools in the San Francisco Bay area where the model was applied and further developed. By Fall 1992–93, 300 schools had embarked on the six-year transitions to accelerated schools in 25 states. The purpose of the two pilot schools was to translate and implement the principles of accelerated schooling while simultaneously providing a basis for building our knowledge on how to implement the changes collaboratively with practitioners.

It is important to note that our estimate of the time required to make the transition from a conventional to an accelerated school is about six years. Since only five years of the six-year period required for a full transformation of our pilot schools have passed, we have not undertaken a summative evaluation. However, the changes in the schools have already been rather remarkable. Parent participation in the two schools has increased dramatically (e.g., 95 percent parent participation in conferences with their children's classroom teachers, in contrast to less than 30 percent before the intervention), and student discipline problems have declined precipitously. Attendance patterns have been improved, and the school environments are very positive. New programs in language, mathematics, and enhancement of student self-esteem have been introduced with great success. *Esprit de corps* among teachers and other staff is unusually high.

The available evidence on student achievement is impressive. Virtually all the schools on which we have evidence have shown rising test scores in comparison with similar schools in their districts. For example, in 1990–91 our pilot school in San Francisco had the largest gains in test scores in all subjects in that city. Other schools have also shown impressive gains in the relatively short periods during which they have implemented the approach. There is evidence of reduced grade repetition and fewer placements in special education, both resulting in the saving of considerable costs to school funding sources.

Pertinence to Primary School Restructuring in Developing Societies

What is the pertinence of the accelerated school model to the issue of primary school restructuring in developing societies? Surely, the setting and challenge are very different, even though many at-risk students in the US are drawn from impoverished rural populations who have immigrated from Asia and Latin America. I think that the message is not in the details of the accelerated school, but in its principles. The accelerated school is based on a number of features that probably are common to all successful restructuring efforts directed at providing more effective schools for disadvantaged students.

- These efforts are based on a philosophy of empowering at-risk populations to have greater control over their life circumstances, both educationally and in other domains.
- They assume that there must be leadership at all levels in order for such a movement to succeed. Teachers, parents and students must be imbued with this philosophy and given the capacities to apply it.
- Effective efforts stress that students, staff and communities must not only have greater involvement in decision making in their schools, but must also take responsibility for the consequences of decisions and must address their own needs through a collaborative, problem-solving process. They place great emphasis on school site responsibility and decision making in contrast to reliance on educational decisions made at highly centralized levels.
- They build on a unity of purpose in school activities and relating the school to community needs and local culture. They require deep community involvement and align themselves with community goals while drawing on the substantial resources that communities can offer their schools in supporting school activities.
- These efforts design their curriculum and instructional strategies to build on the strengths of the students rather than on exposing their weaknesses and failings.
- Educational experiences are based on students' development of active learning patterns (rather than passive ones) through the use of manipulable materials and learning-by-doing activities.
- Once these efforts are beyond the pilot or demonstration level, they require support from higher-level school authorities to assist in the provision of training, materials, and demonstration sites where exemplary practices can be modeled for trainees.

- They view a major source of additional resources as the cost savings from reducing the numbers of students who repeat grades or (in the US) are placed in special education classes.

Many of these dimensions are also characteristic of the Escuela Nueva in Colombia (Colbert, Chiappe, and Arboleda, this volume), which has also reported dramatic improvements in achievement and parsimonious use of resources. It would seem that the discussion of the pertinence of accelerated schools to developing societies should focus on a common set of principles and practices that have emerged in these cases rather than a particular model that is applied to all countries.

References

BERLIN, G. and SUM, A. (1988) *Toward a More Perfect Union: Basic Skills, Poor Families and Our Economic Future*, Occasional Paper 3, Ford Foundation Project on Social Welfare and the American Future, New York, Ford Foundation.

CHASE, C. (1990) 'Releasing the gifted potential of children "at-risk"', in LEVIN, H. (Ed.) *Accelerating the Education of At-Risk Students*, New York, The Falmer Press.

COMER, J.J. (1980) *School Power*, New York, The Free Press.

CUMMINS, J. (1986) 'Empowering Minority Students', *Harvard Educational Review*, **56**, pp. 18–36.

EDMONDS, R. (1979) 'Effective schools for the urban poor', *Educational Leadership*, **37**, 1, pp. 15–24.

EPSTEIN, J.L. (1987) 'Parent involvement: What research says to administrators', *Education and Urban Society*, **193**, 2, pp. 119–36.

EPSTEIN, J.L. and SCOTT-JONES, D. (1990) 'School–Family–Community Connections for Accelerating Student Progress in the Elementary and Middle Grades', in LEVIN, H.M. (Ed.) *Accelerating the Education of At-Risk Students*, New York, Falmer Press, forthcoming.

EVERTSON, C.M. (1982) 'Differences in Instructional Activities in Higher- and Lower-Achieving Junior High School English and Math Classes', *Elementary School Journal*, **82**, pp. 329–50.

GRAVES, D. (1983) *Writing: Teachers and Children at Work*, Portsmouth, NH, Heineman Books.

KNAPP, M.S. and TURNBULL, B.J. (1990) *Better Schooling for the Children of Poverty: Alternatives to Conventional Wisdom*, Study of Academic Instruction for Disadvantaged Students, 2 Volumes, Menlo Park, CA, SRI International.

LEVIN, H.M. (1986) *Educational Reform for Disadvantaged Students: An Emerging Crisis*, West Haven, Conn., National Education Association Professional Library.

LEVIN, H.M. (1987) 'Accelerating schools for disadvantaged students', *Educational Leadership*, **44**, 6, pp. 19–21.

LEVIN, H.M. (1988) 'Accelerating elementary education for disadvantaged students, in Council of Chief State School Officers (Eds) *School Success for Students at Risk*, Orlando, Fla, Harcourt Brace Jovanovich.

LEVIN, H.M. (1989) 'Financing the education of at-risk students', *Educational Evaluation and Policy Analysis*, **11**, 1, pp. 47–60.

McDILL, E.L., NATRIELLO, G. and PALLAS, A. (1985) 'Raising standards and retaining students: The impact of the reform recommendations on potential dropouts', *Review of Educational Research*, **55**, 4, pp. 415–34.

MADDEN, N.A., SLAVIN, R.E., KARWEIT, N.L. and LIVERMON, B.J. (1989) 'Success for all: Restructuring the urban elementary school', *Educational Leadership*, **46**, 5, pp. 14–20.

NATIONAL ASSESSMENT OF EDUCATION PROGRESS (1976) *Functional Literacy and Basic Reading Performance*, Washington, DC, US Office of Education, Department of Health, Education and Welfare.

NATIONAL COALITION OF ADVOCATES FOR STUDENTS (1985) *Barriers to Excellence: Our Children at Risk*, Boston, Massachusetts.

NATIONAL COMMISSION ON EXCELLENCE IN EDUCATION (1983) *A Nation at Risk: The Imperative for Educational Reform*, Washington, DC, US Department of Education.

OAKES, J. (1985) *Keeping Track: How Schools Structure Inequality*, New Haven, Yale University Press.

OAKES, J. (1990) *Multiplying Inequalities: The Effects of Race, Social Class, and Tracking on Opportunities to Learn Mathematics and Science*, Santa Monica, CA, The Rand Corporation.

PALLAS, A.M., NATRIELLO, G. and McDILL, E.L. (1989) 'The changing nature of the disadvantaged population: Current dimensions and future trends', *Educational Researcher*, **18**, 5, pp. 16–22.

PETERSON, P.L. (1986) 'Selecting Students and Services for Compensatory Education: Lessons From Aptitude-Treatment Interaction Research', paper prepared for Conference on Effects of Alternative Designs in Compensatory Education, US Department of Education, Washington, DC.

ROMBERG, T.A. (1986) 'Mathematics for Compensatory School Programs', paper prepared for Conference on Effects of Alternative Designs in Compensatory Education, US Department of Education, Washington, DC.

SLAVIN, R.E. (1983) *Cooperative Learning*, New York, Longman.

SLAVIN, R.E. (1987) 'Ability Grouping and Student Achievement in Elementary Schools: A Best-Evidence Synthesis', *Review of Educational Research*, **57**, pp. 347–50.

SLAVIN, R.E. and MADDEN, N.A. (1989) 'What works for students at risk: A research synthesis', *Educational Leadership*, **46**, 5, pp. 4–13.

US DEPARTMENT OF EDUCATION (1984) *The Nation Responds: Recent Efforts to Improve Education*, Washington, DC, US Government Printing Office.

US DEPARTMENT OF EDUCATION (1985) *Indicators of Educational Status and Trends*, Washington, DC, US Government Printing Office.

WORLD BANK (1988) *Education in Sub-Saharan Africa*, Washington, DC.

WORLD BANK (1990) *Primary Education*, Washington, DC.

Index